BLACK FUNDAMENTALISTS

# Black Fundamentalists

*Conservative Christianity and Racial Identity in the Segregation Era*

Daniel R. Bare

NEW YORK UNIVERSITY PRESS
New York

NEW YORK UNIVERSITY PRESS
New York
www.nyupress.org

© 2021 by New York University
All rights reserved

References to Internet websites (URLs) were accurate at the time of writing. Neither the author nor New York University Press is responsible for URLs that may have expired or changed since the manuscript was prepared.

Library of Congress Cataloging-in-Publication Data
Names: Bare, Daniel R., author.
Title: Black fundamentalists : conservative Christianity and racial identity in the segregation era / Daniel R. Bare.
Description: New York : New York University Press, [2021] |
Includes bibliographical references and index.
Identifiers: LCCN 2020034737 (print) | LCCN 2020034738 (ebook) |
ISBN 9781479803262 (cloth) | ISBN 9781479803279 (paperback) |
ISBN 9781479803255 (ebook other) | ISBN 9781479803293 (ebook)
Subjects: LCSH: African Americans—Religion—History—20th century. | Fundamentalism—United States—History—20th century.
Classification: LCC BR563.N4 B36 2021 (print) | LCC BR563.N4 (ebook) |
DDC 280/.408996073—dc23
LC record available at https://lccn.loc.gov/2020034737
LC ebook record available at https://lccn.loc.gov/2020034738

New York University Press books are printed on acid-free paper, and their binding materials are chosen for strength and durability. We strive to use environmentally responsible suppliers and materials to the greatest extent possible in publishing our books.

Manufactured in the United States of America

10 9 8 7 6 5 4 3 2 1

Also available as an ebook

*For Dad,*

who made me write;

*and for Mom,*

who saw this coming long before I did.

CONTENTS

Introduction — 1

1. "Filled to Overflowing": Black Weeklies and the Fundamentalist Presence — 25

2. Formulating the Faith: The Five Fundamentals across Racial Lines — 56

3. Polemics from the Pulpit: Antimodernist Preaching and Racial Applications — 87

4. Religious Education and Interracial Cooperation: The American Baptist Theological Seminary — 121

5. Contested Identities: Fundamentalism, Race, and Americanism — 158

Conclusion — 185

*Acknowledgments* — 189

*Notes* — 193

*Selected Bibliography* — 235

*Index* — 247

*About the Author* — 261

# Introduction

On Tuesday, June 13, 2017, a wave of chaos and indignation broke over the Southern Baptist Convention's (SBC's) annual meeting. The fumes of the nation's acrimonious 2016 presidential contest still lingered in the air. The recently concluded election season had, among other things, generated a spike in the visibility and influence of the "alt-right" movement, a small but vocal white identitarian group championed by the likes of noted white nationalist Richard Spencer. Hence, as the 2017 SBC meeting approached, a black Southern Baptist pastor determined to take this opportunity to express his concern about the recent increase in the alt-right's visibility. To this end, he introduced what he expected to be an uncontroversial resolution for the convention to firmly denounce the racism and white nationalism of the alt-right. The pastor, Dwight McKissic of Cornerstone Baptist Church in Arlington, Texas, was taken aback when the resolutions committee declined to forward his proposal to the convention floor. The committee explained this initial decision by noting that they were "very aware that . . . feelings rightly run high regarding alt-right ideology," but "we just weren't certain we could craft a resolution that would enable us to measure our strong convictions with the grace of love, which we're also commanded by Jesus to incorporate." This stance released a tidal wave of protest both on social media and from messengers at the convention. For his part, McKissic called it "a mystery how you can so easily affirm standard beliefs about other things, but we get to white supremacy . . . and all of a sudden, we've got a problem."[1]

In the face of this backlash, the committee scrambled to correct its misstep, and so on June 14, the last day of the annual meeting, the convention adopted a resolution that denounced "every form of racism, including alt-right white supremacy, as antithetical to the Gospel of Jesus Christ."[2] Yet from a public relations perspective, the SBC was still left with the lingering optics of having ignored an antiracism resolution offered by one of its black members. Many people, including McKissic, maintained reservations in the face of the hastily passed resolution, arguing that the entire episode "showed a fault line. It showed that maybe, just maybe, you aren't where you're supposed to be on this."[3] Other Southern Baptists bristled at the resolution itself, holding that it was unnecessary and smacked of political virtue signaling: "If there are those in the SBC who have embraced [white supremacy] ... issuing a resolution isn't going to produce repentance. Scripture already condemns it. If Scripture won't convince them, what chance does a resolution have?"[4] Ultimately both the original hesitation to broach the resolution and the divided reaction to its eventual adoption left some black Americans wondering, along with McKissic, how the black and white members of one of the most visible conservative evangelical denominations in the United States could find agreement on many other issues, including doctrinal confessions, and yet still argue about how to address the topic of racism.

This particular issue is by no means a new development, and its recent manifestation in such obvious fashion in the midst of the relatively theologically conservative ranks of the Southern Baptist Convention serves simply to point to its persistence in American religious life—particularly in conservative Protestant circles.[5] Indeed, a full century prior to the SBC's alt-right resolution, this trend was apparent in the emergence of one of the most famous conservative religious movements in modern American history—Protestant fundamentalism. In the early decades of the twentieth century, the fundamentalist movement arose as a reaction against the "modernist" or "liberal" theology gaining popularity in many churches and intellectual centers. Modernist theology sought to adapt Christianity to fit with the growing rationalistic and naturalistic sensibilities of the modern age—thus jettisoning or redefining doctrines such as the virgin birth of Christ or the divine inspiration of the Bible, which were seen as incompatible with a modern, scientific understanding of the world. In response, fundamentalists rose up to affirm the centrality of these "fundamental" theological positions to historic Christianity and to denounce modernists as insidious threats to the Christian religion itself.[6] Eventually, major white fundamentalist leaders built up institutional networks of schools, conferences, newspapers, and the like—networks that, in accord with the prevailing mores of a society structured by Jim Crow, were forged and populated almost exclusively by a white membership. But while these particular institutional networks may typically have been circumscribed by the color line, the theological ideas, ecclesiastical concerns, intellectual arguments, and rhetorical labels were not.

In the years between the world wars, when the fundamentalist-modernist controversy burned the brightest and fundamentalism was making a name for itself as a major force in the American religious landscape, the theological convictions underlying fundamentalism straddled the color line to the extent that some African Americans began to publicly self-identify as fundamentalists and to discuss the importance of "the fundamentals" to the black community. Yet despite this reality, these black actors are for the most part noticeably absent from the historical accountings of fundamentalism, and in turn fundamentalism rarely engenders much discussion in the realm of African American religious history. The story of fundamentalism has thus often become the story of white institutional leaders who take on Brobdingnagian proportions—men such as Minnesota Baptist pastor William Bell Riley, founder of the World's Christian Fundamentals Association, or sensationalist Texas Baptist firebrand J. Frank Norris, whose dominance in the narrative implicitly paints fundamentalism as a pugilistic white enterprise confined to white social circles. For instance, historian David Harrington Watt's evaluation of the demography of interwar-era fundamentalism concludes that it was essentially restricted to "native-born white Americans," while noted sociologist Nancy Ammerman suggests that the term "fundamentalism" itself is broadly inapplicable to the black community both historically and in the present, because "although they share many beliefs with other evangelicals, those beliefs function quite differently in their very different social world" in which black religion offers "a racially based separation in which church and community are bound tightly together."[7] Here again arises the persistent question of racial differentiation in the midst of substantial doctrinal alignment.

Yet, what of those black conservative Protestants who *did* explicitly name themselves fundamentalists, or who undertook a traditionalist defense of the fundamentals? This is the driving question that this book aims to explore. It argues that there were indeed fundamentalists among African American Protestants who not only claimed the title for themselves but also aligned with the theological heartbeat of fundamentalism. In making this case, I especially emphasize the series of ninety articles, compiled and widely distributed between 1910 and 1915, which comprised the theological work from which the movement eventually gained its name—*The Fundamentals*. Sometimes referred to as the sourcebook of fundamentalist theology, *The Fundamentals* represents an early, forthright, and centralized source for fundamentalist doctrinal expression. Comparing the writings and sermons of certain black authors and ministers with the language and arguments of these articles offers one fruitful avenue for exploring and demonstrating fundamentalist convictions and identity across racial lines. The completion of *The Fundamentals* also provides a starting date for this study at 1915, the year in which the final articles of the series were published. Hence, the periodization from 1915 to 1940 discussed in this book stretches from the publication of *The Fundamentals* through the height of the fundamentalist-modernist controversy in the 1920s and 1930s, leading up to the emergence of the neo-evangelical movement in the 1940s.[8]

But beyond simply chronicling the existence of black fundamentalists, this book further argues that black fundamentalists displayed a type of social engagement markedly different from that typically associated with fundamentalism. Rather than spending the majority of their time and energy on fighting against the teaching of evolutionary theory in public schools and similar issues, black fundamentalists advocated social action and religious application that emphasized racial equality, justice for all people regardless of skin color, and the social advancement of the African American community from marginalized minority to full participants in American citizenship. Black fundamentalism was thus not a mere carbon copy of white fundamentalism superimposed onto black churches. Even considering the substantial congruence of theological conviction and exegetical argumentation across the color line that we will examine in this book, black fundamentalism nonetheless represented an internal formulation and expression of religious thought and experience from within black church traditions. Especially as they addressed the topic of race, black fundamentalists applied their conservative religious beliefs in more progressive ways than did their white counterparts.[9] This study of fundamentalism across the color line shows how religious expression is influenced by racial context, as well as how racial prejudice in society can obscure those very same dynamics.

As much as this book challenges the traditional conceptualization of American Protestant fundamentalism, it also shows that theologically conservative religion offered an avenue for African Americans to address racism in ways that are often popularly associated with more theologically liberal (or even secular) traditions in the black community.[10] Black fundamentalists managed to combine a traditional brand of theological fundamentalism with a race-conscious, progressive attitude toward social engagement—two perspectives that are usually considered to be profoundly disparate, if not mutually exclusive.[11] This is not to say that the ideas or approaches of black fundamentalists were identical to those of their more theologically liberal or secular brothers and sisters in the African American community; like any social or political movement, the quest for black freedom evinced plenty of internal diversity. However, it is to say that they were engaged with the struggle for freedom, justice, and citizenship and that their racial context significantly influenced how they applied their religious convictions. These black fundamentalists of the early twentieth century would undoubtedly have empathized with Dwight McKissic's frustration during the 2017 SBC annual meeting at the mystery of "how you can so easily affirm standard beliefs about other things, but we get to white supremacy . . . and all of a sudden, we've got a problem."

Despite the fact that numerous African Americans affirmed fundamentalism or identified explicitly as fundamentalists during the interwar period, the historiographies of fundamentalism and African American religion have, for the most part, failed to intersect. One recent book, Mary Beth Swetnam Mathews's *Doctrine and Race*, marks a noteworthy exception to this trend, offering a much-needed consideration of the relationship between fundamentalism and the black community.[12] She rightly notes that "historians of [fundamentalism] have not engaged fully with how fundamentalists understood race and race relations in general" and further points out that "the extent to which African Americans interacted with white fundamentalists . . . and with fundamentalist theories in general has also received scant attention."[13] Mathews argues that both whites and blacks racialized fundamentalism and modernism in ways that excluded the black community from direct involvement in the controversy—with white fundamentalists painting fundamentalism as an exclusively white movement and conservative black Protestants casting modernism as an essentially white problem.[14] While she does devote substantial space to discussing some of the expressly theological aspects of fundamentalism, Mathews nevertheless excludes blacks from among the ranks of the fundamentalists, maintaining that (among other reasons) their willingness to entertain and employ certain racially progressive social ideologies and strategies, including a general emphasis on racial justice, precluded such an association or identification.[15] African Americans, she contends, were positioned "outside the debate being held by white Protestants—both the fundamentalist/modernist debate and the debates among the fundamentalists themselves," making black Protestants "free to interpret the Bible and current events without the restrictions of the debates that raged around them."[16] Hence, Mathews draws a consistent terminological distinction between "fundamentalists," who were necessarily white, and "black Protestants" (or various parallel descriptors), who "declined to self-identify as fundamentalists." In this vein, she argues that "African American Baptists and Methodists did not explicitly embrace or reject fundamentalism," and that black Baptists and Methodists "would not side with modernism, but they could not live with fundamentalism either."[17]

Unfortunately, this perspective fails to fully account for not only the black Protestants who were overtly embracing the fundamentalist label in the 1920s and 1930s, but also the assertion coming from both proponents and opponents that fundamentalism was, for good or for ill, a widespread phenomenon in the black Protestant community. I argue, in accordance with Mathews, that black Protestants did often embrace various sorts of racially progressive applications and strategies that distinguished them from white fundamentalists, but in many cases they actually grounded these social positions in their fundamentalist theology and identity. Hence, the discrepancy in social application across the color line should not prompt us to dismiss black fundamentalists as inauthentic or even nonexistent. Rather, it should cause us to recognize that fundamentalist American Protestantism, considered from a historical-theological perspective, may have had a wider range of social commitments and cultural applications than has usually been assumed, if we take into consideration the disparate racial, social, and cultural contexts in which fundamentalism was manifested.

While Mathews's book represents an undeniably important step forward in considering the confluence of fundamentalism and racial identity, its novelty also reveals and reinforces the historiography's generally exclusionary trend when it comes to African Americans and fundamentalism.[18] Although she does not go so far as to affirm that "black fundamentalists" was a meaningful category, Mathews does convincingly demonstrate that blacks were self-consciously engaged with certain ideas surrounding the fundamentalist-modernist controversy—at least among the four major denominational newspapers that structure her study. Yet in the majority of historical scholarship, black Americans have typically been excluded from considerations of American Protestant fundamentalism, based either on explicit denials that African Americans could even *be* fundamentalists or on implicit neglect in historical analysis. Moreover, when African Americans do expressly appear in the scope of historical narratives relating to fundamentalism, they often represent either a small sympathetic group to be quickly mentioned and passed over or a bogeyman that white fundamentalists could leverage in consolidating their coalitions. Unfortunately, these sorts of exclusionary perspectives fail to account for those African Americans who consciously self-identified as fundamentalists in the very midst of the fundamentalist-modernist controversy, as well as those whose theological and polemical arguments reflected a doctrinal commitment to fundamentalist principles—not to mention those in the black press who presented claims about the widespread presence of fundamentalist convictions and identity among the black Protestant populace. One of the main goals of this book is to incorporate these marginalized black fundamentalist voices into the historiography.

This marginalization of African Americans in relation to fundamentalism in the scholarly literature reflects at least two notable historiographical trends. First, fundamentalism is often understandably construed as an essentially *institutionalized* political or social movement rather than as a primarily theological undertaking. This position marginalizes those who might have been theologically (and possibly even ideologically) aligned with the movement but whose cultural context and social circumstances precluded overt participation in the movement's institutional structures. Indeed, many of the most visible and influential fundamentalist institutions and networks, established amid Jim Crow and run by powerful white leaders, often reflected (or even reified) the segregationist and racist sensibilities of the predominant white culture. Thus, analyses that treat these institutional structures as definitional to fundamentalism per se tend to obscure the possibility of black participation. Black fundamentalism, in contrast, was not institutionally defined, but rather existed within extant denominational boundaries and other religious structures. In this sense, it was more a perspective than an institutionalized movement. As a result, the fundamentalist outlook among black Protestants was by necessity significantly less separatist in nature than was the institutionalized fundamentalism of whites, and it often existed side-by-side (albeit sometimes uncomfortably so) with more liberal perspectives within organizations such as the National Baptist Convention (NBC) or the African Methodist Episcopal (AME) Church. Such dynamics were for instance evident, as we will see, in the NBC's seminary in Nashville.

The second relevant historiographical trend is that most academic treatments of fundamentalism consider a militant posture toward certain social and cultural changes that were often associated with the modernist worldview, such as an increasing acceptance of evolutionary biology, to be definitional.[19] Yet this perspective naturally excludes African Americans who may have expressly identified themselves as fundamentalists, but whose social focus was often, and necessarily, directed in various ways toward racial issues. In short, if fundamentalism is conceptualized as a movement closely tied to a narrow spectrum of culturally conservative political and social objectives important to conservative white Protestants, and if it is likewise defined by virtue of formal institutional structures, then it follows that African Americans can be safely ignored because they were typically far from the cultural centers of power and the social center of the institutionalized movement, even if they were doctrinally aligned with the fundamentalist perspective.

An example of the first trend—treating fundamentalism as an institutional movement over against the theological specifics of the fundamentalist-modernist controversy—comes in Ernest Sandeen's *The Roots of Fundamentalism*, one of the earliest modern scholarly treatments of the subject. Sandeen carefully distinguishes between the "fundamentalist movement" and the more limited "fundamentalist controversy" of the 1920s, noting that "the movement existed independently of the controversy." He describes the movement as "a self-conscious, structured, long-lived, dynamic entity with recognized leadership, periodicals, and meetings," possessed of a "self-conscious identity and structure similar to the Republican party, the Knights of Columbus, or (probably the closest parallel) the Puritans." For Sandeen, the central concern that gave "life and shape to the Fundamentalist movement," including its institutions, was millenarianism and its attendant focus on the imminent return of Christ.[20] Sandeen's emphasis on the self-conscious identity and institutionalized structure of this millenarian Fundamentalist movement—on a level with a major political party, no less—clearly sets the focus on those citizens with relatively unfettered access to the social and cultural mainstream. Consequently, it is not entirely surprising that African Americans, a group that was constantly pushed to the margins of society in the Jim Crow era, are absent from Sandeen's narrative. The comparison of the fundamentalist movement with a political party is a striking one when considered from this angle; African Americans were routinely marginalized in the political sphere at this time through disfranchisement efforts, and so perhaps it should not be a surprise to see them excluded from Sandeen's evaluation of a movement he considers to be similar to a political party in its institutional makeup. For similar reasons, other studies containing a strong institutional focus—such as Joel Carpenter's *Revive Us Again*, which admittedly "devotes most of its attention to the internal affairs of the fundamentalist movement"—largely omit African Americans because of their marginality relative to the institutional forms, though perhaps not to the doctrinal commitments, of the movement itself.[21]

This perspective is likewise often inculcated in biographical portraits of individual fundamentalist leaders, such as Barry Hankins's biography of J. Frank Norris, *God's Rascal*, or William Trollinger's study of William Bell Riley, *God's Empire*.[22] It is pertinent, though rather obvious, to point out that such prominent fundamentalist institutional leaders were white. Figures such as Riley and Norris rightly receive a significant amount of historical attention because they were men of enormous influence—superstar preachers, Bible college founders, radio personalities, conference organizers, and on and on. They were in many ways larger-than-life characters heading sprawling networks of fundamentalist churches and organizations, and as such their biographies naturally tend to paint fundamentalism as a social movement intrinsically tied to these institutional structures. When, as Ernest Sandeen suggested in 1970, the "fundamentalist movement" is seen as possessing "self-conscious identity and structure similar to the Republican party," the historian's focus will naturally gravitate toward the most influential and "self-conscious" leaders of the movement, just as political pundits tend to focus a disproportionate amount of attention on highly influential party leaders. Furthermore, an emphasis on the formal institutional structure of the movement naturally draws attention to the individuals who created and oversaw the schools, colleges, radio stations, churches, conferences, newspapers, and associations that comprised the fundamentalist institutional networks; and of course any such "top-down" institutional approach is going to tend to exclude socially marginalized groups such as African Americans.

Trollinger admits in his biography of William Bell Riley that top-down thinking has too often characterized the study of fundamentalism: "William Ellis' observation, made in 1981, still rings true: while the revisionists 'have provided a valuable service to historiography by describing the intellectual base of fundamentalism,' they have failed to give 'the grass roots of fundamentalism . . . the full attention it deserves.'"[23] While his statement was not intended as commentary on the paucity of racial analysis within the literature, there is certainly a sense in which it can be applied to the much-neglected subject of black fundamentalists. An emphasis on fundamentalism as an institutionally defined social movement tends to ensure that the most attention is inevitably drawn to the elite white leaders of the movement. And although such attention does at times touch on issues of race and ethnicity—Trollinger discusses Riley's anti-Semitic urge to make Jews the ubiquitous "social scapegoat," and Norris's well-known fondness for segregation and white supremacy prompted Hankins to devote a chapter to Norris's utilization of "the race card" in defending both fundamentalism and the South's social status quo—this nevertheless does little to illuminate the question of fundamentalist expressions *within* black religious communities.[24]

Much as Hankins examines J. Frank Norris's rhetorical connection of the fundamentalists' institutional fight against modernism with the fight to preserve the segregationist status quo, so historian William R. Glass's

*Strangers in Zion* likewise ties institutional fundamentalism in the South to segregationist ideals. Glass explains that it is helpful to view fundamentalism as an institutionalized "movement with a specific agenda," rather than as "a set of [theological] beliefs."[25] For Glass, whose study centers on the development of fundamentalism in the American South, southern fundamentalism was essentially concerned with preserving the doctrinal fidelity of churches and denominations because the movement leaders saw their churches as the moral guardians of their culture and the organizing institutions of their communities; thus, the movement was in large part concerned not merely with doctrinal issues but with preserving the South's social order. A significant part of that social order, of course, centered on race relations, and the prominence of Jim Crow loomed large as the fundamentalist movement was establishing its roots in the South. Consequently, aside from a passing reference or two to a minimal black presence at a few southern Bible conferences, Glass's study includes African Americans only insofar as they appeared in white fundamentalist rhetoric. For example, Glass recounts how the fundamentalist opponents of the reunion of southern and northern denominations played on racial fears and prejudices to consolidate support for their cause, demanding that no consideration of reunion would be feasible unless the northerners provided "an explicit statement that the reunited denomination would maintain a policy of racial separation."[26] Thus it seems that Glass's understanding of southern fundamentalism as "a movement with a specific agenda" rather than "a set of beliefs" limits the degree to which (and the roles in which) African Americans appear in the history of fundamentalism. Given that the movement is presented as one that sought in many respects to preserve the prevailing social and racial hierarchies of the South, African Americans are naturally excluded. There is no room for any conception of black fundamentalists within this particular vision of the "movement."

Political scientist Michael Lienesch, setting his sights specifically on the anti-evolutionist portion of the fundamentalist phenomenon, argues that anti-evolutionists made similar use of racial prejudice by intimating that "acceptance of evolution would encourage racial equality and the eventual mixing of the races."[27] Lienesch goes further than Glass, however, in at least acknowledging some noticeable degree of black support for fundamentalist positions. He notes that black churches of the

1920s "tended to be theologically orthodox, and many of their ministers were biblical literalists who held strong dispensationalist sympathies," and further points out that at the Scopes trial "large numbers of black believers rallied behind William Jennings Bryan."[28] Drawing chiefly on the work of historian Jeffrey Moran to argue that shared anti-evolution sentiments caused some black church leaders to ally with white fundamentalists, Lienesch concludes that "while African Americans remained on the outside of fundamentalism's strictly segregated organizations, many . . . may have considered themselves to be fundamentalists."[29] In this brief statement, Lienesch appears to concur that a strictly institutional focus might obscure connections between fundamentalism and African American religion. Yet although it is commendable that he at least offers some degree of explicit consideration of black support for fundamentalist causes, it is also notable that Lienesch devotes less than one full page to the subject.

In addition to the conceptualization of fundamentalism as an institutionalized movement rather than as a set of particular doctrinal positions, the definitions used to identify the most central aspects of the fundamentalist perspective can likewise tend toward racial exclusion. Most notably, an emphasis on certain types of conservative cultural militancy permeates the historiography of the last several decades, thanks in large part to evangelical historian George Marsden's seminal work *Fundamentalism and American Culture*. Marsden defines fundamentalism as "militantly anti-modernist Protestant evangelicalism" and posits that militant opposition to modernism, in both its theological and cultural expressions, was the single mark that "most clearly set off fundamentalism from a number of closely related traditions."[30] Marsden recognizes fundamentalism as a movement that, though largely driven by theological convictions, was most clearly defined by its fiercely oppositional attitudes toward not only modernist theology but also the social and cultural changes that fundamentalists associated with a modernist worldview. Fundamentalists, then, were not engaged merely in ecclesiastical battles for control over their denominations or spiritual battles for the salvation of souls; they necessarily also took part in protracted social and cultural confrontations designed to preserve the society's status quo—perhaps most famously in the anti-evolution movement and the Scopes trial.[31] Indeed, this brand of conservative cultural militancy is so prevalent in the literature as to be nearly axiomatic. And in fact there is little doubt that such cultural militancy was a key element of the formally institutionalized, white-dominated fundamentalist networks. Moreover, for the most visible and influential movement leaders militant cultural antimodernism was clearly a nonnegotiable priority, as when Baptist journalist Curtis Lee Laws, who coined the term "fundamentalist" in 1920, famously proposed "to do battle royal" against modernist foes.[32]

Apt as this emphasis may be in the context of fundamentalism's institutional history or the study of major (white) movement leaders, a single-minded focus on this brand of cultural militancy can unfortunately also serve to obscure the presence of those African Americans who self-identified as fundamentalists or championed the theological convictions of fundamentalism, but whose political and social attention may have been occupied with social concerns that hit closer to home—issues such as segregation, racial violence, and unequal access to education and voting rights for black citizens. Consequently, such people receive little consideration in the prevailing historiography.[33] For instance, in arguing that fundamentalism was in essence a "lily-white" undertaking, historian David Harrington Watt points to the fact that "few African Americans threw themselves fully into the fundamentalists' campaign to keep evolution from being taught in the nation's public schools."[34] For his part, George Marsden contends that "'fundamentalist' has seldom been a self-designation" for African Americans due to the movement's segregationist heritage.[35] Yet although it is unquestionably true, as William Glass demonstrates in *Strangers in Zion*, that many fundamentalist institutions (particularly in the South) have at times been intimately intertwined with segregation and racial prejudice, there nevertheless remain unexplored in the historical record any number of black figures who *did* in fact call themselves "fundamentalists" or who took up the pen or ascended to the pulpit to stridently defend "the fundamentals" and to decry the insidious threat of modernism. The ubiquitous emphasis in the historiography on anti-evolution activism and other similar forms of socially conservative cultural militancy serves to obscure the presence of self-identified black fundamentalists and to marginalize claims such as that of one *Norfolk Journal and Guide* editorialist who declared, within mere weeks of the famous Scopes trial, that "Afro-Americans are fundamentalists, for the most part."[36]

This is not to say that the approaches outlined above—specifically the emphases on institutional networks or campaigns of conservative cultural militancy—are invalid or useless. On the contrary, these scholarly endeavors have shed enormous light on numerous elements and expressions of twentieth-century fundamentalism. It is merely to say that they are incomplete, because no single approach can adequately capture every facet of the topic—and the particular facet of black participation has remained heretofore largely unexplored. Thus, the approach that I offer here is not intended as a wholesale replacement or repudiation of the perspectives that have come before. However, this book does insist that there is a history of black fundamentalism, and that lifting new voices from the documentary record helps clarify a heretofore opaque chapter in the story of American fundamentalism.

In contrast to the earlier institutional or political approaches to the topic noted above, my analysis in this book aims to seriously incorporate the fundamentalist elements within the black church by taking a historical-theological approach that treats the specifics of doctrinal commitments and doctrinal attitudes—understood and rightfully situated within their historical contexts—as central in identifying and defining fundamentalism. This approach assumes theology qua theology to be a meaningful analytical category and understands the content of religious belief to be important in and of itself, rather than being simply a reflection or manifestation of other underlying driving forces. Indeed, much of American history is so tightly bound to religious paradigms and ideas that some scholars argue that it is *incomprehensible* without considering religious context and praxis, as well as the theological and narrative content of American religious traditions.[37]

It is important to note from the outset that this approach does not entail that the theological content of religious belief is the only meaningful analytical category, or that religious beliefs are entirely unrelated to other commitments. On the contrary, it is an undeniable fact that social circumstances and religious beliefs often inform and influence one another, especially in the essential sermonic (and also more generally religious) task of practically applying theological convictions to everyday life. In this vein we might profitably reflect on what evangelical scholar Mark Noll calls the "social history of theology." Noll's approach admits that theological developments and historical developments, far from being partitioned and compartmentalized, must be understood as mutually influential. Theological changes must be considered within their "ecclesiastical, social, political, intellectual, and commercial" contexts. Noll asserts that incorporating this contextual perspective on theological history is "especially useful for explaining why Christian belief evolved along different lines" in disparate social contexts (for Noll, the contexts were the Protestant United States and Protestant Europe).[38] My analysis in this book reflects, in part, this "social history of theology" perspective. Recognizing that theological developments take place within the always complex, often knotty, and sometimes discomfiting realities of day-to-day life—rather than in some ethereal vacuum—is the very reason that the topic of "black fundamentalists" is meaningful at all. When we examine the fundamentalist ideas and impulses that manifested themselves in the African American community, social and political and intellectual context matters a great deal, especially in conjunction with the pervasive reality of *racial* context in American life. So, in line with Noll's own evaluation of his method, my application of this approach helps to explain the similarities and differences in the evolution of a very particular type of Christian belief in disparate social contexts—in this case, specifically American racial contexts. In the chapters that follow, I argue that the different social and cultural circumstances facing the black and white communities often led to substantially different social actions and applications, even among those who would commonly agree on the most important fundamentalist doctrines.

At the same time, we must also be careful to ensure that the pendulum does not swing too far in the other direction. The theological convictions underlying "fundamentalist" thought (on either side of the racial divide) ought not be boiled down to *mere* expressions of underlying social, cultural, political, or economic ideological positions. Rather, these bedrock doctrinal convictions should be treated as significant and meaningful in themselves, as markers of legitimately deep-seated belief about the nature of reality and, in many cases, also markers of personal or corporate identity. The historical-theological approach in this book seeks to heed noted historian Albert Raboteau's warning of the dangers that exist when historians fail to take seriously the theological content of religious belief. Reducing religion to "an epiphenomenon of economic or political ideology," he cautions, demonstrates both "an inadequate grasp of religion and a simplistic understanding of history."[39] Moreover, the fact remains that many of the historical figures who appear in the following pages considered theology in general, and their own theological positions in particular, to be intrinsically meaningful in defining their identity, and therefore the historical-theological approach seeks to take these religious devotees seriously on their own terms.

One result of this commitment is that some space is devoted to nuanced aspects of doctrinal analysis and comparisons between religionists from across the racial spectrum. While social circumstances and social application unquestionably play a large role in the analysis, similarities and differences in doctrinal positions are also treated as important building blocks for constructing a religious identity. Consequently, while other treatments might focus largely on institutional statements and actions in defining and evaluating fundamentalism, this book utilizes the ninety articles of *The Fundamentals* as an important reference point for theological and exegetical analysis of fundamentalist theology. These collected essays offer a starting point for evaluating the doctrinal content of fundamentalist religious convictions as "fundamentalism" emerged as an identifiable part of American religious nomenclature from the mid-1910s forward.

Another corollary of this emphasis on religious and theological thinking as intrinsically meaningful is that it helps to illuminate the power of religious ideas to shape, drive, and interpret people's actions and experiences in this world. In this respect, my examination of black fundamentalism intersects with the topic of black intellectual history. Historians Keisha N. Blain, Christopher Cameron, and Ashley D. Farmer, in their recent volume *New Perspectives on the Black Intellectual Tradition*, point out that intellectual history not only studies how people of the past used "ideas and symbols . . . to make sense of the world" and "what [historical subjects] thought about what they were doing," but also allows us to gain a deeper understanding of the world with which our historical subjects were grappling. Such examination "deepens our understanding of social and cultural history, forcing us to investigate the ideas that undergird political and social life and grapple with the theories and ideologies that inform historical actors." From this vantage, studying the theological ideas of black fundamentalists has the potential to tell us quite a lot about the world in which they lived. This is certainly true when comparing fundamentalist groups across the color line. Shared theological convictions had the power, in some cases, to bridge social gulfs and drive interracial fellowship, but divergences in social application, especially on issues of race, also showed how theological ideas and their consequences were utilized to address contextually specific social and racial concerns. Likewise, with respect to the field of *black* intellectual history in particular, detecting the voices of black fundamentalists reinforces Blain, Cameron, and Farmer's argument that the history of black intellectual engagement is "by no means monolithic." Identifying a fundamentalist facet within the black intellectual tradition, then, adds to "the range and depth of the ideological and social traditions upon which black intellectuals drew in their efforts to address key issues in black communities."[40] This tack illuminates the "sometimes overlooked fact" that, in the words of Albert Raboteau, "African-American opinion has never been unanimous."[41]

The historical-theological approach also allows for a sense of the *religious* variety, diversity, and dynamism among African American congregations and individual religionists. Recognizing that real, substantive theological divisions and conflicts existed within African American communities helps to avoid the temptation to treat "the black church" as a singular, monolithic, undifferentiated whole. Even as many African Americans on opposing sides of the fundamentalist-modernist conflict shared a broad concern for the advancement of the race—and while they may have been inclined to embrace different strategies, some of them were also willing to work side by side in seeking to achieve those goals—they still expressly drew lines of distinction and differentiation on essentially theological grounds. Their commonality in the one arena did not necessarily dictate a congruence in the other; a level of complexity and diversity within "the black church" in general, and often even within a single denominational structure, is apparent. That black fundamentalists sought to balance their recognition of the common oppression facing all black people in a Jim Crow world with their conviction about the spiritual centrality of the traditional "fundamental" doctrines of Christianity also helps to illuminate how and why black fundamentalists tended to be less separatist than their white counterparts. In this respect they represent at once both a theologically distinct facet of a diverse black church tradition and a specifically black manifestation of fundamentalist sentiments.

This situation further reinforces the value of treating theological conviction as a meaningful identity-shaping factor in and of itself, rather than simply, as Raboteau noted, "an epiphenomenon of economic or political ideology." After all, if that were the case, then there would seem to be little reason for black religionists who faced the common sociopolitical foe of Jim Crow oppression to draw any sharp theological dividing lines over such doctrinal issues as biblical inspiration or the divinity of Jesus. Indeed, if theology were merely a utilitarian expression of underlying political and social motivations, then such doctrinal divisions would be utterly confounding, since they would functionally hinder the utility of religion in accomplishing its principal and elemental sociopolitical goals. In and of itself, the persistence of these theological distinctions demonstrates their deep significance to the practitioners themselves, while the fact that these very same practitioners at times showed a spirit of ecumenical cooperation for common racial goals (an ecumenical approach that white fundamentalists would generally have rejected out of hand) speaks to the power and ubiquity of racial identity as a motivating factor for many African Americans—even fundamentalists and modernists—in the context of Jim Crow America.

With the historical-theological approach in mind, then, the difficult task of defining "fundamentalism" remains. Approaching this endeavor from the vantage of theology and identity, I propose four conditions: (1) the embrace of an overarching supernaturalist and biblicist worldview, including an attitude of continuity with historic Christian traditions, (2) a personal commitment to the central doctrinal essentials of the movement, consonant with the theological convictions reflected in *The Fundamentals*, (3) a readiness to explicitly criticize and overtly condemn modernist theology, and (4) the willingness to utilize expressly fundamentalist language and terminology in defining one's theological positions and religious identity. The first three conditions, which are primarily theological, build upon one another to form the doctrinal and attitudinal content of fundamentalism, such that the removal or denial of any one of them would clearly set someone outside of the fundamentalist realm. The fourth condition, which has to do with self-identification, is more subjective and therefore, by necessity, more elusive.[42] The three theological tenets together are the essence of what I would define as "doctrinal fundamentalism"—that is, regardless of whether or not a historical actor explicitly claimed the fundamentalist moniker, these tenets reflect a fundamentalist posture from a historical-theological perspective, though of course not necessarily from an institutional one.[43] The first three chapters of the book identify and examine these three elements in the black community.

The fourth element, self-identification as a fundamentalist, is rather more difficult because of the inherent subjectivity involved, but it remains important in demonstrating that some major black ecclesiastical leaders sought to overtly position themselves *within* the cultural maelstrom that was the fundamentalist-modernist controversy. When such self-identification appears in conjunction with the three aspects of "doctrinal fundamentalism," as laid out above, it becomes difficult to deny that a significant historical-theological congruence between white and black Protestants has seemingly slipped through the cracks of the historiographies of fundamentalism and of African American religious history. Of course, self-identification as a definitional criterion has its own inherent limitations—most notably, that divorced from explicit theological affirmations, the term "fundamentalist" might well carry different connotations to each person who uses it. Two caveats, then, are in order. First, many of the figures in the following pages who sought to elucidate and defend "the fundamentals" or to identify as "fundamentalists" did so in light of their clear doctrinal affirmations, thus adding their self-identification to the already established contours of their "doctrinal fundamentalism" (as defined above). Second, those who designated themselves "fundamentalist" in the absence of a robust, detailed theological or doctrinal context may present more tenuous connections to the historical-theological formulation of fundamentalism, and thus the conclusions we can draw from their examples are somewhat more limited. Nevertheless, the existence of the raging religious controversy between fundamentalists and modernists during the interwar period meant that blacks' very usage of the terminology implied a willingness to be identified in some respects with the common public perception of fundamentalism. So, while self-designation is obviously a limited criterion, it is nevertheless an important element of dealing with historical figures on their own terms, and it will recur throughout the following chapters as both an important marker in the process of identity construction and, in many cases, as a parallel affirmation of the other three theological elements of "doctrinal fundamentalism" as laid out above.

While consideration of this self-referential aspect of fundamentalism recurs throughout this book, the first three theological elements receive specific consideration in the first three chapters, since they progressively build upon one another. Chapter 1 explores the claims by commentators in the black press (on both sides of the theological divide) that fundamentalism was a widespread force *within* the black community. Using these weekly newspaper accounts to examine the contours of the basic fundamentalist worldview that was understood to exist among African Americans, this chapter both identifies a professed fundamentalist presence among black Christians and analyzes the theological and racial connotations of these black weeklies' considerations of fundamentalism. In terms of broad theological characteristics, this fundamentalist worldview was characterized by a supernaturalist presupposition connected to the traditional beliefs of "the old-time religion," a commitment to biblicism that was often termed "biblical literalism," and a doctrine of creation that denied the rising tide of evolutionary thought. To deny a supernaturalist and biblicist worldview would, automatically and obviously, preclude a fundamentalist identity. Yet while many African Americans recognized a major fundamentalist contingent among themselves, the broad theological commonalities between black and white fundamentalists did not necessarily manifest in a similar overlap in social worldview, especially regarding issues of race. The fact that the black community was subject to ubiquitous structures of racial oppression meant that the press's discussions of fundamentalism were also often tinged with questions and implications about the relationship of fundamentalist religion to racial identity and upright social action. In this case, a historical-theological perspective illuminates a self-identified fundamentalist contingent within the African American community, while an institutional perspective might obscure such a connection.

While a supernaturalist and biblicist worldview obviously constitutes the sine qua non of fundamentalist thought, it just as obviously needed to be joined with specific Protestant doctrinal propositions that formed the "fundamentals" of the faith that fundamentalists undertook to defend. To deny any of the basic doctrinal essentials that comprised the majority of the argumentation in *The Fundamentals*—such as, for example, the full divinity of Christ—would virtually axiomatically set someone apart from the "fundamentalism" of the early twentieth century.[44] Chapter 2, therefore, focuses on the so-called five fundamentals, which consist of biblical inspiration, Christ's divinity, the virgin birth, substitutionary atonement, and Christ's literal resurrection and second coming, and examines these doctrines as they were commonly taught by conservative black clergy and religious leaders. In terms of the positive affirmations attending the basic "fundamental" theological propositions, conservative African Americans very much resembled white fundamentalists. For both, the Bible represented the inerrant words of God Almighty, and Christ was as fully divine as he was fully human—he was literally born of a virgin, his bloodshed was necessary to effect the forgiveness of humanity's sins, and he physically arose from the grave in anticipation of a literal future second advent. The doctrinal formulations, the accompanying argumentation, and the common appeal to solidarity with both biblical and church-historical sources demonstrated substantial similarity between members of different races who sought to champion the fundamentals.

But even possessing a supernaturalist/biblicist worldview and also embracing the core "fundamental" doctrines fail to fully encapsulate the fundamentalist perspective. These commitments might be sufficient to make one a theological conservative, but perhaps not a fundamentalist. Characterized not only by what it affirmed but also what it opposed, historic Protestant fundamentalism entailed an overt resistance and explicit opposition to the rising modernist theology in early twentieth-century churches and denominations. The most famed modernist preacher of the era, Harry Emerson Fosdick, drew this distinction: "We should not identify the Fundamentalists with the conservatives. All fundamentalists are conservatives, but not all conservatives are Fundamentalists. The best conservatives can often give lessons to the liberals in true liberality of spirit, but the Fundamentalist program is essentially illiberal and intolerant."[45] The fundamentalist posture of overt polemical opposition to modernism, which Fosdick characterized as "essentially illiberal and intolerant," constitutes the focus of chapter 3. Even more pointedly, the chapter deals with African American clergymen's polemical repudiations of modernism from the pulpit—a location that (along with its associated ecclesiastical office) holds a place of special authority and influence in both the Protestant tradition in general and the African American Protestant tradition in particular. While chapter 2 notes the many similarities between blacks and whites in formulating and arguing for the fundamental doctrines, chapter 3 goes even further, examining not only the congruence in antimodernist polemics across racial lines but also the significantly different applications that African American preachers drew from these same pro-fundamentalist and antimodernist positions. In some cases, black fundamentalist preachers launched immediately from their fundamentalist doctrines or polemics into social considerations—the need to subvert Jim Crow, the promise of black racial advancement through religion, the promotion of interracial marriage—which would likely have been inconceivable to many of their white counterparts. Thus chapter 3 continues the argument from previous chapters that certain African Americans could rightly be considered fundamentalists on the basis of both their positive doctrinal affirmations and negative polemical repudiations, but it also shows that the expression and application of that fundamentalist faith could differ enormously from one side of the color line to the other.

While racial context unquestionably affected the way fundamentalists understood their faith's relationship to the culture, there were nevertheless instances of confluence and cooperation across racial lines that are worth noting. Chapter 4 examines in detail one such interracial endeavor, the establishment of the American Baptist Theological Seminary (ABTS) in Nashville, Tennessee. As a school affiliated with the nation's leading black Baptist denomination (the National Baptist Convention, USA), ABTS represented National Baptists' desire to bolster the availability of conservative Baptist theological training for black ministers across the nation. Partnering with the National Baptists in this project was the white Southern Baptist Convention, which helped fund the school and shared in the control of the institution's governing bodies. The seminary's early leadership, doctrinal statements, founding documents, and early controversies testify to a pro-fundamentalist and antimodernist outlook within this institution and allowed (in some cases) for a remarkable degree of interracial cooperation on the basis of shared religious identity. ABTS is a particularly noteworthy case due to the fact that it was much more than the paternalistic exercise that one might expect in the context of the early twentieth-century South. In fact, although white Baptists obviously exercised much influence, the seminary project was designed for African Americans to maintain primary control over the institution by holding majorities among the governing bodies, the faculty, and the administration. The first few decades of ABTS's existence testify to both the unifying power of a common religious confession as well as the tragic dividing walls erected by a culture of Jim Crow, which even a shared commitment to "the faith once delivered" could not breach.

Chapter 5, in turn, examines another aspect of fundamentalist identity as it came to be expressed and experienced in the African American context—the contested relationship between fundamentalism and Americanism. The chapter serves to highlight some of the divisions *within* the black community over this brand of religion, as pro- and anti-fundamentalist forces maneuvered on the rhetorical battlefield of American identity to cast fundamentalism as either supportive of or injurious to various American ideals (and hence blacks' full participation in the American experiment). In this context, fundamentalism was treated not only as a religious issue, but also as a racial and political issue. Both sides admittedly sought to attain for African Americans the full extent of American citizenship and the rights and privileges thereof, but they vociferously disagreed as to whether fundamentalist religion and identity constituted a help or a hindrance in such a quest. But even as opponents attempted to portray fundamentalism as an albatross around the neck of the race, fundamentalists within the black community sought to weave together these various elements of their identity—as black, as fundamentalists, and as true Americans—in ways that were unique and particular to their cultural experiences in their time and place, as African Americans living under the threateningly watchful eye of Jim Crow.

Thus the progression of the chapters points to the dual reality facing black fundamentalists in the interwar years. On the one hand, they embraced and propounded fundamentalist doctrines, arguments, and polemics, even to the point that some African Americans explicitly donned the controversial mantle of fundamentalism for themselves. Yet on the other hand, their place in American culture as a whole was subject to the overarching white supremacy of Jim Crow, and as a result the actions, attitudes, and activism that stemmed from their religious convictions took on a very different cast from that of their white counterparts. The task of applying their theological convictions to the most pressing issues facing their community entailed that issues of racial justice and equality took a level of precedence unfamiliar to white fundamentalists, and the institutionalized racial prejudice of the Jim Crow era led black fundamentalists to eschew strict ecclesiastical separatism. And even when the lines of strict racial distinction were momentarily blurred by a common religious confession, as in the ABTS project, the strictures of American society drastically circumscribed the boundaries of interracial cooperation, because the single most defining characteristic of any black person in the eyes of the dominant white society remained his or her race. Due to the tensions that arose from these two intersecting realities—the theological reality of their fundamentalist religion and the social reality of the second-class citizenship imposed upon them by Jim Crow—black fundamentalists remained largely ignored by their white counterparts and, until recently, also by historians. The pages that follow seek both to examine this tension and to understand these people on their own terms, thereby offering another level of complexity and variety to the experiences of African American religionists in the twentieth century and suggesting an American Protestant fundamentalism united in essential doctrinal attitudes but variegated in its hues of social action, cultural application, and activist fervor.

1

"Filled to Overflowing"

Black Weeklies and the Fundamentalist Presence

In the weeks leading up to the July 1925 trial of John Scopes in Dayton, Tennessee, the topic of fundamentalist Christianity was much on the mind of the American public. The trial, centering on John Scopes's teaching evolution in a public school in violation of Tennessee state law, drew national attention from across the ideological spectrum, ranging from fundamentalist giant William Bell Riley to famed cultural critic H. L. Mencken. Just as the trial ultimately functioned as a referendum on fundamentalist Protestantism itself, so the summer of 1925 represented an opportunity for religionists across the country to reflect on the merits of the fundamentalist perspective and to assess their relationship to it. Into this charged cultural context, less than a month before the proceedings began—on Saturday, June 13, 1925—the editorial page of the *Norfolk Journal and Guide*, a historically black newspaper based in Norfolk, Virginia, published a column lauding "fundamentalism" as a significant element of African American faith and practice. Having made clear his thesis by titling the column "Our Group Are Fundamentalists in Religion" and confident in his proclamation that "Afro-Americans are fundamentalists, for the most part," the Norfolk editorialist concluded his piece with the assertion that "Yes, the Afro-American people are Fundamentalists, and they can give a reason for the faith that is in them by pointing to what they have become in this free Nation from what they began in the days of the Colonies."[1]

More than simply a declaration regarding the perceived religious conservatism within the African American culture of the day, this editorial drew an explicit connection between the purported fundamentalist proclivities of the black populace and the issue of racial advancement in the legal, social, and political realms. Religious fundamentalism and racial identity, it implied, were intimately intertwined within the African American community in 1925; both were indivisibly linked by the longsuffering quest for freedom that united black Americans across the centuries-long sweep of American history. Yet this editorialist's claim that African Americans were "for the most part" fundamentalists represents a perspective that has, with a handful of welcome exceptions, received far too little scholarly attention.[2]

Theologically speaking, American Protestant fundamentalism was marked from its very beginning by its opposition to the emerging theological modernism of the early twentieth century. Modernist theology typically aimed to bring Christianity into line with the most current patterns of rationalist thought, embracing higher-critical methods of biblical scholarship and often eschewing supernaturalist biblical interpretations that rested on the reliability or historicity of the miraculous events narrated in the text. For example, in his famous lectures from 1899 and 1900 on the nature of Christianity, renowned German liberal scholar Adolf Harnack argued that Christianity's true "Easter faith" was not dependent on the uncertain historical claims of the apostles' original "Easter message" of physical resurrection: "Either we must decide to rest our belief on a foundation unstable and always exposed to fresh doubts, or else we must abandon this foundation altogether, and with it the miraculous appeal to our senses."[3] Such modernist attitudes engendered fiery reactions from religious conservatives—both white and black—who undertook to defend the doctrines that they considered to be the "fundamentals" of the faith. Nevertheless, historical scholarship has often associated fundamentalism with certain cultural and social forms that tend toward excluding African Americans. George Marsden's formulation of fundamentalism as a militant opposition to both theological modernism and "the cultural change associated with it" lends itself to emphasizing protracted cultural battles of a conservative and reactionary nature—most notably on issues such as evolutionary theory and public school curricula—waged by high-profile fundamentalist leaders and their institutional networks.[4] The ubiquity of Jim Crow, as well as the overtly segregationist and racist positions of certain towering fundamentalist leaders such as J. Frank Norris, meant that many highly visible fundamentalist institutions emerged from a basically white social context empowered by American segregation.[5] As a result, fundamentalism also often carries with it an association with the white racial politics of segregation, and therefore, in Marsden's words, "'fundamentalist' has seldom been a self-designation" for black Americans.⁶

In contrast to that assessment, the Norfolk editorialist's argument during the weeks leading up to the infamous Scopes trial that black Americans were "for the most part" fundamentalists—even if we account for the likely hyperbole in that statement—offers an interesting historical counterpoint. In fact, amid the vicissitudes of the fundamentalist-modernist controversy, debates and discussions about fundamentalism were prevalent in the black press. This was true not only of explicitly religious or denominational papers, such as the *Star of Zion* or the *National Baptist Union-Review*, but even of "secular" black weeklies such as the *Norfolk Journal and Guide*, the *Afro-American*, the *Chicago Defender*, the *New York Amsterdam News*, and many others.⁷ An examination of these black weekly newspapers helps to show that the perception of fundamentalism as a significant internal expression of black religiosity was not limited merely to one editorialist in Virginia; on the contrary, many voices in the black press, on both sides of the debate, considered fundamentalism to be (for good or for ill) a widespread phenomenon within the black Protestant community. Such discourse demonstrates that there were numerous black Protestants who overtly embraced an expressly fundamentalist identity amidst the heat of the fundamentalist-modernist controversy.

Since black newspapers were both shapers of public opinion and instruments for cultivating a shared culture, the discourses revealed in their pages can yield instructive insight into the perceptions of race, religion, and fundamentalism within the wider African American community. While localized papers certainly played a part in this process, so too did the growth of a national press. With the population mobility brought on by the Great Migration in the early twentieth century, the national circulation of several popular black weeklies also expanded, meaning that the conversations and ideas advanced in the pages of, for example, the *Chicago Defender* or the *Afro-American* often reached well beyond the newspapers' local or regional settings.⁸ The disputes over fundamentalism in the black weeklies of this era not only demonstrate that partisans on both sides of the issue understood "fundamentalist" to be a meaningful analytical category for *black* religious expression, but also illuminate some of the broad elements associated with these black fundamentalists' worldviews. Writers in the weeklies regularly associated a common array of characteristics with fundamentalist religious expression—including, as one might expect, such conservative theological bellwethers as supernaturalism, divine creation, and biblicism. Moreover, the pages of the black weeklies also tackled issues of racism, segregation, and social oppression in the context of their debates over fundamentalism, revealing racial considerations that undoubtedly influenced both pro- and antifundamentalist writers. The testimony of these black newspapers, then, demonstrates not only a robust debate *about* fundamentalism, but also a debate whose terms assumed that a substantial "black fundamentalist" presence within the community was a basic fact of life.

## "They Are Everywhere and in Everything"

The *Journal and Guide*'s editorial declaring the race to be "for the most part" fundamentalists was by no means alone in presenting fundamentalism as either widespread within or characteristic of the black community, though the scope of its claim to encompass nearly the whole of "the Afro-American people" was undeniably ambitious, if not somewhat hyperbolic. Still, the pages of black weeklies testify to a sense that fundamentalism was, if perhaps not the predominant view, then at least a noteworthy religious influence among African American Christian bodies. Even as these newspapers published editorial perspectives about fundamentalism that spanned from wholehearted support to vehement vituperation, both sides implicitly (and sometimes explicitly) affirmed that this religious perspective was one that had to be reckoned with *inside* the black community.

Among those sympathetic toward the movement, some asserted a widespread devotion to Christian fundamentalism within their own particular denominational bodies. For instance, more than a year before the Scopes trial captivated the nation, a 1924 column in Wichita's *Negro Star* exhorted that "all loyal members of evangelical churches and especially the Missionary Baptist Church watch close the insinuating forward movement of modernism in its attacks on many of the fundamentals of Christianity and combat such movement whenever detected by a more close adherence to The Church." In the eyes of this columnist, theological modernism was no mere distant threat, nor was it a problem circumscribed to white churches, but rather it represented an "insinuating" adversary to all loyal gospel-loving churches—a looming, steadily advancing peril whose assaults on the Christian fundamentals not only required Christians to maintain a watchful eye and a vigilant mind, but also demanded an active and combative rebuke. Missionary Baptist Churches were singled out as particularly concerned with "the fundamentals of Christianity" and "the Old Time methods of repentance, regeneration, and absolute compliance to the every command of The Christ."[9] It is worth noting that the fundamentalism in view here, identified by the editorialist as the proper remedy to modernist encroachments, consisted of both theological propositions and personal conduct; the method given to combat modernism was a close personal adherence to the church and its traditional "Old Time" teachings—a category that would presumably include such doctrines as divine creation, the divinity of Christ, and biblical inspiration, which often came under fire from modernist theologians. Even the language that the editorialist employed—warning of the "insinuating forward movement" of the modernist perspective in Christian circles—offered not only an approving nod toward fundamentalism as representing traditional Christian fidelity, but also a recognition of this fundamentalist-modernist conflict as a profoundly significant issue on which black churches and denominations had to take a stand.

In similar fashion, several years later the *Atlanta Daily World* reported on Bishop Noah W. Williams's identification of the African Methodist Episcopal (AME) denomination as fundamentalist in its outlook and traditions.[10] Williams was serving in South Carolina as the presiding bishop of the AME's Seventh Episcopal District, and in this capacity he displayed a concern for black educational institutions both through his involvement with Allen University in Columbia, South Carolina, and, as reported in the *Atlanta Daily World*, through his desire to establish a new AME divinity school in this region.[11] As he lobbied for the creation of a new school, Williams argued that rigorous denominationally specific theological education was necessary because the AME's "principles, traditions, organization and fundamentalism" placed it squarely in the position "to do as much for the cause of the Master as any Christian organization in America, whether that organization be composed of white or colored people."[12] So for Williams, who himself wrote publicly in the national press about his affirmations of biblical inspiration and the literal return of Christ, the fundamentalism that he perceived to characterize the AME denomination was foundational in its positioning as a highly influential exponent of the cause of Christianity.[13] While the AME Church never explicitly identified itself as fundamentalist, and while there was certainly a wide variety of ministerial perspectives within the denomination, we can see in the doctrinal statements of various AME publications such as the *A.M.E. Shield* and *The Doctrines and Disciplines* why Williams might make such an identification on strictly theological grounds. These publications expressly affirmed numerous essential doctrinal elements of the fundamentalist worldview that constituted central battleground issues in the fundamentalist-modernist conflict, including divine creationism, biblical inspiration, the deity of Christ, substitutionary atonement, and propitiation.[14] Interestingly, in Williams's statement the typical brand of cultural militancy so often identified with fundamentalism seems to have been absent, as the denominational approach in view was directed toward internal educational improvements and a "more uniform" ministerial teaching.

Claims about widespread fundamentalist proclivities within the black community emerged in the pages of black weeklies not only from sympathetic voices, but also from vehement opponents of the movement. Among the most notable and interesting in this regard was popular labor organizer and cultural commentator Ernest Rice McKinney. Though he was the grandson of a West Virginia Baptist minister—his grandfather, Lewis Rice, reportedly even baptized Booker T. Washington—McKinney nonetheless retained a sense of skepticism toward religion in general, and a particularly overt hostility toward the brand of theologically conservative fundamentalist Christianity that he observed in the black community.[15] In a scathing 1925 article that cast Christian fundamentalism as "an obstacle to civilization to climb over and batter down," McKinney lamented that "the Negro race is filled to overflowing with these 'Fundamentalist' gentlemen. They are everywhere and in everything. They keep us poor, ignorant, and weak."[16] Revisiting the subject in his newspaper column just months later, McKinney excoriated fundamentalists as backward-gazing "imbeciles" for their rigid commitment to biblical inerrancy and their "persecution of . . . Dr. Fosdick and Prof.

Scopes." His rhetorical bite went so far as to imply that the numerous blacks who embraced the fundamentalist perspective were not really fully or authentically part of the race at all; they were "white southerners with Negro mothers [and] Negroes with white fathers."[17] Aside from the startling depiction of black fundamentalists as enemies of "the Negro race"—a topic that will warrant further discussion later—McKinney's characterization of the race as "filled to overflowing" with fundamentalists is a striking image in its own right. Such a characterization seems to echo, albeit from a polar opposite viewpoint, the Norfolk editorialist's grandiose claim that "Our Group Are Fundamentalists in Religion."

Such a sense of extensive theological fundamentalism within the black community, even if perhaps exaggerated at times for dramatic effect, was nevertheless borne out by the presence of individual black churches and individual black leaders, both clerical and otherwise, who were identified in the black press by the express use of the term "fundamentalist" or "fundamentalism." Walker's Tabernacle Baptist Church in Atlanta publicly embraced such an identity. The public announcement of their cornerstone-laying celebration in late 1932 unabashedly publicized that the principal address at this defining ceremony "will emphasize the importance of Fundamentalism in the church."[18] Significantly, the ceremony celebrating the laying of this church building's literal foundation included exposition highlighting the similarly foundational role of fundamentalist convictions in the church at large, thereby indicating the gravity and import of the topic for the clergy and laymen of Walker's Tabernacle Baptist. It is difficult not to see here a symbolic association of fundamentalism with the very bedrock of the church's foundation; just as the brick-and-mortar church building could not stand apart from its architectural foundation, so the church as a spiritual entity could not stand apart from the affirmation of the essential truths of fundamentalism.

Major leaders in the wider African American community likewise identified themselves in this manner. In one of the more intriguing self-identifications in this vein, AME pastor William David Miller termed himself a "progressive Fundamentalist" in an interview reported by the Topeka *Plaindealer*, though unfortunately he offered no further explication of that tantalizing phrase aside from his conviction of the centrality of evangelism for the church.[19] But regardless of what Miller might have intended the qualifying adjective "progressive" to signify, his forthright use of "fundamentalist" bespoke an apparent willingness to identify with the *theologically* conservative tradition widely connoted by that terminology during this era of turbulent religious conflict. Miller's career through the 1930s, pieced together through various publications, suggests that this particular fundamentalist, at least, possessed a high degree of charisma and influence. Arriving in 1908 at Wesley Chapel AME Church in Houston, Miller helped the church take on "new strength and growth," swelling membership to more than 800 during his six-year tenure.[20] In each of four assignments after Wesley Chapel, Miller was able to either oversee the completion of church buildings or substantially pay down the church's debt while also increasing congregational giving, apparently through increased attendance. His arrival at Oklahoma City's Avery Chapel AME Church in 1929 presaged rapid growth: in his eleven years at the church, Miller was able to rebuild and expand the church building, establish an old folks' home, and increase membership from 364 to 1,545—all in the midst of the Great Depression. He also held the distinction of being the only black clergyman in the state whose sermons were broadcast over the radio.[21] Clearly Miller must have exhibited significant personal charisma and magnetism in order to achieve such success in so many venues, but his avowed position as a "progressive Fundamentalist" also indicates that a great many people in the black communities in Houston, Waco, Los Angeles, and Oklahoma City were ready and willing to lend their ears (and their money) to a man overtly claiming to preach some brand of fundamentalist Christianity.

Some members of the black press found their thoughts turning to the topic of fundamentalism even apart from the exclusively ecclesiastical realm. A correspondent for the *Pittsburgh Courier* found this to be the case as he covered a graduation event at Howard University in June of 1928. He reported that the school's president, Dr. Mordecai Johnson, proudly "proclaimed his beliefs in fundamentalism" to Howard's graduating class, warning them that "religion . . . is the only thing that can give morale" and, in the reporter's words, commending "'the old-time religion' as a cure for broken morale and a panacea for present day evils."[22] The interpretive spin injected by the reporter is in this instance perhaps more revealing than the speech itself. It is unclear whether Dr. Johnson himself used the term "fundamentalism" to describe his beliefs or whether this constituted an editorial addition from the reporter; considering Johnson's educational pedigree, his connection to social gospel theologian Walter Rauschenbusch, and Harlem minister Adam Clayton Powell's characterization of Johnson as a "modern . . . and emphatically not fundamentalist" minister, in addition to the lack of explicitly quoted material in this portion of the article, the much more likely explanation is that this was an editorial insertion.[23] What is clear, however, is that while Johnson in all likelihood failed to use the term himself, the *Courier*'s reporter found the idea of "fundamentalism" sufficiently pressing on his own mind that he apparently erroneously associated Dr. Johnson's appeals to religion's utility and immediate moral significance with the fundamentalism that Ernest Rice McKinney had previously decried as "everywhere and in everything." The influence of this religious perspective, it seems, was felt beyond the pews and the pulpit.

Among the ranks of self-proclaimed black fundamentalists, few were more widely recognized and regularly heard in their day than the Henry Brothers, a nationally renowned traveling revivalist troupe. The ensemble was prominent in the early to mid-1930s, headed by the family patriarch, J. I. Henry, who was accompanied by his sons, J. L. Henry, O. D. Henry, N. G. Henry, and W. W. Henry.[24] Best known in the print media for employing a showman's flair to "put over their fundamentalism," the Henrys attracted both enormous crowds and nearly constant controversy wherever they spoke.[25] Capacity crowds of around 1,600 people turned out for their revival services in Norfolk in September 1933, and even when numbers were not precisely reported, phrases such as "packing them in" and "filled to capacity" often peppered the newspaper accounts of the Henry Brothers' revival stops. Even in death the Henrys drew massive crowds, as thousands reportedly came to pay their respects at the sudden and unexpected passing of O. D. Henry from "acute indigestion" in July 1935 following a series of revival services in Roanoke, Virginia. Such was the brothers' fame that in 1933 a Baptist pastor resolved to draw a crowd to his church on Sunday by falsely advertising that one of the Henrys would be speaking.[26] On another occasion, the brothers' notoriety put them in physical danger, as they needed a police escort in Washington, DC, after being repeatedly threatened by a group of armed men who were unhappy that "You g–d–preachers think you run this town"; the same men tried to assault the brothers outside their revival meeting the following night, sparking a near riot

Figure 1.1. A photograph of the Henry Brothers from a September 1933 edition of the *Afro-American*, reporting on the brothers' revival services in Norfolk. Used with permission from the *AFRO American Newspapers*.

in which the church members chased away the would-be assailants.[27] The Henry Brothers' popularity and renown also elicited criticism from certain ministers and members of the black press. They were painted by detractors as "religious exploiters" and "racketeers" due to their revival style, which was characterized by a great deal of ecstasy and emotion, the regular utilization of music to periodically build and ebb emotional fervor throughout the services, the collection of a "sacrificial dime" offering, regular congregational shouting, and occasional fainting spells.[28]

Beyond the particulars of their revival ministry, the family achieved a sort of celebrity status because controversial elements of their personal lives—occasionally ignominious and sometimes downright strange—regularly invaded the headlines of major black newspapers, earning them the moniker "the Headline Henrys."[29] The evangelists received a cold reception from the ministers in Boston, for instance. They were "treated as racketeers" because their lifestyle was perceived to entail "too much commercialism, unclean living, drinking, and immoral conduct." This perception among the Boston ministers was undoubtedly reinforced by the fact that the brothers traveled about in their own "custom built Peerless limousine." Owning such a luxury car served as a noteworthy status symbol among certain commercially successful black celebrity preachers of the 1920s and 1930s, a way of authenticating their celebrity ministry and reinforcing their social standing in the community; yet for their critics among the Boston clergy, the luxury vehicle represented a level of materialism unbefitting of the ministry.[30] This particular controversy remained firmly ensconced on the mundane end of the spectrum for the Henrys, however. On one occasion, Nathaniel G. Henry fell mysteriously and violently ill, leading him to accuse a local female schoolteacher of feeding him a poisoned sandwich.[31] At other times, W. W. Henry added his own series of personal indiscretions to the headlines: shortly after leaving the troupe in 1934 to accept the pastorate of Holy Trinity Baptist Church, he was arrested (and eventually found guilty) for drunkenness and destruction of property; a matter of months thereafter he was accused (and ultimately convicted) of impregnating a fifteen-year-old girl; the following year he was found to have fathered a child with an eighteen-year-old white girl—an incident that caused some of his congregants to padlock the church door in an attempt to prevent him from returning to preach, and subsequently prompted the formal revocation of his pastoral position at Holy Trinity.[32] As a group of traveling fundamentalist preachers, this family evidently attained a high level of celebrity and notoriety, as they garnered both approbation and opprobrium from the media.

Interestingly enough, the content of the Henrys' "fundamentalist" preaching was never laid out in the newspaper articles covering their revival meetings. Even as the brothers outright declared that "all of us are fundamentalists," the theological particulars of their message were routinely ignored in favor of discussion about their style and methods of working a crowd.[33] Yet it was widely understood that the Henry Brothers self-identified as fundamentalists, and they were repeatedly presented as such in the black weekly newspapers. The *Afro-American*, for instance, expressly labeled the Henrys as "Baptist Fundamentalists."[34] And as professed fundamentalists, these revival preachers received raucous welcomes and capacity crowds nearly everywhere they appeared. That type of reception for a group of itinerant revivalists demonstrates that, at the very least, large segments of the black population were *open* to hearing a purportedly fundamentalist message. This fact, combined with the black weeklies' testimony to the substantial fundamentalist sympathies within many black churches and denominational structures, suggests that Ernest Rice McKinney may not have been too far off after all when he opined that the black community was "overflowing" with fundamentalists.

## Characteristics and Connotations

Inasmuch as these newspapers offered a venue for debating the merits and value of black fundamentalist religion, they also painted the picture of a religious worldview largely consonant with that typically associated with the fundamentalist movement as a whole. Staples of this worldview included an emphasis on supernaturalism, biblical literalism, and a belief in divine creation (typically contrasted against evolutionary views), which aligned with two of George Marsden's three "most distinctive" doctrines of fundamentalism—biblicism and divine creation.[35] But despite this significant congruence, the reports and discussions in the weeklies also indicated that some African American fundamentalists tended to connect their religious convictions with issues of racial advancement, and so evinced racially distinct social concerns that differentiated them from their white conservative counterparts. So whereas a seemingly ubiquitous conservative cultural militancy characterized the institutionally driven white "fighting fundamentalists," African American fundamentalists were more hesitant to make such culturally conservative battles (even on issues about which they may have agreed in principle with their white counterparts, such as evolution) their raison d'être. Yet, at least in terms of their overall religious worldview, black fundamentalists had quite a bit in common with their white brethren.

Amid discussions of fundamentalism in the pages of black newspapers, the rather ambiguous terminology of "old-time religion" was apt to appear with relative frequency, usually without explicit definition. However, the surrounding context typically indicated that the authors or the speakers being quoted used it to refer to at least two general religious views: a firm continuity with the religious traditions of the past and an emphasis on the supernatural aspects of religion. Both of these positions set the fundamentalist worldview in opposition to that of modernism, which embraced religious innovation and a generally naturalistic (as opposed to supernaturalistic) approach to the world. The terminology of "old-time religion" was employed in this way in order to portray a movement tied to past tradition and essentially supernaturalist in character—though, of course, the value judgments surrounding such identifications varied widely based on the author's perspective.

The manifestation of supernatural elements in the natural world was an oft-implied connotation of "old-time religion," especially in the context of revivalism and the Christian's struggle against the sin and evil evident in the modern world. The Henry Brothers' gatherings, for example, were twice referred to as "old-time revival" services in a 1933 issue of the *Afro-American* in the context of their stated desire to "wipe out sin and conquer the devil."[36] The supernaturalism of this sort of "old-time religion" entailed not only the purposeful working of God in his creation, but also the nefarious and malevolent presence of an evil spiritual power—the devil—intent on leading men into sinful behavior. The Henrys' equation of "wiping out sin" with "conquering the devil" indicates the degree to which the immoral and sinful *actions* of men in the natural world—actions necessitating endless revivals and calls for moral reform, spearheaded by professional revivalists like the Henry Brothers themselves—were tied to the idea of a supernatural tempter who was at the root of the natural sinful actions of humanity.

The supernaturalism of "old-time religion," however, did not exclusively or necessarily entail explicit recognition of evil spiritual powers in the world; often it was connected simply with the possibility of God intervening in society or in the lives of individuals. In an instance of a somewhat more theologically specific belief in supernatural intervention, a Wichita writer for the *Negro Star* insisted in 1924 that the Missionary Baptist Church's ability to combat modernism rested on "a hurried beating back to the path of the Fathers and the Old Time methods of repentance, regeneration, and absolute compliance to the every command of The Christ." This author's explicit recognition of "regeneration"—an expressly miraculous work of the Holy Spirit to turn the heart of an individual away from his or her sin and toward Christ—as an essential piece of the "Old Time" religion, as well as his identification of the need for "a fully consecrated ministry prepared in heart by the Holy Spirit," clearly testifies to the supernaturalism that was in view when the term "old-time religion" was applied to the question of fundamentalism versus modernism. Not only might the devil be constantly on the prowl, as the Henrys preached, but God the Holy Spirit was also considered to be actively and intimately at work in the world. Only those Christian leaders "prepared in heart by the Holy Spirit" represented the hope of the black church to rebuff modernism's assault on the Christian "fundamentals" and repudiate the modernists' faithless embrace of such naturalistic ideas as "high criticism of accepted biblical truths." Indeed, the specific and personal supernatural work of the third person of the Trinity himself, evidenced by the church and its Spirit-led ministers "beating back" to the old-time religious doctrines, was here presented as the only means to "combat" the "insinuating forward movement of modernism in its attacks upon many of the fundamentals of Christianity."[37]

It is also notable that the Wichita editorialist's language and arguments demonstrated remarkable alignment with the sentiments being concurrently expressed by white fundamentalists. Less than two months after the publication of this *Negro Star* editorial, the fundamentalist contingent of the Northern Baptist Convention (a predominantly white denomination) sent a letter to their convention pressing for the denomination to adopt a stringently conservative statement of faith. The similarity in language between the January 1924 editorial and the March 1924 letter reveal a commonality of concerns between fundamentalist partisans across racial lines. Whereas the Wichita editorialist warned about the "insinuating forward movement of modernism," the Northern Baptist fundamentalists sounded the alarm about "the subtle and disastrous inroads of modernism"; while the *Negro Star* writer urged "a hurried beating back to the path of the Fathers," the white Baptists pressed the need "to restate, re-emphasize, and reaffirm the historic faith of Baptists"; and just as the Wichita author highlighted the necessity of "regeneration" and "a fully consecrated ministry prepared in heart by the Holy Spirit" to combat the modernist threat, the Northern Baptists likewise argued that this task centrally involved not only doctrinal principles such as biblical inerrancy and Christ's deity, but also a recognition of "the power and sufficiency of the gospel to produce under the operation of the Holy Spirit that regeneration necessary to the salvation and to the spiritual life of our fellow-men."[38] For pro-fundamentalist contingents on both sides of the color line, the supernatural intervention of the Holy Spirit—operating in both the regeneration of individual hearts and the spiritual maturation of the church as a whole—stood as a significant bulwark in their resistance to modernist incursions. In this respect, the supernaturalism that newspaper articles like the *Negro Star* editorial evoked by associating fundamentalism with "old time" religion, including doctrines such as supernatural regeneration, reflected wider currents of fundamentalist thought that stretched across denominational (and even racial) lines.

Similar sentiments found expression in other African American denominational contexts as well. James M. Nabrit, a National Baptist and the fourth president of the American Baptist Theological Seminary, overtly warned against "liberalism in religion" as one of the greatest "foes" facing black ministers due to liberals' rejection of "old-fashioned regeneration and spiritual power" in favor of naturalistic ideas of "morality, human goodness and mere culture."[39] The old-time religion once again was linked with both an explicit rejection of modernist theology and an express embrace of such supernaturalistic concepts as the regenerating work of the Holy Spirit. This work of the Spirit was connected in turn with the idea of a type of "spiritual power" that lay well beyond the reach of modernists and liberals. Combatting the modernist threat, it seemed, entailed a direct reliance on the supernatural power of the triune God—an idea encapsulated in the appellation of "old-time" or "old-fashioned" religion.

Even the disparaging comments of modernists and religious skeptics pertaining to fundamentalism's "age-old fetishes" and its stark opposition to modern science indicate that the "old-time religion" was characterized by a belief in the penetration of the supernatural realm into the natural world. In 1930 the *New York Amsterdam News* saw fit to inform its black readers of a mass meeting featuring an assortment of white speakers, but held by the black Hubert Harrison Memorial Church, intended to advance the position that the tenets of "fundamentalism," "orthodox Christianity," and "the old-time religion" (all three terms seemingly used interchangeably) were outdated and antithetical to the modern world. "The spiritual, 'Old-Time Religion' is a delightful song," one Unitarian minister at this meeting argued, "but the idea is intellectually fallacious. Why should a religion that was good enough for Moses be good enough for us?" The teachings of the fundamentalists, he argued, brooked "no reconciliation [with] the known facts of science," and all the speakers agreed that Christianity must rid itself of its "age-old fetishes" in favor of the "freedom and recognition of science."[40] From this point of view, the "Old-Time Religion" of the fundamentalist was irreconcilably at odds with modernity because it entailed supernaturalist presuppositions that necessarily conflicted with modern science, thus relegating old-time religious fundamentalism to the realm of mere superstitious fetishism.

In addition to connoting a broadly supernaturalist worldview, the "old-time religion" label was also at times applied to black fundamentalism as a means of conveying a perceived continuity with religious traditions of the past. For one AME minister, Bishop Heard, it entailed doctrinal faithfulness to the historical beliefs of the AME Church and by association also to the racial heritage represented by the denomination's revered founder—renowned preacher, uncompromising abolitionist, bold political activist, and lifelong racial justice advocate Richard Allen.[41] The *Atlanta Daily World* reported that the bishop "made a plea for the church to make a return to fundamentalism as laid down by the founder, Richard Allen, in other words return to the 'old time religion.'" Just as this report seems to indicate that Heard himself associated his fundamentalism with a harkening back to historical tradition, so the *Daily World*'s reporter associated Heard in much more opprobrious terms with "obsolete ideas" and a dangerously backward-looking intolerance for new doctrines that were being "laid down by young men."[42] Though the relative value ascribed to such a backward-gazing position differed radically from Bishop Heard to his *Daily World* critic, it is notable that both men recognized continuity with historical tradition to be essential to Heard's promotion of "old time" fundamentalist religion. Similarly, a short 1925 column in the *Cleveland Gazette* lamented the lack of "middle-ground" in the fundamentalist-modernist controversy; in doing so, the *Gazette* painted fundamentalism as, among other things, "old-timeism," which was seen as "conservative" and "reactionary" and clearly presented fundamentalists, whether white or black, as people tied to—and usually actively looking to—the past.[43] Such an orientation of looking for continuity with past church tradition as a justification for their current theological convictions was often shared by both black and white fundamentalists in their defenses of what they understood to be the long, historically orthodox faith tradition that subsisted through all ages—what the Epistle of Jude termed "the faith once delivered to the saints."

The broad supernaturalism and traditionalism associated with the appellation of "old-time religion" carried along other particular theological associations as well. Among such common traits ascribed to African American fundamentalists, noted and attested by partisans from both sides of the fundamentalist-modernist conflict, was the conviction that the Bible, as the inspired word of God, ought to be interpreted "literally."[44] Unsurprisingly, a propensity for anti-evolutionism also stemmed from the literal understanding of the universe's divine creation as described in the opening chapters of Genesis.[45] Literalism, belief in special divine creation, and anti-evolution attitudes thus all hung together as a major component of the black fundamentalist worldview as it was presented in the black weeklies.

Perhaps the most intriguing example of the widespread association of fundamentalism with biblical inerrancy and biblical literalism in the black community appeared not in the form of a hard-hitting news report, a golden-tongued soliloquy, or a high-minded public disputation. Instead, it came as a tiny question-and-answer tucked away deep within the children's section of the October 8, 1927, *Chicago Defender*. The weekly *Defender Junior* featured a regular segment of simple trivia questions for kids to answer. This particular edition offered such questions as "What is the 'initial sack' in baseball?" and "What is the official abbreviation for Colorado?" It also included the question "In religion, what is the essence of fundamentalism?" The answer, provided at the bottom of the page, was "the literal interpretation of the Bible."[46] The identification of biblical literalism with the "essence" of Christian fundamentalism, without any racial qualifiers attached, speaks to the pride of place that this conviction held as an identifying mark for fundamentalists, black or white. That disputations over the nature of the Bible were central to the fundamentalist mindset is, of course, no grand revelation. More interesting and notable is the relatively unusual context in which this assertion appeared. The fact that the *Defender* (itself no bastion of religious fundamentalism, by any means) utilized this topic as a part of its *children's* trivia game illustrates the universal, indeed almost elementary, nature of this information in the minds of the newspaper's editors. Whether or not the *Defender's* young African American readers around the country knew anything else of the particulars or the nuances of the fundamentalist-modernist controversy, they were presumably expected to know that biblical literalism constituted the "essence" of religious fundamentalism just as they should easily know that first base was the "initial sack" in baseball.

Just a week after the *Defender* printed the trivia question in its children's section, the paper published a column by George A. Singleton entitled "Religion Worth Having," lamenting that the black man's fundamentalist religion, as a mere "hand-me-down . . . from the American white man," was not fitting for the race: "The form of Christianity as worshiped instead of practiced by the gloriously orthodox and the manifestly fundamentalists is not the type which has abidingness. The Negro group needs religious leaders who will extricate them from the meshes of a crass superstition, literalism and formalism."[47] Chastising black fundamentalists not only for the "crass superstition" of their supernaturalism but also for their devotion to biblical literalism, Singleton identified these two major components of fundamentalism as snares entangling the race. Also worth noting is Singleton's overarching theme that black religion ought to be deliberately geared toward advancing racial interests—a quality that he considered to be lacking in black fundamentalism and black Christianity more generally. Yet as we will see later on, this idea that religion could be a useful avenue for seeking racial advancement was by no means absent among pro-fundamentalist African American voices.[48]

Lest we are tempted to conclude that biblical literalism was merely a stereotyped charge leveled at fundamentalists by their less-than-sympathetic contemporaries, we should note that the weeklies also testified that African American proponents of fundamentalism were pleased to claim biblical inerrancy and biblical literalism as badges of distinction. Take for example Lacey Kirk Williams, the president of the National Baptist Convention (NBC), USA, who in an address to the 1928 Baptist Ministers' Conference in Washington, DC, undertook "an affirmation of fundamentalism." In so doing, Williams raised two points of doctrine in particular: the deity of Christ and the "belief in a literal interpretation of the [N]ew [T]estament," including Jesus's virgin birth and works of miraculous power.[49] Nor was Williams new to this particular battle. Three years prior, he had taken to the floor of the NBC's September 1925 annual meeting to deliver his presidential address, mere weeks after the furor surrounding fundamentalism and evolution had captivated the nation during John Scopes's trial. Given the summer's events in Dayton, Williams felt obliged to adjudicate the hot-button topic of the fundamentalist-modernist controversy. "The differentiation," he proclaimed to the convention, "between the Modernists and the Fundamentalists has been very clearly and fairly drawn, and ... I believe that we should take our stand with those who believe in the full, sufficient authority of the Scriptures in matters of religion."[50] The fact that Williams made such arguments while in a position of great authority in one of the most prominent African American denominations of the day reflects the gravity and the centrality of biblical inerrancy and biblical literalism among black fundamentalists; this issue was evidently no less central to them than it was to their white counterparts.[51]

Moreover, black weeklies also testified that the emphasis on biblical literalism and divine creation, particularly as such literal interpretation affected their exegesis of the creation narrative in Genesis 1–3, brought the fundamentalist perspective ineluctably into conflict with the rising tide of evolutionary thought.[52] Floyd J. Calvin, writing in the *Pittsburgh*

*Courier* on the occasion of William Jennings Bryan's death in 1925, lauded the text of Bryan's final (undelivered) speech as "a clear exposition of the case against evolution and the cardinal principles of the Fundamentalists' creed." Keeping in mind Bryan's role as a prosecutor in the recently concluded Scopes trial, Calvin proceeded: "Thousands refuse to believe that man is descended from an ape, and we are one of them. As for the whole fight between science and the Bible, we stand with the Commoner and the Bible."[53] Calvin's anti-evolutionism was thus erected, as he saw it, on the foundation of the Bible—and presumably, given his affirmation of William Jennings Bryan's fundamentalist argumentation, this foundation also entailed the necessity of a literal interpretation of the Bible's inerrant words in the early chapters of Genesis.

Of course, such rejections of evolutionary theory on the basis of a literalist hermeneutic attracted critical rejoinders geared toward reproving both biblical literalism and fundamentalism per se. While historian Mary Beth Swetnam Mathews has observed that black Baptist and Methodist denominational papers "did not tie the antievolution effort to the fundamentalists in their discourse," nonreligious black publications displayed no such reservation.[54] The very same edition of the *Pittsburgh Courier* that carried Floyd Calvin's praise of William Jennings Bryan also included an article from the other end of the ideological spectrum, rebuking the fundamentalists on this very score. "Fundamentalists insist that God created man at one-stroke," the author wrote, "but how can they explain the fact that man was once as hairy and Simian in appearance as an ape?" Fundamentalists had evidently earned this rebuke by choosing to "stand by the Adam and Eve story," which was a "Bible story [that] has no facts to support it, while the Evolutionary theory has." In direct contravention of the fundamentalist appeal to the Genesis creation narrative and the divine inspiration of scripture, this particular editorial posited to the contrary that "God chose to write the story of creation on the face of the whole earth instead of on the printed page."[55]

The very same month, an article in the *Afro-American* took aim at William Jennings Bryan's outlook in the Scopes trial, criticizing the trial itself, as well as fundamentalism more generally, as simply "phases of the age-long conflict between science and religion," noting that the same Bible that fundamentalists invoked in opposition to evolutionary theory also "teaches us that the sun moves [around the earth]" while "science claims that the earth moves [around the sun]."[56] Such argumentation, taking aim at the biblical literalism that underpinned fundamentalists' opposition to evolutionary theory, has echoes of another article published the year prior to Bryan's death in the *Journal and Guide*, derisively comparing Bryan and other anti-evolution fundamentalists to Don Quixote—"church leaders whose bodies live in the 20th century, but whose minds are still in the 15th century." The author proceeded to preempt the fundamentalists' appeal to their "inspired" Bible by declaring that in reality "every stratum of the earth crust is a vast lead in the 'inspired book' of Evolution."[57] Clearly biblical literalism and inspiration—manifested most concretely in what one critic panned as "the ridiculousness of the literal interpretation of the early chapters of Genesis"—were recognized by both friends and foes to be at the heart of the anti-evolution attitude common among the fundamentalists, including those advancing such attitudes from within the black community.[58]

At the same time, however, African American fundamentalists do not seem to have been as prone to the brand of cultural militancy that characterized the white fundamentalists who have garnered the vast majority of scholarly attention. White standard-bearers such as J. Frank Norris or William Bell Riley elicited the stereotypical image of the "fighting fundamentalist" by their willingness to engage in protracted cultural battles over whether evolution should be taught in public schools, while black fundamentalists hesitated to do so. One reason that historian David Harrington Watt, for instance, excludes blacks from his analysis of the fundamentalist movement is that "few African Americans threw themselves fully into fundamentalists' campaign to keep evolution from being taught in the nation's public schools."[59] Likewise historian Jeffrey Moran has identified "white fundamentalists' emphasis on aggressive cultural battles" as a dividing line.[60] While we have seen that numerous African Americans *did* in fact identify as fundamentalists, and while newspaper pundits on both sides likewise identified a substantial fundamentalist presence in the black community, a common commitment to the basic religious tenets of fundamentalism (or even more specific doctrinal definitions) did not necessarily dictate identical types of political and social involvement.

In the context of the Jim Crow era, amidst radical abuse and widespread racial oppression—and in a segregated society that automatically defined black individuals first and foremost by their race—it should come as no surprise that black fundamentalists may have had a different social agenda than their white counterparts, an agenda geared more toward concerns of racial advancement. After all, as renowned sociologist C. Eric Lincoln has noted, the black church has historically functioned as a custodian of African American identity, constituting "in a real sense a universal church, claiming and representing all Blacks out of a tradition that looks back to the time when there was *only* the Black Church to bear witness to 'who' or 'what' a black man was."[61] So while black fundamentalists in the interwar period certainly encountered theological conflicts with other segments of the black Christian community, they also applied their fundamentalism and directed their cultural energies to addressing the common issues of racial oppression and inequality that faced the black community as a whole.

At times, fundamentalist voices construed racial progress as actually being a primary motivator *driving* religious decisions and religious activity. Contrary to the idea advanced by the likes of Ernest Rice McKinney and George Singleton that fundamentalism was antithetical to racial progress, some fundamentalists presented their theological conservatism as a clear means of advancing specifically racial interests. Consider once again the *Norfolk Journal and Guide*'s 1925 editorial "Our Group Are Fundamentalists in Religion." This column grounded the continuation of racial progress on the "simple faith" that could help achieve that end: "It has brought us thus far, and the belief is general that it is sufficient to carry us further. . . . We have seen so many radical changes to our advantage in the gradual evolution of the past half century, and we are seeing so much of the like sort from day to day that we see no good and sufficient reason to waver in the Faith." One cannot help but wonder whether the editorialist would have condoned "wavering" in the faith if the "radical changes to our advantage" that he evidently observed in day-to-day life had begun to slow or cease altogether. In this arrangement racial progress was given a pride of place such that racial considerations were intimately and inextricably tied to religious identity. Continuing in this vein, the editorial concluded with the sentiment that black fundamentalists "can give a reason for the hope that is in them by pointing to what they have become in this free Nation from what they began in the days of the Colonies." Racial progress was here again linked explicitly to religious identification. Notably, the editorialist also obliquely lent credence to the idea that black fundamentalists' time and energy was by necessity devoted more to issues of race than to anything else; the race's tendency to resist the "new paths" that cast doubt on "the Bible as our sufficient guide," and the tendency to more generally avoid speculation on issues of religious modernism, in the eyes of the editorialist, "may be due in large measure to the fact that we have so many other problems to contend with that absorb our time and dominate our thoughts."[62] So we see here not only evidence of racial advancement being rhetorically connected to religious fidelity, but also an indication that black fundamentalists consciously acknowledged the need to devote their mental and social energy to addressing racial concerns rather than to more stereotypically fundamentalist issues like cultural battles over evolutionary curricula in the public schools.

African American fundamentalists were also shown at times as leveraging their religious identities for racial ends. Such was the case with the aforementioned L. K. Williams, president of the NBC, USA, from 1922 until his death in 1940. In February 1928 several black weeklies published a report on Williams's attendance at a Baptist ministers' conference in Washington, DC, at which Williams addressed issues of theology, the church's social responsibility, and racial interests. The *Afro-American* made no secret of its evaluation of his theological stance; atop the story's third paragraph, which began summarizing Williams' conference address, the paper inserted a very straightforward subheading: "Fundamentalist." Inasmuch as the speech focused on theological issues, it was "an expression of Baptist doctrines and an affirmation of fundamentalism." As noted previously, Williams's "fundamentalist" emphases in this address included his affirmation of "a literal interpretation" of the Bible, as well as his belief in the divinity of Jesus, the virgin birth, and the literal reality of Jesus's miraculous resurrection of Lazarus (John 11). Williams also lauded the superiority of Baptist church structure, which gave individual churches the freedom to do "whatever there is that ought to be done for the community for which the church exists." He enjoined that all such needs within a community ought to fall "under the tutelage, management and control of the church," and in turn every church "ought to form a program to cover the entire complex needs of its membership." Regarding the specific need to press for the social interests of the black community as a whole, Williams opined that black Baptists possessed "a larger opportunity" as well as "a larger responsibility" than other groups—a responsibility that motivated Williams to travel across America "to promote the interests of the Negro race through the Baptist denomination."[63]

Williams's comments in 1928 closely echoed those he made in his NBC presidential address three years prior, in which he had likewise joined affirmations of fundamentalism and condemnations of modernism together with a sense of the Baptist church's preeminence and an exhortation that the black church must actively press for social and political gains.[64] In both cases, Williams was seen as commingling his fundamentalist theological convictions with his love for Baptist church polity, all while keeping an eye on the need, in the words of the *Afro-American*'s 1928 report, "to promote the interests of the Negro race" by virtue of his religious position. Similarly, Williams was closely involved with the effort to establish, in cooperation with the white Southern Baptist Convention, a black Baptist seminary in Nashville; at the dedication of the school's first building, he sincerely thanked his Southern Baptist brethren for their assistance while simultaneously explaining that their people's debt to the black race had not yet been fully paid.[65] Williams's activity offers another example of black fundamentalists linking religious identity and racial advancement in ways that their white counterparts would not have conceived. Such a perspective was a product not only of racial pride and solidarity on the part of African American fundamentalists but also of the ubiquitous racial prejudice and discrimination that they faced on a daily basis, emanating from the white supremacist social structures of early twentieth-century America and institutionalized most visibly in the legal edicts of Jim Crow.

In addition to this connection to the general ethos of racial advancement, two other common perceptions, which were at times voiced in the pages of the black weeklies, may have also played some role in the apparent disjunction between white fundamentalists' brand of conservative cultural activism and black fundamentalists' focus on issues of racial import. The first of these was an association of fundamentalism with white southerners, thus linking their battles for cultural conservatism with the concepts of racism and white supremacy. This connection was propounded with some regularity in the black weeklies throughout the

1920s and 1930s, which may help to further explain black fundamentalists' tendency to apply their religion to racial issues (in contrast to the other cultural concerns driving their white fundamentalist counterparts). Voices in the black press, for instance, would at times link fundamentalist religion per se with southern racial violence and intolerance in particular, even going so far as to conjoin considerations of fundamentalism with the practices of the Ku Klux Klan.[66] In 1926 the *Pittsburgh Courier* reflected on a recent outbreak of racial violence in Texas by proclaiming that Texas "has always been the perfect paradise for the fundamentalist and barbarian." Another article in the same edition of the *Courier* held up Georgia as the quintessence of "arrogant bigotry," full of people "obsessed with Fundamentalism, Ku Kluxism, and colorphobia."[67] A piece in the *Afro-American* a year earlier, penned by famous Howard University dean Kelly Miller, had identified the Ku Klux Klan as "composed mainly of Fundamentalists."[68] At roughly the same time, soon after the Scopes verdict, an editorial in the *Crisis*, published by the National Association for the Advancement of Colored People, equated the religious fundamentalists of Dayton, Tennessee (where the Scopes trial had been held) with those "who permit lynching and make bastardy legal in order to render their race 'pure.'"[69] Drawing a similar rhetorical link between fundamentalist religion and legalized racism, newspaperman Wendell Dabney expressed joyful amazement that "a Negro who shot a white man in Georgia for stealing his chicken was cleared by a jury"; the triumph of justice in this instance signaled to Dabney that "surely Fundamentalism is about to bid 'farewell, a long farewell to all its greatness.'"[70]

Even when the fundamentalist perspective was not directly tied to the South or the Klan, it was often disparaged by opponents as being tightly intertwined with historic racism. In a rhetorical strategy that was not entirely uncommon, Ernest Rice McKinney pointed his readers back to the days of antebellum America, arguing that "it was the heterodox who destroyed slavery in America and England. The Orthodox Fundamentalists wanted slavery to continue."[71] Likewise, in 1926 a Norfolk reporter, having already expressly associated fundamentalism with religious intolerance, concluded that "intolerance and race prejudice sleep in the same bed and are all but indistinguishable."[72] At the close of the decade such religious "fundamentalism," still largely associated with conservative clerics in the South, continued to be criticized in outlets such as the *Chicago Defender* as "sectional bigotry opposed to human freedom and adult conscience."[73]

Outspoken proponents of fundamentalism within the black community were not exempt from attacks. These old-time religionists were at times accused of holding back the entire African American race. Ernest Rice McKinney, as discussed earlier, railed against the ubiquity within the black community of fundamentalists who worked to "keep us poor, ignorant and weak." For McKinney, the hope for the race rested in the idea that "some day, we will revolt [against fundamentalist clergy] and then someone will have to get another job or starve."[74] In this brief column, responsibility for the race's poverty, ignorance, and political weakness was laid largely at the feet of a single group: black fundamentalist clergy. Other writers even went so far as to identify particular religious teachings that were holding the race back. Edward Arbor, writing for the April 1935 issue of the *Crisis*, was quoted as saying that "being guided by such principles that make one love one's neighbor, turn the other cheek and 'take it to the Lord in prayer,' avails little when opposition is found in masked men with shotguns, closed factory doors, and farmland without seeds to plant." As multiple news outlets picked up this story, they noted that Arbor contended that racial progress was undermined by the "fundamentalist teachings" of some black preachers in the South who "consigned to hell" militant racial activists.[75] That such declamations awaited those who permitted (or were even perceived as permitting) their religious convictions to stand in the way of racial progress and racial solidarity might easily have served as motivation for fundamentalist black Christians to prioritize their racial struggles and racial applications of their conservative doctrine.

A second widespread perception that may have helped motivate black fundamentalists to devote more energy to progressive racial causes than conservative cultural wars was the idea prevalent among many black Christians that *true* religion required right social action, not merely right theology.[76] This theme reverberated all through the 1920s and 1930s, especially in the trendsetting, socially minded *Chicago Defender*. In December 1923, for instance, popular columnist Roscoe Simmons sardonically observed, "Maybe the Modernists and Fundamentalists arguing about creeds will stumble upon true religion. . . . They may not be much on Christianity, but they are up on theology." Simmons was convinced that upright social conduct was the essence of "true religion," which seemed beyond the theologically minded disputants, as evinced by his biting critique: "Suppose they fought sin half as hard as they fight among themselves over creed. This would be a pleasant world, would it not?" Social action, here represented as "fighting sin," took clear precedence in Simmons's mind over doctrinal disputations. He resumed the same drumbeat two weeks later, imagining that "looking down from heaven Jesus will say: 'Look at my children, fighting over faith, when they know that faith without works is as ships without water.'" Without question, social action easily trumped theological considerations in Simmons's evaluation of "true religion," as he drew upon the poetry of nineteenth-century Englishman Roden Noel to drive home his point: "What if men take to FOLLOWING where He leads, / Weary of mumbling Athanasian creeds?" Simmons continued on this track in the months that followed, drawing support for his position particularly from John 14:15: "If you love me, keep my commandments."[77]

Simmons and the *Defender* were by no means alone in promoting an emphasis on upright social action. Other figures across the spectrum—from defenders of fundamentalism to its skeptics and critics—likewise saw this as an imperative. As discussed earlier, on the fundamentalist side of things L. K. Williams, president of the NBC, determined in 1928 to travel through the country "to promote the interests of the Negro race through the Baptist denomination" *even as* he was undertaking an affirmation and defense of fundamentalism. Whereas Roscoe Simmons might have looked askance at this abiding theological emphasis, Williams saw no contradiction. His theological convictions in this context were joined closely with social action designed to advance racial interests, and his concept of upright social conduct was closely connected with explicitly racial concerns.[78]

Yet even while Williams saw social action and racial advancement as congruent with his theological fundamentalism, other ministers, such as Adam Clayton Powell Sr., pressed for racial interests from a position much more skeptical of fundamentalist proclivities. As the famous minister of Harlem's Abyssinian Baptist Church, Powell was, in the words of historian Wallace Best, "one of the earliest African American exponents of the Social Gospel" and one of Harlem's "chief exemplars of theological modernism."[79] From this position of notoriety, Powell warned in the pages of the *New York Amsterdam News* that the institutional church was collapsing due to its failure to speak out against "present day Philistines" afflicting the land: "the profit system, intolerance, selfishness, racketeering, exploitation, race hatred, mob violence, unbrotherliness, and every form of injustice." He concluded morosely that "the preachers are feeding the people on fundamentalism and religious traditions instead of telling them how to get food and fundamental human rights."[80] Where Williams saw a congruity between fundamentalist religion and racial progress, Powell saw a disjunction. Clearly Powell believed that practical solutions to social problems—namely, food and human rights—not the exposition of the theological content of "religious traditions," ought to be foundational to the church's faith and practice. Likewise J. Raymond Henderson, a Baptist minister in Atlanta, chastised the "great many folk who are gluttons for what they believe to be fundamentals" yet who possessed merely a "convenient faith" that remained aloof of politics. In reality, Henderson argued, true religion dictates that "the church cannot stay out of politics and be true to its mission."[81] True Christianity, it seemed to many in the black community, was just as dependent (if not more so) on right social conduct in the arena of racial justice as it was on creedal specifics.

At times the premium placed on racial militancy was even more obvious, as in the *Chicago Defender* piece by George A. Singleton in October 1927, which argued that African Americans needed a new type of religion: "The form of Christianity that is generally embraced by the Negro group makes them servile. The type of religion needed by the black man is militantly aggressive. . . . A religion that makes for manhood, group cohesiveness, solidarity, racial self-esteem, brotherhood, shot through with the very life of Jesus is the religion worth having."[82] The purpose of African American religion, in Singleton's mind, was to advance the interests of the race, replacing servility with racial militancy, racial solidarity, and racial self-esteem. Indeed, in the context of Jim Crow, the notion of social action on the part of the African American community almost necessarily pointed to the prospect of explicitly *racial* activism. The pervasiveness of such attitudes within the black community—especially attitudes that promoted social action for racial progress as the test of "true religion"—adds another dimension to the black fundamentalists' precar-

Figure 1.2. Reverend John L. Henry leading his congregation to sign a petition for anti-lynching legislation. Used with permission from the *AFRO American Newspapers*.

ious position. That is, their continuous experience of racial oppression, in conjunction with both their community's emphasis on social action as a mark of true religion and the potential association of fundamentalism with anti-black racism, led them to contextualize their religious convictions within the necessary and ever-pressing task of promoting the interests of the race as a whole.

A parting image may serve to reinforce the point. On March 30, 1935, the *Afro-American* printed a photograph on its front page captioned

"Churchgoers Sign Up," showing the Reverend John L. Henry, formerly of the Henry Brothers' traveling revival troupe, who had since accepted the call to become the pastor of Tenth Street Baptist Church in the nation's capital. In the photo, Henry was leading a long line of his congregants out the door of Tenth Street Church and toward a petition booth in front of the building. There the reverend and the rest of his congregation readily signed a petition in favor of the Costigan-Wagner antilynching bill.[83] While J. L. Henry had very conspicuously identified himself as a fundamentalist during his days as an itinerant revivalist, on this day he made the front page of the paper not for his preaching or for his theology but rather for his willingness to lead his congregation to jointly engage in progressive social action on behalf of the race. Henry stood ready to proclaim a brand of "fundamentalism" in his family's revival meetings, and he may well have done the same from the pulpit of Tenth Street Baptist, yet on this day this purportedly fundamentalist clergyman led his congregants to stand up and fight also for racial justice.

* * *

There is little doubt that the African American community has received far too little attention in the historiography of American Protestant fundamentalism. Indeed, the very existence of black fundamentalists has been overlooked by a good many commentators. According to the testimony of the black weekly newspapers, not only did a number of African Americans claim for themselves the "fundamentalist" label, but they also shared some notable characteristics with their white counterparts: a supernaturalist perspective, an emphatic continuity with religious traditions of the past, a belief in biblical inspiration and inerrancy, a "literalist" hermeneutic, an emphasis on divine creation, and an attitude of hostility toward evolutionary thought. Yet as we have seen, one major difference lay in the fact that the conservative brand of cultural militancy so long held to be an essential defining characteristic of fundamentalism—that is, the willingness among white fundamentalists to engage in protracted and heated cultural battles against the perceived cultural changes that accompanied modernism, such as the struggle to keep evolution out of public school curricula—was often absent (at least as a first-order concern) among conservative black Christians. Instead, for black fundamentalists the pressing racial issues facing them from all sides often meant that their social outlook centered more on the progressive politics of racial advancement than on the conservative social and political agendas of white fundamentalists. If the broadly conceived religious worldview of fundamentalism offered a degree of commonality for its adherents across racial lines, the oppressive disparities imposed on black Americans by Jim Crow racism assured that social accord was not so readily forthcoming.

2

# Formulating the Faith

*The Five Fundamentals across Racial Lines*

As the fundamentalist-modernist controversy reached its zenith in the 1920s, few people cast a longer shadow across the landscape of fundamentalism than Texas Baptist churchman J. Frank Norris, whose pugnacious ministry garnered him both fame and infamy. A figure who commanded the attention of thousands as a preacher and the publisher of the *Searchlight*, a major fundamentalist newspaper, Norris also captivated the nation as he stood trial for murder, and was ultimately acquitted, for shooting an unarmed man in his church office in 1926. If he was a larger-than-life character in some respects, Norris nevertheless reflected the sensibilities of the culture around him in many ways, not least of which was his outlook on race. He stood squarely in the southern mainstream as a proponent of Jim Crow segregation, and he was warm to the Ku Klux Klan. Like many white fundamentalist leaders, Norris considered African Americans to be simpleminded and intellectually inferior, easily led astray on matters religious, and more responsive to superstition than intellectual appeals. On one occasion, when Norris resolved to amuse himself at the expense of several black men who were working in his church, he went to great lengths to fabricate a haunting in the church in order to frighten the workers. Laughing at their obvious distress, Norris justified his action as an opportunity to "get in conversation with them about the end of the world and when they are going to be earthquaked." This was, he said, "really a righteous act to shake them up and have them forget their troubles." From the perspective of this preeminent white fundamentalist, black intellectual inferiority precluded the possibility of thoughtful or rigorous theological engagement; they just needed a good haunting to "shake them up" and get them talking about when they might be "earthquaked." For Norris and others like him, this infantilizing view meant that black people had no part in the doctrine-heavy enterprise of fundamentalism.[1]

Contrary to such racist presumptions, however, we have seen that African American observers from across the theological spectrum claimed that the black race was "for the most part" fundamentalist, was "filled to overflowing" with fundamentalists, and the like.[2] If we are to take their testimony seriously, then a follow-up query naturally arises. Was the *theological* heartbeat of fundamentalism, the doctrinal content that formed the foundation of the fundamentalist perspective, evident among these African American voices? Were their essential theological convictions and formulations regarding the "fundamental" Christian doctrines closely akin to the theological positions being advanced and defended by the better-chronicled white religionists under the banner of "fundamentalism"? While white leaders such as Norris used the era's prevailing racialist social dogmas to deny that blacks possessed the intellectual capacity for nuanced theological reasoning, it is significant that several of the most central theological tenets of the white fundamentalist platform were being taught in black churches with nearly identical content, formulation, and biblical/exegetical backing. This is not to say, of course, that black fundamentalists were simply copying from or blindly emulating a group of white exemplars; rather, fundamentalists on both sides of the color line met the challenge of modernist theological arguments contemporaneously and in parallel, drawing from both a deep church-historical tradition and, even more importantly, the presumed authoritative voice of scripture to validate their positions as the biblically and historically authentic "faith once delivered to the saints."[3]

In the popular imagination, the word "fundamentalist" may conjure images of a person wholly preoccupied with religious minutia—and to some degree, this reflects a historical reality. In order to distinguish themselves from their modernist opponents, fundamentalists focused on quite specific and nuanced theological distinctions. For fundamentalist theologians, it was important to know the difference between plenary verbal inspiration theory and mechanical dictation theory, for instance, or between the penal-substitutionary theory of atonement and the moral exemplar theory of atonement. From the very outset of the modernist controversy, fundamentalist leaders were concerned not only with the inward fidelity of believers, but also with the rigorous doctrinal precision required to combat what they saw as modernist incursions into orthodox churches and denominations. Such theological precision was considered necessary, at least in part, because modernists regularly appealed to feelings, emotions, and inner experience as they argued for ecclesiastical tolerance and lobbied for the acceptance of theological liberalism.[4]

Indeed, in perhaps the most famous modernist sermon of the era, Harry Emerson Fosdick took aim at fundamentalist intolerance, arguing on experiential rather than exegetical grounds that liberal and conservative theologies ought to peacefully coexist: "There are many opinions in the field of modern controversy concerning which I am not sure whether they are right or wrong, but there is one thing I am sure of: courtesy and kindliness and tolerance and humility and fairness are right. Opinions may be mistaken; love never is."[5] For Fosdick, the theological opinions in dispute did not touch the essence of Christianity; they paled in comparison to the need for interpersonal love and tolerance—not to mention ecclesiastical acceptance. Given the contours of modernist arguments such as Fosdick's, fundamentalists aimed to arrest the growing inroads of liberal influence in their churches and traditions by pivoting the rhetorical battleground away from experiential arguments and placing a premium instead on what they considered to be objective revealed truth. Indeed, fundamentalists perceived the foundations of the Christian faith to be deeply at risk if the onward march of liberal theology was not halted with expedience. As a result, those most vocal in their opposition to modernism naturally expected a high measure of theological exactitude in their doctrinal formulations, lest their modernist adversaries use theological imprecision as a cover for smuggling in aberrant or dangerous perspectives.

Of course, a great many white fundamentalist leaders who lived in the midst of, and often explicitly embraced, the culture of Jim Crow America tended not to extend this same expectation of theological sophistication to African Americans. At the same time that some white fundamentalists were embracing religious films as increasingly popular missionary tools, often thereby disseminating the impression of a "white American Jesus" to foreign fields, the religious outlook on the home front was no less racialized.[6] In some cases, southern fundamentalist leaders exploited white Americans' racial fears and prejudices to consolidate white support for their social and ecclesiastical aims and in the process essentially dismissed African Americans as meaningful historical actors altogether.⁷ In other cases, even when black Christians were considered as legitimate individual agents rather than a subversive oppositional monolith, assumptions of moral and intellectual inferiority led white fundamentalists to conclude that conservative blacks lacked the ability, willingness, or desire to properly engage in crucial doctrinal debates. J. Frank Norris's assumption of black inferiority led him not only to dismiss their intellectual capacity, as seen in the opening illustration to this chapter, but also to cast them as especially vulnerable to subversive anti-Christian and anti-American influences.⁸

Similarly, Northern Baptist newspaperman Curtis Lee Laws, the man credited with popularizing the term "fundamentalist," bemoaned that blacks' simplemindedness exposed them to the menace of the Catholic Church: "There is much in Roman Catholicism that has an appeal to the average uncultured Negro. . . . [Catholic practices] are all calculated to work on the credulity of one who is naturally superstitious."⁹ Inherent in such white fundamentalist leaders' perceptions of African Americans was a firm conviction of intellectual inferiority and susceptibility to superstition, which, even when couched in less overtly negative phrases such as "naturally religious," predictably excluded black Christians from conversations of major doctrinal import.¹⁰ After all, if African Americans could not be trusted to resist the wiles of Romanism, how could they be expected to contribute to, or even understand, the precise theological formulations that constituted the fundamentalist bulwark against modernist incursions?

Such racism notwithstanding, many black clergy and laypeople did in fact approach doctrinal discussions with an eye toward theological nuance and doctrinal precision, and by attending to their theological discourses, we not only counter the racist narrative, but also help to rectify the tendency that historians Keisha Blain, Christopher Cameron, and Ashley Farmer identify within the field of intellectual history—namely, that "people of African descent are often marginalized, if not excluded entirely from historical narratives."¹¹ Even as the typical story of the fundamentalist-modernist conflict has fallen prey to this tendency, the intellectually robust definitions and defenses of fundamentalism's theological principles issuing from contemporary black thinkers and churchmen tell a different tale. To demonstrate the depth of thought and precision extant among theologically conservative black thinkers of the era, it is useful to focus on five of the most common doctrinal tenets of fundamentalism: biblical inspiration and inerrancy, the deity of Christ, the virgin birth, the substitutionary atonement, and the physical resurrection and literal second coming of Christ—sometimes together termed the "five fundamentals."[12] Along with a general attitude of skepticism and antipathy toward modernism, these five doctrinal pillars offer a helpful starting place from which to launch a historical-theological examination of conservative black Christians and their relationship to the defining doctrinal characteristics of the "fundamentalist" faith.

This is not to say that every person mentioned in the following pages expressly self-identified as a fundamentalist, though several certainly did.[13] Rather, the point is to demonstrate that typically "fundamentalist" doctrines were being formulated, understood, and expressed similarly in both white and black contexts. For example, when black newspapers such as the *Star of Zion* asserted "the inspiration of the Scriptures" to be the nonnegotiable centerpiece of fundamentalist bibliology (or doctrine of scripture), one might wonder whether that terminology entailed the same essential theological connotations, such as inerrancy and infallibility, as it did for white fundamentalists.[14] By comparing primarily nonsermonic theological sources from black churches with the nonsermonic "sourcebook" of fundamentalist teaching, *The Fundamentals*, we can see that the doctrines most often associated with fundamentalism were understood and taught in much the same way by theological conservatives on both sides of the color line—at times prompting black thinkers to raise their voices in explicit defense of "the fundamentals," or "fundamentalism," or even to expressly label themselves as "fundamentalists."[15] Black and white conservatives drew in parallel from the common streams of church history and biblical exegesis, understanding their own views to be an extension of both what scripture plainly taught and what the church historically believed. This being the case, they also shared a common emphasis on the doctrine of scripture as ground zero for the modernist conflict and as the indispensable root from which an orthodox defense and understanding of the other "fundamental" doctrines must spring.

That concerns about these sorts of theological formulations in the face of modernist challenges—most notably on the doctrine of biblical inspiration—were widespread in the black religious community is evident even in the era's commercial culture. Noted historian of religion Lerone A. Martin, for example, has demonstrated the commercial marketability that at times attended these doctrinal convictions. Martin suggests that widespread concerns among conservative black preachers about the "modernist turn" in theology, specifically touching on issues such as biblical inspiration and evolution, ushered in marketplace shifts as figures like Calvin "Black Billy Sunday" Dixon and William Arthur White put their overtly conservative sermons on phonograph records for the first time in the 1920s. The fact that such sermons, which at times addressed "erudite theological issues," played some early part in the burgeoning phonograph entertainment industry in the black community points to the cultural and social importance of those theological ideas, and should in turn motivate reflection on the particular contours of these "erudite" doctrinal formulations.[16] This is especially true for the subject of biblical inspiration, which achieved a place of primacy (for both white and black apologists) in the quest to defend "the fundamentals" of the Christian faith.

In approaching this topic from a historical-theological perspective, it is also important to recognize that even among such propositionally driven actors as the fundamentalists, there was not necessarily absolute harmony on every nuance of every doctrine. Without question, there was firm unity around the essential nature of the "fundamental" doctrines, and there were lines that could absolutely not be violated without crossing into the presumed outer darkness of modernism. But even so, we would do well to consider the particular gradations of these historical-theological discussions as existing on a spectrum rather than as a static dichotomy.[17] We might conceptualize, for example, the doctrine of scripture as a range with the leftmost polarity representing a view of the Bible as a natural product of the minds of fallible men and the rightmost polarity a view of the Bible as a stenographic dictation from the divine mind. Somewhere in the middle of the spectrum is a point dividing the fundamentalists from their opponents, from which all rightward positions would acknowledge the Bible as being wholly inspired by God in its every word and every claim, and therefore without error; however, even among those right-most positions, there were contestations over exactly *how* God inspired the Bible to be written and whether men were active or passive agents in its creation. Within fundamentalist circles, there were heated conflicts over the distinction between plenary verbal inspiration, which allowed for the active agency of the biblical authors even as they wrote the inerrant words of scripture, and mechanical dictation, which held the biblical authors to be essentially passive scriveners.[18] Even within the four volumes of *The Fundamentals*, the very sourcebook from which the movement gained its name, both perspectives were represented.[19] Likewise, as we examine perspectives on the "five fundamentals" within black churches and publications, it is wise to recognize that there were a variety of expressions that fell on different points of the theological spectrum; the pertinent question is whether they fell within the fundamentalist range.

\* \* \*

The foremost fundamentalist doctrine, which also typically enjoyed pride of place in any listing of "the fundamentals of the faith," was without a doubt the doctrine of biblical inspiration. In fact, nearly one-third (twenty-eight out of ninety) of the essays in *The Fundamentals* were specifically devoted to some aspect of bibliology, or the doctrine of scripture—many specifically addressing issues of inspiration, inerrancy, and the claims of higher-critical scholarship. As laid out in *The Fundamentals*, a commitment to the doctrine of biblical inspiration—or the idea that the very words of the Bible were divinely inspired such that God could properly be described as the author of the biblical texts—also entailed the concomitant ideas of biblical inerrancy (the Bible as being without any *actual* error in its claims) and infallibility (the Bible as being without even the *possibility* of error). Whereas modernist thinkers could speak of the ideas (but not the words) of scripture as being inspired, or even of select portions of scripture as being inspired in some vaguer sense, the fundamentalist defense of inspiration emphasized God as the author of the very words of the Bible in its totality. Moody Bible Institute president James M. Gray displayed just such an approach in his contribution to *The Fundamentals*, affirming that God "caused [every word in the Bible] to be recorded, infallibly and inerrantly recorded, for our profit. In this sense the Bible does not merely contain the Word of God, it *is* the Word of God."[20] Recognizing that modernist denials of other "fundamental" tenets of the faith were first grounded in a denial of the absolute authority and trustworthiness of the scriptures that taught these essential doctrines, fundamentalists committed above all to a defense of their doctrine of scripture.

Contrary to the prejudiced assumptions of many white fundamentalists, black Christians were facing the same modernist challenges to their understanding of the nature of the scriptures, and, in many cases, they were expressing the same doctrinal interconnections, definitions, nuances, and rejoinders. Not content with a mere tip of the hat to the Bible as "the Good Book," numerous African American thinkers aggressively confronted modernist thought in their own cultural contexts, while utilizing religious terminology that would have been perfectly at home in popular fundamentalist organs such as J. Frank Norris's *Searchlight* or Curtis Lee Laws's contributions to the *Watchman-Examiner*. Indeed, some of these defenders of traditional bibliology did so by wielding the pen in their own denominational newspapers—an indication that, while their denominations could certainly not be classed as "fundamentalist" in their totality, an attitude of hostility toward modernist innovations and a pressing drive to uphold the faith's doctrinal fundamentals characterized a substantial number of black Christians' views and cut well across denominational lines. They argued *from* scripture *for* scripture, drawing on both biblical and historical source material to demonstrate that an inspired and authoritative Bible constituted the very foundation upon which Christian orthodoxy rested.

In doing so, black defenders of "the fundamentals" paralleled their white counterparts in contrasting their perspective against what they saw as the modernists' dangerous embrace of higher biblical criticism—a method of biblical scholarship that emphasized human authorship over against divine authorship and approached the biblical texts as the natural products of a long process that had fused together many different streams of prior source material. The higher-critical approach was designed to ascertain a historical reality that lay *behind* the texts—a task that, in the words of one popular contemporary critical scholar, "presupposes that one will acknowledge (and be willing to discover) that there are historical problems with the New Testament: discrepancies, contradictions, historical errors, and factual mistakes."[21] As higher biblical criticism emerged onto the scholarly and religious scenes in the late nineteenth and early twentieth centuries, it cast doubt on the human authorship traditionally ascribed to many biblical texts (for example, the claim that Moses wrote Genesis, or that Daniel wrote the book of Daniel, or that John the Apostle wrote the Gospel of John), as well as on the idea of a unified and consistent biblical corpus. Such conclusions troubled theological conservatives, since they posed a challenge to the concept of divine authorship or divine inspiration. In the face of this challenge many African American Christians, in parallel with their white counterparts, concluded that the modernist approach undermined the highest view of scripture and therefore it likewise undermined the very bedrock of the Christian faith.

One such declamation surfaced in the pages of the African Methodist Episcopal Zion (AMEZ) Church's denominational newspaper, the *Star of Zion*, courtesy of Cambridge, Massachusetts, minister Eli George Biddle.[22] In August 1921, the Sunday School Convention of the AMEZ's New England Conference experienced firsthand the advances of modernism, as a "higher critic" in their own midst "attempted to foist his pernicious doctrines" upon the rest of the members. The incursion of this "un-scriptural, un-sanctified, and harmful teaching" into the convention meeting incensed Biddle, a Civil War veteran and an elder statesman of the denomination. His disdain for the higher-critical perspective, along with his frustration that it might be gaining ground within the AMEZ, prompted him to write an impassioned response in the *Star of Zion* entitled, appropriately enough, "The Fundamentals." In it, Biddle trumpeted "the importance of our tenaciously holding on to the great 'fundamentals' of our Christian faith." For Biddle, such an attitude was constitutive of both membership in the AME Zion Church and Christianity more broadly: "No one can be a Bible Christian or a Zion Methodist unless they hold to these 'Fundamentals.'" His enumeration of these nonnegotiable doctrines included "The Virgin Birth," "The Vicarious Sacrifice of Christ," and "The Divinity of Christ," but in keeping with his concern about his denomination's potential susceptibility to the "pernicious" teachings of higher criticism, Biddle's list of "the fundamentals" was notably headed by the crucial doctrine of "The Inspiration of the Scriptures."[23]

The higher-critical threat to the doctrine of scripture sat square in Biddle's crosshairs as he explained the dangers of modernism and the central importance of the fundamentals. His rebuke of the "would-be leaders and teachers" who were championing higher criticism required

Biddle to highlight the primacy of the doctrine of inspiration, for he saw capitulation on the doctrine of scripture as the very root from which infidelity on the other "fundamental" issues also grew. In contrast to the denomination's general rules, which maintained the sufficiency and trustworthiness of scripture, "the 'Higher critics' and their amateurish followers would have us discard the plain teaching of 'The Holy Scriptures' for their foolish and far-fetched deductions; they deny 'The Virgin Birth,' which the Word of God so plainly and emphatically teaches." Compromise on bibliology likewise cultivated a denial of the "Divinity of Christ," a doctrine so significant that those who rejected it were no longer to be considered true Christians at all. Indeed, if the AMEZ were to compromise on these issues, it would "cease to exist as a Church of Christ." Biblical inspiration was not merely *a* fundamental doctrine to defend; in a real sense it was the *chief* fundamental from which the others received their veracity, as much for Biddle as for the authors and editors of *The Fundamentals*.[24]

Mere months later, Biddle took once again to the pages of the *Star of Zion* to further clarify exactly what "biblical inspiration" entailed and to argue for the "well-established beliefs in the great fundamentals of the Christian religion as drawn from the plain teachings of the Word of God." In addition to the fundamentals he had listed earlier, Biddle added Christ's sinless life, bodily resurrection, literal ascension, indwelling of the believer, and bodily second coming—all, once more, grounded in "a firm, unshaken belief in the infallibility of the Word of God." For Biddle, then, biblical inspiration necessarily entailed biblical infallibility—not only that the Bible *actually* contains no errors (i.e. inerrancy), but also that it *could not* contain errors by virtue of its divine origin. If, after all, God was the author of the very words of the Bible, then those words could not contain error because God can neither lie nor be mistaken. As Biddle's argument proceeded, once again the fundamental doctrines, and especially inspiration, became a litmus test for true Christianity: "All true Christians" believed the Bible to be divinely inspired (and therefore inerrant and infallible), and "only infidels and skeptics" would dare to "deny the inspiration of any book of the Bible."[25] Not only does Biddle's connection of inspiration with inerrancy and infallibility accord with James Gray's explication, as cited above, but his identification of non-inerrantists as "infidels" likewise parallels a well-worn theme found all throughout *The Fundamentals*, whose articles decried those who denied verbal inspiration as "infidel scoffers," identified the roots of the higher-critical movement as "entirely infidel," and considered modernist denials of inspiration and New Testament miracles as "infidel attacks," to name just a few examples.[26]

Continuing his argument, Biddle contended that "we can accept the Holy Scriptures on their face value without any 'ifs' and 'ands'" because any "seeming contradictions" ultimately disappear as "scientific discoveries and conclusions which at first seemed to destroy the validity of the Scriptures eventually are seen to confirm their divine origin."[27] Such an argument displayed further similarities with the fundamentalist sourcebook, strongly resembling Scottish Presbyterian minister James Orr's discussion of science and Christianity, which posited that "the supposed disharmony [of scientific discovery] with the truths of the Bible was an unreal one, early giving way to better understanding on both sides, and finally opening up new vistas in the contemplation of the Creator's power, wisdom, and majesty."[28] Archaeologist Melvin Grove Kyle, whose contribution to *The Fundamentals* highlighted archaeological support for biblical claims, contended in like fashion that "recent testimony of archaeology to Scripture, like all such testimony that has gone before, is definitely and uniformly favorable to the Scriptures at their face value, and not to the Scriptures as reconstructed by criticism."[29] Not only is the argument substantially similar, but Biddle's exhortation to accept "the Scriptures on their face value" used language identical to Kyle's, indicating, if not direct allusion, at least a high degree of congruence and agreement between the parties. Moreover, Biddle also offered words of wisdom from "a great scholar" that "the pick and the spade are unfading witnesses to the truth of the Bible"—possibly echoing James Gray's contention that "the pick-axe and the spade point to the same original as the Bible" or perhaps even alluding to an older book to which Gray himself was likely referring: James Freeman's *Handbook of Bible Manners and Customs*, which claimed that "the pick and the spade are to be the humble instruments of illustrating and authenticating the Word of God."[30] Whether the "great scholar" was Gray himself, or whether Biddle and Gray were simply drawing on shared source material, the parallels between Biddle's arguments and those of leading scholars in *The Fundamentals* remain clear. This congruity also offers a measure of counterbalance to scholarly claims that black ministers did not possess *The Fundamentals*.³¹ Biddle's similarity in argumentation and language to Orr, Kyle, and Gray—while by no means absolutely conclusive—does at least offer the possibility that he possessed and was alluding to these writings.

The parallels to *The Fundamentals* in Biddle's argument and language also extended to his selection and exegesis of biblical texts. Biddle repeatedly invoked John 5:46–47 as evidence that Jesus himself "endorsed and approvingly cited the Old Testament as the very Word of God."³² Christ's words in this passage serve both as an affirmation of the inspiration of the Old Testament and a harsh rebuke of the Pharisees: "For if you believed Moses, you would believe me; for he wrote of me. But if you do not believe his writings, how will you believe my words?" (John 5:46–47 [English Standard Version, ESV]).³³ It is no stretch to see here the pattern for Biddle's own rebukes of modernist higher critics. After all, if Jesus himself viewed the Old Testament writings as authoritative words from God, then modernist higher critics casting doubt on those words should be classed not with Jesus, but with his Pharisaical antagonists. Notably, multiple contributors to *The Fundamentals* used this verse in precisely the same way, to offer Jesus's view of the Old Testament as proof of the inspiration and inerrancy of scripture and concomitantly the falsity of higher criticism.³⁴

Even more centrally, Biddle's tactic of pairing 2 Timothy 3:16 ("All Scripture is breathed out by God") with 1 Peter 1:21 ("men spoke from God as they were carried along by the Holy Spirit") aligns perfectly with one of the fundamentalists' most common exegetical arguments in favor of inspiration. In fact, Biddle even affirmed that the text of 2 Timothy 3:16—the locus classicus for the doctrine of inspiration—"is just as important as John 3:16," the best-known and most-memorized verse in all the Bible. If John 3:16 was self-evidently significant as a certain testimony to God's love for the world and the salvific mission of Jesus, then 2 Timothy 3:16 was equally significant because it provided the basis for such certainty. One of the editors of *The Fundamentals* made a similar point in noting that "to claim that good men wrote the Bible, and deny its inspiration, is on par with the claim that Christ was a good man, while He pretended to be what He was not."³⁵ These and other scriptures that suffused Biddle's articles again indicated profound alignment with and similarity to leading fundamentalist scholars and sources of the day.[36] Both appealed directly to the Bible as the grounding authority in matters of faith, often invoking the very same passages, and both emerged with exegetical conclusions affirming the central and foundational importance of biblical inspiration, inerrancy, and infallibility.

Of course, Reverend Biddle's position was not characteristic of the totality of the AME Zion denomination, which makes his willingness to draw stark doctrinal dividing lines that much more interesting. Not many years after Biddle's vehement defense of inspiration and inerrancy appeared in the *Star of Zion*, the paper's editor W. H. Davenport said of the fundamentalist-modernist conflict that "Methodism has not been seriously disturbed by these discussions." Davenport recognized that "an inerrant Bible" was at the center of the controversy for fundamentalists, but he eschewed the centrality of inerrancy or even the literal divinity of Christ as essential doctrines for Methodist life, quoting with explicit approval a Methodist Episcopal minister who argued that "the only test of doctrine which essential Methodism has is the effect on life.... If the newer views of the Bible ... make for better spiritual results in terms of practical life, the Methodist is likely to accept them cordially as soon as actual tendency becomes clear."[37] This rather utilitarian sentiment is certainly a far cry from Biddle's jeremiad that those who reject the fundamental tenets of the faith "cease to exist as a Church of Christ."

An even more striking contrast with Biddle's fundamentalist apologetic appeared in the *Star* in 1930, as the newspaper reported on an interracial women's conference at Harry Emerson Fosdick's Riverside Church at which Mrs. Ida L. Wallace, the wife of an AMEZ bishop, impressed the attendees with her withering condemnations of the "old beliefs" from which "slavery and racial inferiority" emerged. "Today," she intoned, "the Negro's prestige is gaining in direct ratio to the breakdown of fundamentalism."[38] Drawing a sharp distinction between the God of the Old Testament and Jesus of the New Testament, Mrs. Wallace opined that "the old-fashioned Jehovah was paternal, but Jesus was brotherly."[39] This distinction echoed strains of ancient Marcionism—a second-century view, widely condemned as heretical, which, in positing a similar division between the deities of the Old Testament and the New Testament, led to a rejection of the Old Testament scriptures.[40] Either way, Wallace's contrast of "the old-fashioned Jehovah" of the Old Testament with the Jesus of the New Testament stood diametrically at odds with Biddle's conviction that "He who speaks now to us by His Son is the same Almighty God who spake by the prophets."[41] Along with Wallace's overt repudiation of fundamentalist doctrine, these perspectives would presumably place her among the "infidels and skeptics" from Biddle's point of view. Yet even so, Biddle did not abandon the AME Zion Church; his fundamentalist convictions led him to vociferously defend those central fundamental doctrines and to attack those who would compromise them, but not to separate from a denomination that was, at least in theory and sometimes in practice, willing to entertain modernist theology on a utilitarian basis. Although this posture could be seen as antithetical to fundamentalism, historian Nathan Finn has challenged the absolute centrality of separatism to fundamentalist identity, positing a distinction between "separatist fundamentalists" who stressed organizational separation and "denominational fundamentalists" who were concerned with defending and advancing the cause of the fundamentals within extant denominational structures. Though Finn's analysis focuses on white Baptist fundamentalists in the South, the "denominational fundamentalist" concept seems a useful one to apply to Biddle and similar black fundamentalists who remained within their denominations.[42]

The issue of bibliology was not one to fade quickly from the ranks of the black Methodist ecclesiastical bodies. In 1936 the *Star of Zion* published a piece by J. G. Robinson, the longtime editor of the African Methodist Episcopal (AME) *Church Review*, entitled "Preachers—Modernists and Fundamentalists." At this point Robinson had been the editor of the *Church Review* for twelve years, having taken over in 1924 as the successor to Reverdy C. Ransom. Over his editorial tenure (which eventually stretched to sixteen years) Robinson represented a much more theologically conservative viewpoint than had his predecessor, shifting away from Ransom's focus on the social gospel and toward a greater emphasis on articles about preaching and theology.[43] Such an emphasis was certainly evident in Robinson's article for the *Star of Zion*, which clearly laid out his position in favor of biblical inerrancy, as well as numerous other classic fundamentalist concerns. From the outset of his article Robinson pulled no punches, unabashedly identifying modernist thought as "contrary to the universal belief of the Christian church." Like Biddle before him, Robinson found the central root of the modernists' error to be their proclamation of "the errancy of the Holy Scriptures." This denial of biblical inerrancy was enormously problematic because it placed modernists "entirely out of harmony with the accepted interpretation of the Holy Scriptures," which had been passed on throughout the history of the church. Due to this capitulation, "Many of the doctrines which were believed to be necessary for salvation are found to be non-essentials," including the doctrines of the virgin birth, the deity of Christ, regeneration, the resurrection, and hell. Illustrating the great breadth of difference between Robinson and his markedly more social-gospel-friendly predecessor at the *Review*, Robinson castigated the modernist "Gospel of social service and economic security" not only as a betrayal of both the church historic and the scriptures, but as a profoundly deleterious influence on the spiritual lives of black laymen. This false modernist gospel, he proclaimed, "has well nigh taken all the comfort and sweetness out of the lives of the people and almost emptied the churches."[44]

At this juncture, Robinson represented a stark counterpoint to numerous of his fellow black intellectuals, many of whom expressed a great deal of warmth toward social gospel ideology. At its core, the social gospel understood the chief and central concern of Christianity to be the transformation of the social order toward ever higher and more righteous social ideals. The movement's progenitor, Walter Rauschenbusch, explained that the "doctrine of the Kingdom of God" was the "marrow" of the social gospel and was summed up in the goals of "redeeming the social order" and "the practical proclamation and application of a social morality." Such a reorientation away from more traditional forms of Christianity required a concomitant doctrinal reformulation, agitating fundamentalists who saw this as yet another brand of modernist compromise. In constructing a social gospel theology, Rauschenbusch claimed that "the entire redemptive work of Christ must be reconsidered," that the doctrine of the Trinity was incidental (as the social gospel united "trinitarians and unitarians alike"), that the historic Chalcedonian definition of Christ's divine and human natures was "a false trail," and that the question of whether Christ possessed "a divine essence" was functionally insignificant.[45] Yet even while Rauschenbusch and other white social gospel advocates began to identify social sin and social redemption as major categories of theological reflection, they often failed to incorporate racism as a major consideration in their program of social redemption.⁴⁶ It fell to leading black thinkers, then, to adapt and refocus Rauschenbusch's social gospel ideas to apply specifically to issues of racism and racial oppression.

From W. E. B. Du Bois to Reverdy Ransom, from Adam Clayton Powell to Langston Hughes, many black intellectuals indeed found this to be a useful approach in their campaigns for racial progress and their protests against the obvious injustices and inequities begotten of Jim Crow.⁴⁷ In his 1903 sociological study *The Negro Church*, for example, Du Bois made clear that the central, foremost element of Christianity was its ability to inculcate moral goodness and justice; while younger children in the black community displayed "the clearer and simpler idea of the direct connection of goodness and Christianity," the fact that most older children defined Christianity with some sort of doctrinal reference "to some higher will" showed that these older youths "are not impressed to a sufficiently large extent with the fact that moral goodness is the first requirement of a Christian life."⁴⁸ Feeling "hindered by religious traditionalists," Du Bois adapted a social gospel paradigm that saw black churches as essentially functioning, in the words of one Du Bois scholar, "to inculcate beliefs in justice, liberty, and morality into their parishioners and to create a truly Christian society."⁴⁹ His treatment of religion, then, focused on its this-worldly social effects.⁵⁰ Yet for professed fundamentalists such as J. G. Robinson, by the likes of whom Du Bois presumably felt "hindered," the emergence and increasing popularity of the social gospel within black Christian circles represented a danger for the race because it removed a great deal of the transcendence and ultimacy of religious meaning that had so long provided black people with comfort amid oppression and with communal solidarity amid external forces of division.⁵¹ Robinson believed that AME bishops were among "the greatest factors in the elevation of the Negro Race," and as a result the character of their faith was enormously significant for the African American people as a whole.⁵² If for social gospel exponents like Du Bois the social gospel represented liberation and opportunities for the black community to progress, for Robinson it raised the specter of communal infidelity and threatened to undermine the very religious truth that had so far bolstered African Americans in their communal struggle—emptying the churches and removing all of God's transcendent "comfort and sweetness" from life.⁵³

In contrast to modernist ideas, Robinson pointed to the upright example of "the old line preachers (of which I am one) called 'Fundamentalists.'" Robinson's unambiguous identification as a fundamentalist is particularly notable, as is his immediate description of fundamentalists as those "who unequivocally hold on to the inerrancy of God's Word as it is set down in the Holy Bible from Genesis to Revelation." This formulation reflects the "plenary verbal" idea of biblical inspiration, the conviction that the Bible is divinely inspired so as to be without error both in the totality of its scope (plenary) as well as in its exact words (verbal)—a contrast to modernist conceptions of either partial inspiration or the inspiration of thoughts rather than words (or in some cases, a denial of inspiration altogether). Furthermore, Robinson exhorted that fundamentalists like himself must believe that "the Word of God is infallible"—once again, as with Eli George Biddle and James Gray, inexorably linking the concepts of inspiration, inerrancy, and infallibility—and they must also "hold tenaciously to the apostolic interpretation of the Word of God." The result of this fidelity was that, in contrast to the false "social service" gospel of the modernists, fundamentalists would "preach the Gospel of conviction, Conversion, Regeneration and Sanctification." Invoking the recent testimony of a young layman, Robinson again opened fire on the message of the social gospel, exhorting preachers to "leave off much social philosophy and sociology, and give us the pure unadulterated Gospel of Jesus Christ."[54]

For Robinson, this was no minor matter, but it was in fact an issue of eternal consequence. The fact that modernists and fundamentalists preached essentially different gospels meant that their eternal destinations were likewise different. A person who embraced the fundamentalist gospel "can see God's face in peace," but not so the modernist. In a whirlwind imprecatory paragraph, Robinson conjoined the description of false teachers in 2 Timothy 3:1–4 and the condemnation of rebellious unregenerate man in Romans 1:25 to leave no ambiguity as to the dangers of the modernist foe. Like the false teachers against whom the Apostle Paul warned his protégé Timothy, modernistic preachers exhibited an "eagerness to fit the Gospel to this present wicked age," so that it might be palatable to men who are "lovers of their own selves, covetous, boisterous, proud, blasphemers, disobedient, unthankful, unholy truce-breakers, false accusers, incontinent, fierce, despisers of the good, traitors, highminded, lovers of pleasure more than lovers of God." Accordingly, modernists fit the description of the rebellious God-haters of Romans 1, having "changed the truth of God into a lie" and "serv[ing] the creature more than the Creator." As if to put a bow on this particular philippic, Robinson also placed modernists under the curse of Revelation 22:19, which consigned to eternal damnation anyone who might "take away from the words of this Book of the Prophecy." Modernists, by their embrace of biblical errancy and their commitment to higher biblical criticism, heaped upon themselves the perdition of Revelation 22 on top of everything else.[55]

While undoubtedly inflammatory and arresting, these associations were also not unique or entirely original to Robinson. Numerous articles in *The Fundamentals* made similar arguments, sometimes using identical biblical references. One such article by Swiss theologian Frédéric Bettex, devoted to combatting higher criticism, similarly understood modernism to be a damning error, noting that "the Book of Revelation is only the occasion for derisive laughter on the part of these skeptical critics; and because it is so, the curse mentioned in its last chapter is made applicable to them."[56] German American Methodist minister Arno C. Gaebelein read the apostasy passage of 2 Timothy 3:1–5 as being prophetic of "the present day apostasy," and in the same vein Methodist evangelist and Union Civil War veteran Leander Whitcomb Munhall even invoked the example of wicked Balaam to show the degradation of modernists' false teaching.[57] And just as Robinson's allusion to Romans 1:25 accused modernists of idolatrously serving "the creature more than the Creator," James Gray drew upon similar themes to demonstrate that modernist criticism of verbal inspiration was "just a spark from the anvil on which the race is ever trying to hammer out the deification of itself."[58]

Fervent dispute over the doctrine of scripture also entered the ranks of black Baptists as well as Methodists.[59] J. H. Frank, the stridently antimodernist editor of the *National Baptist Union-Review*, provides a compelling example. Historian Mary Beth Swetnam Mathews describes Frank as embracing "a dichotomy between the forces of biblical inerrancy, on which side he placed the majority of African Americans, as well as the leaders of the fundamentalist movement, and the forces of modernism, in which camp he included black intellectuals like Kelly Miller and William Pickens, as well as the majority of white Americans."⁶⁰ Frank, in fact, identified himself and the majority of black Baptists as "fundamentalists," in contrast to the "so-called 'Intellectuals' of our race." On the doctrine of scripture specifically, Frank wrote that the Bible "is not false but true [when dealing with history and science], true to fact and true to the truth founded upon the facts." Following in the footsteps of George Biddle and many others before him, Frank invoked 2 Timothy 3:16 to support this position, but at the same time he also noted that the Bible's purpose was not "to be authority in history, in science, in art, in philosophy—but to teach life and how to live."⁶¹ Mathews concludes that this "refusal to categorize the Bible as the ultimate historical document ran counter to fundamentalist understanding of the text," which was presumably, according to Mathews, to see the Bible as "the sole source of knowledge on ancient history."⁶²

Yet the fundamentalist doctrine of scripture in no sense necessitated that the Bible be "the sole source of knowledge" for history or science; to the contrary, Frank's remarks sound very much like those that might be found in *The Fundamentals* itself. Fundamentalists held the Bible to be the ultimate epistemological *authority* to which all other epistemological sources were subordinate, but it was not in itself the only source of knowledge. In fact, in his contribution to *The Fundamentals*, Arthur Tappan Pierson, one of the consulting editors on the famous Scofield Reference Bible, assumed that there are means of discovering scientific and historical truth outside the pages of the Bible, while still maintaining that all truth so derived will of necessity be consistent with the scripture's teachings: "The Bible is not a scientific book.... Like an engine on its own track, it thunders across the track of science, but is never diverted from its own." In a claim here almost identical to that of J. H. Frank, Pierson affirmed that the Bible's essential *purpose* is not to be an authoritative scientific manual. Yet while "no direct teaching or anticipation of scientific truth is here found," nevertheless "God led inspired men to use such language, as that without revealing scientific facts in advance, it accurately accommodates itself to them when discovered."⁶³ Thus, contrary to Mathews's claims, J. H. Frank's position on biblical authority and inspiration (particularly relative to scientific exploration) is very much in accord with the position advanced in *The Fundamentals*. As a result, her argument that Frank should be excluded from the fundamentalist ranks rings rather hollow; on the contrary, Frank's willingness to self-identify as a fundamentalist and his commitment to aggressively defending biblical inspiration illustrates once again the reality of a self-attested fundamentalist presence within the black community—an element of the historical record that has heretofore been largely ignored by historical scholarship.

Concerns over safeguarding the doctrine of scripture emerged not only from the editorialist's typewriter but also from the pastor's study. AME minister John Albert Johnson, whose ministry spanned from the 1870s through the 1920s, saw dangerous pastoral implications in the historical-critical rejection of biblical inspiration. Johnson characterized historical criticism as a "vitally defective" approach that "has made the figure of Christ utterly uncertain" to its acolytes.[64] Yet the central purpose of the faithful minister, indeed the central purpose of God's activity in this world, Johnson contended, was the proclamation of "salvation to ruined man"—salvation from the guilt and condemnation of sin through the propitiatory, redemptive work of Christ on the cross. To dwell on moral duties or Christian virtues "in any other light than that which streams from the cross is *not* a testimony of the gospel"; indeed, "if Christ and him crucified are not the theme and the glory, there is injury inflicted upon man, and there is dishonor done to the majesty of mercy on high." For this very reason did "the finger of Inspiration write the Bible and the arm of Omnipotence defend it"—for an errant Bible would make Christ and his work utterly uncertain, and how then could the gospel be proclaimed?[65]

Further evincing his desire for doctrinal specificity and commitment to historically orthodox argumentation, Johnson continued to link the veracity of the doctrine of biblical inspiration (and the concomitant characteristics of inerrancy, infallibility, and authority) to the words and works of the Christ of scripture. Invoking the person of Christ as a rhetorical support for the divine inspiration, veracity, and trustworthiness of the Bible was indeed a well-worn practice in Christian history (from second-century Irenaeus to sixteenth-century Calvin and beyond), and Johnson understood his own arguments as resting squarely within this longstanding "orthodox" tradition, in direct contrast to the modern "rationalists" who clung to a potentially error-ridden Bible.[66] In a paper written to clarify and adjudicate the contentious issue of biblical inspiration, Johnson concluded that the testimony of "the Messiah, the great

Prophet, the infallible Teacher" on this matter should settle the question once and for all; whatever view Jesus took of the scriptures ought to constitute "the end of our inquiries." Thus focusing on the teachings of Christ himself in the gospels, Johnson found that Jesus "everywhere spoke of... the scripture as the word of God; that he regarded the whole in this light; that he treated the scripture and every part of it, as infallibly true, and as clothed with divine authority—thus distinguishing it from every mere human production." Therefore the inspiration and infallibility of the text applied to the whole of the canon and to every specific constitutive part. This contradicted both the "Latitudinarian" theory adopted by the "entire school of Rationalists and so-called advanced thought," which posited that "there may be error in facts stated, or sentiment uttered," and the "Commingled" theory, which held that "when the essentials of Religion are introduced there is truth" but "when the matter is historical there may be great mistake," an approach "most destructive since it makes man the Judge of what is inspired and what is not."

The testimony of Christ, consistent as it was with the testimony of other scriptures such as 2 Timothy 3:16, settled the matter for Johnson.[67] The divinity of Christ the incarnate Word ensured the divine origin of the written word of God, such that scripture would be "proved merely human [only] when Christ Himself is proved so."[68] On this point in particular Johnson's argument paralleled James Gray's work in *The Fundamentals*, which contended that since Jesus's claim to the divine status of "incarnate Word" entailed that he was "absolutely without sin," the scriptures' claim to be the "written Word" likewise necessitated that they be without error.[69] Drawing on a common historic tradition, which Johnson called the "orthodox view" and which extended back to the early church and the apostles themselves, both black ministers such as John Albert Johnson and J. G. Robinson and white conservatives such as the contributors to *The Fundamentals* produced parallel defenses and explications of the doctrine of inspiration in response to modernist challenges.[70]

Considering how closely bound Johnson's formulation and defense of biblical inspiration was with his convictions about the person and work of Jesus Christ, it should come as no surprise that insofar as conservative black churchmen formulated a doctrine of scripture that ran closely parallel to that of their white fundamentalist counterparts, the same would be true of their Christological doctrines. Johnson himself demonstrated as much, for example, in his pointed written critique of Adolf Harnack's *Christianity and History*. While acknowledging Harnack as "the leading church historian of Germany" and "unsurpassed" in his knowledge of early church history, Johnson leveled a barrage of criticism at Harnack's position on the basis of its "discarding the old definitions of Christ's person." By denying Christ's deity and offering basically the moral exemplar theory of the cross, Harnack's attempt to preserve Christ as "the Lord and Saviour of mankind" collapsed Jesus into "a Savior merely by His teaching and example," whose "words and example supply the ideal of the perfect life, and . . . stimulate the realization of the ideal." The fact that this school of thought "ascribes such unique attributes to [Christ] and yet refuses to speak of anything unique in His person" amounted to, in Johnson's words, a "fatal defect" and an "extraordinary inconsistency." The "weakness and inconsistency" of Harnack's position was that historical criticism offered an "utterly uncertain" Jesus whose gospel was likewise utterly insufficient to save; the biblical claims about "the birth and infancy of the Lord, the Easter story, many things told of His life are discarded as mere husk." This "vitally defective" view was self-evidently false to Johnson, almost even without need of rebuttal, because it was so far out of step with the testimony of the church all the way back to the first century: "How far short [Harnack's position] falls of what the Church has always believed on the subject is obvious."[71] Identifying Christ's deity, miraculous birth, atonement, and resurrection as central not only to his own experience or even to his denominational tradition, but to historic Christian orthodoxy throughout the ages, Johnson unabashedly decried the fatal errors of modernist thought and historical criticism.

Of course, while Johnson saw the age-old testimony of the church as an essential element in establishing the veracity of these doctrines (and, hence, demonstrating the falsities of modernism), once again the final authority, as usual, rested with the God-breathed scriptures. Reflecting on the doctrine of the incarnation and the hypostatic union (that is, the unity of the two natures—divine and human—in the single person of Christ), Johnson argued that the doctrine is "founded upon and rendered necessary by facts divinely revealed," the validity of which rests upon nothing less than "the Authority of the Holy Scriptures." In a lengthy description echoing the orthodox formulation laid down at the Council of Chalcedon in the fifth century, Johnson distinguished between divine nature, human nature, and the personhood of Christ, arguing that the perfect unity of the two natures was to be found in the person of Christ, but without any mixture or confusion of the natures that might undermine their perfect distinction. This formulation was "rendered necessary" to sufficiently account for the biblical facts, which included the "miraculous conception" of Christ and the prophecies attending his birth, the "ordinary and natural development" of his humanity during his boyhood, his unhesitating claim to "unity and equality with the father," his many miracles displaying power over both natural and spiritual forces, his death, and his literal resurrection and ascension to heaven.[72] With the exception of any in-depth discussion of atonement, this one paper explicitly affirmed the five fundamentals on the basis of the trustworthiness and authority of scripture. Fidelity to the biblical testimony, supplemented by a submission to the historic doctrines of the church, grounded Johnson's strident convictions about the doctrinal fundamentals and the folly of modernist, higher-critical innovations. Moreover, setting such claims in the twin contexts of biblical testimony and church history may also have served in a sense to decenter the theological question from a strictly American context, thus implicitly repudiating the idea advanced by some critics that black fundamentalists were mere purveyors of a paternalistic hand-me-down religion from the American white man.[73]

Similarly grounding the orthodox fundamental doctrines about the person of Christ in biblical necessity was Edward Franklin Williams, a Congregationalist minister from Chicago. To be sure, "fundamentalist" would be an anachronistic designation for Williams, who died in 1919, after the publication of *The Fundamentals* in 1915 but prior to the 1920 advent of Curtis Lee Laws' "fundamentalist" moniker in the *Watchman-Examiner*. Still, Williams was a theological conservative who was involved in arranging revival meetings for such conservative celebrities as Dwight L. Moody and Ira Sankey in the mid-1870s, and later for the editor of *The Fundamentals* himself, R. A. Torrey.[74] Williams's doctrinal convictions on such topics as the five fundamentals evidently led to antimodernist sentiments as well, such that in initial discussions about potentially bringing Torrey's evangelistic meetings to Chicago in

1906, a fellow minister sought to assure Williams that Torrey's teachings were untainted by "the modern viewpoint," which might "threaten the very ground-work" of the faith.[75] With these considerations in mind, we might describe Williams as a "doctrinal fundamentalist" or even, perhaps, a "proto-fundamentalist" since, though his ministry extended into the time period in view for this study, he died before any person or movement was precisely so named.

Like Johnson, Williams turned to the scripture's testimony and example in affirming the Christological fundamentals, such as the deity of Christ. In a lecture on "The Practical Nature of the Christian Religion" he turned to Colossians chapter 1 for an example of true faith and Christian life. The very first characteristic, which rooted all the manifestations of Christian virtue that were evident in the Colossian church, was that "they had faith in Christ. They recognised his Deity, cherished hope through Him and received the truth of the Gospel." Here Williams painted the recognition of Christ's deity as unequivocally essential for true Christian faith on the basis of the teachings and examples laid down in scripture. As was his wont, Williams went on to heavily emphasize social and ethical application, reminding his congregants that "we are not only permitted to believe for our own good, but for the sake of others," and urging them toward a life that is "wholly Christlike, where there is a strong and honest desire to do what Christ wishes us to do" in terms of personal conduct, service to others, and wholesome moral living.[76] Yet the strong and extensive exhortations about Christian living and moral action that characterized his writing and preaching were grounded in the doctrinal propositions of his gospel—in this case, specifically, the deity of Christ.

The fact that Williams's commitment to the spiritual, theologically conservative doctrines of the historic Christian tradition was conjoined with a consistently strong emphasis on practically emulating Jesus's example challenges the strict division that scholars sometimes assume between "otherworldly" doctrine and "this-worldly" activity.[77] Community engagement and religiously motivated work in the social realm is often conflated with a "social gospel" religious outlook, thus putting at odds religious emphasis on "otherworldly" spiritual doctrines (such as Christ's divinity or the heavenly afterlife) and the practical emulation of Jesus's acts of care and mercy toward people in the here-and-now.[78]

Yet the practice of emulating Jesus's example and actively engaging with the community was neither solely restricted to the social gospel movement nor inherently antithetical to an emphasis on teaching spiritual doctrines. Edward Franklin Williams regularly urged his listeners toward active community engagement and service as a means of honoring Christ, in concert with his emphasis on the centrality of certain fundamentalist doctrines—such as the deity of Christ in the example above—to "the truth of the gospel." On another occasion, Easter festivities led Williams to undertake a defense of Christ's literal resurrection from the dead (and the attendant promise of eternal heavenly life with Christ for all who believe); in explicating this rather "otherworldly" doctrine, Williams exhorted that the reality of Christ's physical resurrection and the believer's promise of eternal life ought to motivate Christians to "go to the house of mourning, to give comfort and help when we enter homes of poverty[,] not to rebuke, but to cheer and stimulate and give aid, join the ranks of reformers and earnest workers who seek to improve the moral condition of the city and of our homes . . . [and] do whatever we can to make life better for the toiling millions around us or to prepare a better world in which the millions yet unborn shall live after we have left it." Though he was no social gospeler, Williams's commitment to "otherworldly" fundamental doctrines such as the deity and resurrection of Christ was by no means disconnected from social acts of care and mercy toward the "toiling millions" in this world.[79]

Even as conservative black theologians expressed their convictions about the supernatural nature of the Bible and of Christ himself, the other fundamentals also gained hearings as defining elements of the Christian faith. As noted previously, both Eli George Biddle and J. G. Robinson listed a variety of "fundamental" doctrines in the midst of their vociferous defenses of biblical inspiration and inerrancy. These included not only Christ's divinity and virgin birth, but also his literal resurrection and ascension, his second coming and final judgment, and his substitutionary atonement. On the subject of atonement specifically, Biddle used the interchangeable terms "Vicarious Sacrifice" and "Vicarious Death" to describe Christ's work on the cross on behalf of fallen man.[80] Both phrases indicate that the biblical testimony demands that the death of Christ be in some sense substitutionary, that he was atoning for human sin by *taking the place* of sinful men—the central feature of the fundamentalist doctrine of atonement.[81] This was the essential question dividing fundamentalists and modernists regarding the atonement: Was Christ's death in some respect vicarious or substitutionary, so as to achieve some sort of objective atoning remedy or payment for the sin of mankind?

While the penal-substitutionary view ultimately came to dominate fundamentalist (and later, neo-evangelical) thinking, fundamentalism initially left room for differing substitutionary theories. For example, *The Fundamentals* declared that "the Christian world as a whole believes in a substitutionary atonement," though it may not "regard any existing theory of substitution as entirely adequate." Any theory of substitutionary atonement must necessarily flow from biblical testimony, but it was "not absolutely necessary" to have a specific theory at all, so long as one professed a broadly substitutionary view of Christ's work on the cross.[82] The real danger, from this point of view, was the modernist's moral example theory of atonement, which held that Christ's death served only as a moral example to stir up love and self-sacrifice in human hearts. This concern surfaced, as we have already seen, in John Albert Johnson's criticism of Adolf Harnack's "fatal defect" of presenting a Christ who is "a Savior merely by His teaching and example."[83] Both black and white conservatives sometimes used language that seemed to reflect a governmental (as opposed to penal) theory of substitution, but they still fell into the fundamentalist range of the spectrum by virtue of a commitment to substitution over against bare moral example.[84]

Such commitment to the centrality of substitutionary atonement, as well as another compelling example of congruence with *The Fundamentals*, was evident from the pulpit of Isaac Reed Berry, a black Methodist minister who was ordained in 1917. In a sermon titled "God's One Essential for Salvation" Berry vociferously defended substitutionary atonement, arguing that Satan's goal was to neuter the gospel message by convincing people to deemphasize the atoning power of Jesus' blood:

> Satan's masterpiece today is to bring men to believe that the blood of Jesus is non-essential, unnecessary to man's salvation. His gospel is a gospel of works and is being preached by a lot of salvation-by-character infidels today. . . . [On judgment day] the Lord will say, 'I never knew you.' Now who could these people possibly be? They were splendid people, the ma-

jority of them doubtlessly sincere. All of them with a splendid record of good works to their credit. But they were the dupes of Satan. They drifted out on the tide of eternity without the blood of Jesus Christ, God's one essential of salvation.[85]

In contrast to his own understanding of Christ's atoning blood as being paramount to Christian salvation, Berry lifts up to scorn a perspective that sounds very much like moral example theory, as well as being reminiscent of the social gospel attitudes that elicited such vociferous condemnation from J. G. Robinson in the pages of the *Star of Zion*. It is not difficult to hear Berry's disdain for what he sees as an anemic view of salvation—a reliance on good works bereft of the atoning blood of Jesus—ultimately amounting to nothing more than a hopeless attempt at "salvation-by-character." Purveyors of such a bloodless view likewise turn out to be "dupes of Satan," unwittingly assisting the prince of darkness in his plan to expunge from Christianity the infinite atoning value of Christ's shed blood on the cross. This argument offers a striking similarity, both in vocabulary and rhetorical force with the treatment of the same topic in *The Fundamentals*:

> Satan's religion has always one clearly defined mark in the *omission of the Gospel of Calvary*. And by this test all "gospels" that are not the Gospel may be recognized! The atoning death of the Son of God; His propitiation for sin; His blotting out of sin; His deliverance from the power of sin by the severing power of the Cross; His call of the blood-redeemed soul to the Cross in humiliation of self, and sacrifice for others—in brief, *all that Calvary means*, is emphatically repudiated, or else always carefully omitted, in the doctrines of the seducing spirits which are evolved in hell. . . . [Satan] knows that it is only the real acceptance of the death of Christ—or Cross of Christ—which saves from sin and delivers the soul from the power of Satan.[86]

Thus, both in his emphasis on the absolute necessity of a substitutionary understanding of Christ's atoning work on the cross, and in the rhetorical force of identifying other non-substitutionary perspectives with the work of Satan, Berry reflects a notable congruence here with the testimony of *The Fundamentals*.[87]

Just as the commitment to substitutionary atonement in *The Fundamentals* was broad enough to accommodate several different perspectives within the fundamentalist range of the theological spectrum, the same also held true regarding the eschatological expectation of Christ's second coming. The fundamentalist position, at its core, diverged from the modernist's at the point of declaring the second advent to be a literal bodily end-times event. As seen above, Christ's return was included in lists of "fundamentals" to be accepted on the basis of, in J. G. Robinson's words, "the apostolic interpretation of the Word of God."[88] Yet this doctrine does not seem to have been a heavy point of detailed exposition for these black conservatives, especially in comparison with the time devoted to the doctrine of scripture or the divinity of Christ. Even as Eli George Biddle, for example, briefly cozied up to dispensationalism in a series of articles in 1922, he quickly returned to a vaguer premillennial eschatology and shifted his focus to other topics.[89] To be certain, Biddle still listed Christ's "literal bodily resurrection," "His glorious ascension," and "His promised imminent triumphal return" as indispensable fundamental doctrines of the "faith of our fathers," but he failed to give much ink, in the long run, to the particularities of the dispensational brand of end-times theology. Similarly AME Bishop Noah W. Williams, reporting in 1935 about his visit to the Holy Land, took a moment to discuss eschatology. He predicted "a war of world-wide proportions" to be on the horizon, "more destructive than the last World War," and that this new world war would usher in "the battle of Armageddon . . . and the Second Advent of Jesus the Christ." From this stance, he admitted, "it can be seen at once that I am a Pre-Millennialist." But rather than going into lengthy apocalyptic interpretations, Williams instead turned his attention, and that of his readers, back to the doctrine of scripture. To learn about the Second Coming, he said, "Just read your Bible, if you believe it is the Inspired Word of God, and if you do not believe it is the Word of God then quit pretending."[90] Eschewing extended eschatological speculation and ignoring dispensational particulars altogether, Williams affirmed to his readers that the physical return of Christ was a simple fact to be gleaned from just reading the inspired Bible.

Dispensational premillennialism has come to be almost axiomatically identified with fundamentalism in the minds of many observers—and indeed, this specific end-times perspective did eventually become, for some fundamentalists, an uncompromising point of faith—but it was not always so. In 1924 Baptist minister Robert Ashworth, seeking to chronicle the development of fundamentalism among Northern Baptists for the *Journal of Religion*, noted that although many of the movement's leaders were premillennialists, "this view of the second advent . . . is not made a test of fellowship." Ashworth went on to quote a Northern Baptist fundamentalist who argued that "there are as many varied views about the return of our Lord among Fundamentalists as will be found among other bodies of Christian people. The thing upon which we insist concerning the second advent is that Christ will come back to the earth 'according to his promise.'"[91] Likewise Eugene Perry Alldredge, a fundamentalist leader in the Southern Baptist Convention, strenuously criticized what he saw as a dangerous overemphasis on premillennial theorizing coming from the dispensationalist ranks of J. Frank Norris and other institutionalized voices of fundamentalism.[92] *The Fundamentals* also affirmed this approach to the topic, allowing for significant latitude regarding eschatological specifics and end-times theories. Its article titled "The Coming of Christ" identified the Second Coming not only as a "fundamental doctrine" and a "Scriptural doctrine . . . held universally by all who admit the authority of Scripture," but also as a doctrine admitting substantial "difference of opinion among even the most careful and reverent students" as to its specific details. While there existed "many varieties of opinion" between various millennial perspectives, these differences of opinion were related mainly as to "the order, rather than as to the reality of events." Hence, the editors of *The Fundamentals* saw Christian unity about the *literal reality* of Christ's second coming as constituting the central fundamentalist conviction on the matter, and this essential Christian unity marked the present day as a time "not for disputing over divergent views, but for united action."[93] The line of demarcation on this fundamentalist doctrine concerned one's willingness to affirm the literal bodily return of Christ, not a specific millennial or eschatological theory. On this point as on all the others examined heretofore, black and white exponents alike fell into the fundamentalist range of the theological spectrum, grounding their convictions on their understanding of church-historic tradition and their view of the infallible testimony of the sacred scriptures.

\* \* \*

As we have seen in this chapter, many black conservative theologians placed themselves within the fundamentalist range of the spectrum with respect to some of the most central doctrinal disputes of the day, representing in some instances an intriguing counterpoint within the black intellectual tradition to the popular "social gospel" ideas that prevailed among many popular race leaders of the era. In many cases, these black conservative voices addressed and affirmed the central tenets of fundamentalist theology by offering arguments, imprecations, biblical exegesis, and sometimes even linguistic formulations that were highly consonant with the content of *The Fundamentals*. Yet even so, this doctrinal similarity did not mean that African American fundamentalists were carbon copies of their white counterparts in either thought or deed; in fact, the next chapter will illustrate some of the different applications that black preachers were apt to draw on the basis of their racial identity and experience.

It must also be noted that to assert a close doctrinal correspondence between black and white fundamentalists on these central issues is not to imply either a subordination of black theologians to their white brethren or even a necessarily causal relationship between the positions and arguments of the two groups, such that black believers might be construed to have been somehow paternalistically reliant on their white counterparts to show them what to say and how to think. In fact the arguments coming from both groups, often so similar in their form and substance, actually pointed as much to a parallel reliance on older church-historical and biblical streams of thought as to a contemporary borrowing from one another. Both black and white fundamentalists saw themselves as relying for their language, doctrinal formulations, and arguments firstly on the text of sacred scripture itself and secondarily on the testimony of the church through the ages. Hence they did not see themselves as engaged in theological innovation, a charge that they often leveled against their modernist opponents. Rather, they were commonly (if often separately) engaged in the task of preserving the "faith once delivered to the saints" to which both God's word and two thousand years of church history attested—a perspective that comports with the regular appeals to "old time religion" we saw earlier.

This shared perspective, however, in no way rendered black and white fundamentalists indistinguishable from one another. Indeed, the fact of this common theological ground in some ways serves only to highlight the very real differences between them. The cultural context in which they lived made improbable, if not impossible, the complete elimination of the "dividing wall of hostility" (Ephesians 2:14) between Christian brethren of different races. As segregation and racial division demarcated the boundaries of normalcy in Jim Crow America, unity in fundamentalist doctrine certainly did not beget unity in all things. Even as preachers of both races used their pulpits to advance clear antimodernist polemics, black ministers also had to balance and intertwine a religious identity that envisioned twenty centuries of orthodox historical solidarity with a racial identity that modern society demanded be treated as their single most defining characteristic. The polemical content of this sort of preaching, including its expressly antimodernist contours and its overtly racial applications, is the subject of the next chapter.

3

Polemics from the Pulpit

*Antimodernist Preaching and Racial Applications*

In June 1963 a cadre of black civil rights activists, nearing the end of an all-night bus ride from South Carolina to Mississippi, were arrested in Winona, Mississippi, for sitting on the "white" side of the bus depot. Among them was civil rights heroine Fannie Lou Hamer, whose experience in the Winona jail would, quite literally, leave lasting marks. Beaten to within an inch of her life by two of the jailers, Hamer was left with partial blindness and permanent kidney damage from the brutal assaults. Even amid her excruciating suffering in the Winona jail, however, Hamer still managed to elicit a religious conversation with the wife of one of the jailers, a professing Christian woman who came to bring water to the prisoners. In the course of the exchange, Hamer turned the woman's attention to Acts 17:26 to illustrate the injustice of the current moment: "[God] hath made of one blood all nations of men for to dwell on all the face of the earth" (King James Version [KJV]). Hamer's utilization of this biblical passage, singular and heroic as her actions were in this circumstance, was no novelty in making the argument for black equality. Just such a reference leaped to the lips of black Methodist minister Isaac Reed Berry, whom we met in the last chapter. His ordination in 1917 initiated a ministry that was marked in part by the era's fundamentalist-modernist controversy. When Berry rose to his pulpit to undertake an exposition of this same text, the Apostle Paul's speech to the Athenians in Acts 17, he touched on several theological points typical of a fundamentalist mindset: This passage demonstrated that God is the Creator who "created the world and all things therein," that God is the Giver "who giveth to all life breath," and that God will judge all men for their sins at the end of time, proven by the literal historical fact of "the resurrection of Jesus." In the midst of this discourse, Berry took the occasion to mention another aspect of God's character revealed in this text: "God is the Unifier." Quoting Acts 17:26, he noted that the idea of unifying all people was offensive to the Athenians, "who considered themselves a super race, a unique race, and all other races were just a little lower, for they were made out of a little lower dust." In contrast, Paul's "doctrine of One Creator carried with it the doctrine of the oneness of mankind." Applying the text to the present, Berry offered a criticism of racial superiority that struck at the heart of the Jim Crow–white supremacist conception of human nature: "Every man on earth is my brother, no supermen, no super race, we are one in nature and we all need to be saved from sin. He has made of one all nations to dwell on the face of the earth." Along with the variety of theological emphases in this sermon that evidenced strong fundamentalist convictions, Berry paired a racial application bearing directly on the segregation of his day.[1]

Such was the position in which black clergy who embraced fundamentalist tenets found themselves, seeking to proclaim and defend the theologically conservative "fundamentals" against perfidious attacks, while also offering race-conscious applications springing from their particular social context. As we have seen, baseline elements of fundamentalist dogma were by no means delimited by racial boundaries. While the socially constructed racial strictures of the Jim Crow era attempted to absolutely divide "black" from "white," religious commonalities across such border lines were a reality of life, especially in the realm of Christian theology, which not only predated this American segregationist context but also sought to address spiritual problems of eternal and universal significance. In the early twentieth century, theological conservatives from both sides of the color line offered highly congruent formulations and biblical defenses of such central doctrinal pillars as the deity of Christ, Jesus's literal resurrection and return, and especially the commitment to biblical inspiration and inerrancy. Affirming in parallel their alignment with both church-historical orthodoxy and the apostolic teachings of scripture as validation for their doctrinal stances, both black and white conservative Protestants identified these "fundamental" doctrines as definitive of the true Christian faith.

Yet neither the profession of a broadly fundamentalist worldview nor the affirmation of these key points of conservative doctrine were, on their own, sufficient to make what we have termed heretofore a "doctrinal fundamentalist" in a historical-theological sense. Because fundamentalism in its historical onset was a reaction against the emerging modernist theology of the late-nineteenth and early twentieth century, the necessary flipside of the positive affirmation of the fundamental doctrines of the faith was its negative corollary—the willingness to openly and publicly rebuke and condemn modernist theology as a threat to true Christianity. This constituted another common theological trait among white and black fundamentalists. But even in the face of this commonality, black preachers often advanced racially conscious applications of their fundamentalist and antimodernist convictions that would have been foreign to most of their white counterparts.

Perhaps nowhere did the public rebuke of modernism carry more cachet than from behind the sacred desk itself. From the very beginning of the Protestant Reformation, the preached word had functioned as the central focus of the Protestant worship service; no less a Protestant authority than Martin Luther remarked that "the preacher's mouth and the words that I heard are not his; they are the words and message of the Holy Spirit."[2] The Reformation's emphasis on the authoritative nature of the preached word was passed down and preserved among its black progeny as well as its white. Indeed, the role of African American ministers in this era as influential and authoritative voices, both in religious and social terms, has been widely attested.[3]

With this in mind, it is well worth noting that black fundamentalist clergy were at times willing to use their position not only to expound on the age-old doctrines of the faith, but also to expressly attack in vivid terms the encroaching dangers of theological modernism. Preachers from a variety of Protestant backgrounds—Methodist, Baptist, Congregationalist—stood before their local congregations and sometimes even before their entire denominational bodies to decry the infidelities of modernist thought as a sure means to shipwreck the faith of those whom it ensnared. A pronounced antimodernist streak ran through many of the same voices that, as we saw earlier, gave fullthroated positive defenses of the fundamentals. In fact, the pulpit proved to be a place where the two sides of this particular coin—positive affirmation of fundamentalist doctrine and negative polemics against the dangers of modernism—could come together at once, with the authoritative backing of the word of God as faithfully proclaimed by the servant of God from behind the sacred desk.

That an antimodernist polemic existed alongside fundamentalist doctrine is perhaps no major surprise, although in the context of our exploration here, which defines fundamentalism on the basis of both positive affirmations and negative denials, it is undeniably important. But even more interesting in this context are the applications that black ministers could draw from their considerations of fundamentalist doctrine and polemics. As with white fundamentalist ministers, there were of course calls to holy living, jeremiads against the moral ills of society such as drunkenness and violence, exhortations to steadfastness in the faith, and appeals urging constant fidelity to historic biblical orthodoxy and orthopraxy. But another strain of application turns up in a number of the doctrinally fundamentalist sermons delivered by African American clergymen—a willingness to bring the fundamentals to bear on questions of racial equality and to position modernism as a threat not only to Christianity in general but to African Americans in particular. And while normally these sorts of applications were not necessarily the central crux of the sermon itself—after all, application is typically a subsidiary element of the expository task—that they exist at all provides a point of marked contrast between these conservative black preachers and their white fundamentalist counterparts, who would likely never have considered making such points from the same texts and doctrines. In fact, while fundamentalism is often associated with social and political conservatism, the racial applications advanced by these black fundamentalist ministers complicate this paradigm in that they incorporated major challenges to the social and political status quo on matters of race.[4] Thus as we consider the fundamentalist polemics emanating from behind the pulpits of black ministers, we see at once doctrinal affirmations and antimodernist arguments that crossed the color line as well as divergences in application stemming from segregation in the era of Jim Crow.

## Confronting Modernism from the Pulpit

As fundamentalist ministers considered the rising tide of liberal theology within American Protestant churches, they concluded that modernism's challenges to traditional conservative orthodoxy were multitudinous. Modernism offered a naturalist alternative to traditionally supernatural presuppositions, it embraced higher critical methods at odds with the doctrine of divine biblical inspiration, and it presented a merely human Christ who in his life and death functioned primarily as a moral exemplar rather than a divine atoning sacrifice. But from the fundamentalist perspective, the many errors of modernist theology—whether about the nature of scripture, the divinity of Christ, the reality of miracles, the literal resurrection, or the atoning work of Christ—all converged on a central problem, which was modernism's denial of the biblical gospel. Without a divinely inspired revelation, fundamentalist preachers argued, no one could know the salvific truth of the gospel; without a divine Messiah, God's holy law could not be truly fulfilled on behalf of fallen mankind; without an atoning sacrifice, sinful man could not have peace with God; and without a literal resurrection, in the words of Paul the Apostle, "we are of all people most to be pitied" (1 Corinthians 15:19 [ESV]).

One of the recurring charges fired from conservative pulpits was that in denying central theological tenets of historic Christianity modernists in fact undermined the Christian gospel itself. Modernists were accused of preaching an entirely *different* gospel than that of Christ and the apostles, a gospel that was unable to save anyone. Perhaps no occasion could be more apt for just such a critique than Easter morning, as pastor Edward Franklin Williams prepared to proclaim the resurrection of Jesus to his congregation from a very familiar gospel text in Luke 24:5-6, which recounted the angels' proclamation to the women at Jesus's tomb, "Why seek ye the living among the dead? He is not here, but is risen."

This particular Easter morning, Williams came to the church with the apparent intent to unload both barrels at the modernistic "doubters of the resurrection" who seemed to be so commonplace in the modern world. Quickly incorporating two more of the five fundamentals in addition to the literal resurrection, he further qualified these "doubters" as those who also "criticize the Gospels" (raising the issue of biblical inspiration) and who "reject the Saviour as a Redeemer" (invoking the issue of atonement). After such an astringent introduction, Williams allowed for a brief moment of commonality, admitting that all shared a "substantial agreement that the teaching of Jesus reaches the high water mark of excellence, that in morals he has no superior, that in example he should be accepted as the only worthy moral leader of men." The problem for Williams was not that modernists believed that Jesus was a great moral teacher or the supreme example for moral behavior; Williams himself, and indeed all fundamentalists, believed this to be true as well. The problem was that this was *the extent* of what the modernists believed about Jesus, and therefore their doctrine of Christ was anemic and insufficient to save. Hence, Williams lamented: "For them, there is no Easter Day. Christ did not rise from the dead. THEY would not go to the tomb to see if it were empty. That would for them be only seeking the dead among the dead. . . . THEY are ethical followers of Jesus, nothing more." Holding up modernists as a sharp contrast to the disciples, who came to the empty tomb to see it firsthand, Williams made clear their shortcomings relative to his interpretation of the biblical testimony.[5]

Not content to conclude his critique there, however, Williams went on to declare to his congregation that the "Christ" of the modernists was in fact a false and powerless Christ, unable to actually sustain or fulfill the promises of the gospel: "The ethical does not exhaust Jesus. He is ethical because he is something more. If Christ is not risen your faith is vain. . . . Such a Saviour can be nothing more than a dead unrisen Saviour for us. He is no Saviour from sin. He cannot forgive. He cannot purify the heart." Theological liberalism, then, was not merely errant on a few pedantic points of doctrine, but was in reality an entirely false system without hope for salvation, forgiveness, or purification—indeed, without a true "Saviour" at all. Modernists "refuse to give [Christ] their confidence or to accept his aid or to credit him with any supernatural power," and therefore "people like these have no real acquaintance with the living Jesus." Undeniably tied up in Williams's opposition to the modernist denial of biblical inspiration, denial of supernaturalism, denial of the atonement, and denial of the resurrection was the single overriding conviction that these theological innovations constituted an essential denial of the gospel itself and therefore placed modernist adherents *outside* the fellowship of true Christian believers. The fact that such people might claim to follow Jesus made no difference to Williams. As far as he was concerned, their denials of essential gospel elements demonstrated that they were absolutely separated from the true Christ and served only a "Christ of their own creation, a creation who has never existed on earth or in heaven." Such was the modernist's hopeless estate.[6]

Williams returned to this theme many times from his pulpit. Another Sunday morning he took the text of 2 Corinthians 11:3 to paint modernists as the modern-day analogues of the "super-apostles," the Apostle Paul's bitter antagonists in the Corinthian church. They were "false teachers then, [and] now," seeking in their "wickedness" to "pervert men from the ways of truth" so that souls might perish. These men "assumed to be Christian teachers," but in reality sought to undermine the essential message of the Christian faith. "If you can destroy the deity of Christ," Williams proclaimed, "you can discredit his message." The siren song of these modern-day false teachers calling men to "be liberal, be advanced thinkers" echoed the serpent's insidious appeal to human pride and vanity in the Genesis creation narrative—"you will be like God, knowing good and evil." In just the same way that the Apostle Paul compared the deception of the super-apostles with Satan's deception in the Garden of Eden (2 Corinthians 11:13–15), so Williams carried the same idea forward into the twentieth century: "So Eve was persuaded. So are men now." And just as Paul mourned that some of the Corinthians had fallen prey to the "different gospel" of the super-apostles, so Williams warned that the modern-day false teachers sought to deny the divinity of Christ and in their "air of superior learning" tried to convince people not to "narrow [themselves] down to the old gospel." Thus Williams exhorted his congregants to "Be on guard lest your minds be corrupted from the simplicity of the gospel that is in Christ."[7]

Williams' "simple gospel" also entailed a harsh rebuke of the era's nascent social gospel message, which was being developed in the late nineteenth and early twentieth centuries by the likes of Baptist minister Walter Rauschenbusch and progressive Congregationalist pastor Washington Gladden. Such modernist "false teachers," he warned, not only rejected the divine personhood of Christ but also eviscerated the true gospel of personal salvation through faith in Christ. Their "liberality" and "advanced thinking," Williams noted in exasperation, offered a spiritually hollow message centered on the idea that "man could save society without saving its units" and that society could "get new and salutary institutions without regenerating the men who make them."[8] This salvo seems to have been aimed directly at the social gospel perspective that Rauschenbusch, among others, had been formulating since at least the 1890s during his time as a Baptist pastor in Hell's Kitchen, New York. In his eventual systematic theology of the social gospel, Rauschenbusch summarized the movement's key tenets, one of which was that the message of Christianity must be adjusted to effect the "regeneration of the social order" in lieu of focusing on individual salvation. To "keep Christian doctrine unchanged" was to "ensure its abandonment" in the modern world. This being the case, Rauschenbusch practically bristled when theological conservatives argued that "regeneration is what men need" and that "we cannot have a regenerate society without regenerate individuals."[9]

This was, of course, exactly the critique that E. F. Williams was leveling at the social gospel in his sermon, for he believed that the supernatural regeneration of the individual was the primary foundation upon which any meaningful social action and moral reform must be built. Williams declared that this social gospel, whose proponents styled themselves "advanced thinkers" who were not "narrowed down to the old gospel," was simply another illustration of how those who imbibed the wisdom of the world "knew not God." The theological admissions of men like Rauschenbusch, casting doubt as they did on Christ's deity and preaching a gospel that privileged social salvation above individual regeneration, placed social gospel advocates in the lineage of wicked deceivers stretching back through the first-century Corinthian super-apostles all the way to the devil himself in the Garden of Eden. The polemical bite from Williams' pulpit assured his hearers that modernists worshiped a false Jesus, preached a false gospel, and sought to devour the souls of their prey. In short, they had far more in common with Satan than they did with Christ.[10]

Others of Williams's ministerial colleagues took a similar tack. Just as Williams drew on 2 Corinthians 11 to castigate the modernist "false teachers" of his day, so Bishop John Albert Johnson turned to a closely related text in the same letter—2 Corinthians 4:1–2—in order to expound both the proper role of the Christian ministry and the problems of false teaching within the church. A slightly younger contemporary of Williams, Johnson had a ministerial career that stretched from 1875 to 1928 and took him around the globe. Born in Canada, his early career included time in Canada, Bermuda, and the United States. Later he also served as the African Methodist Episcopal (AME) Church's resident bishop in South Africa from 1908 to 1916, and when he returned to the United States, he served as the presiding bishop of the AME's Second Episcopal District, encompassing portions of the upper South from Maryland, Virginia, and North Carolina.[11] Johnson, then, was no unsophisticated provincial preacher; rather he was an influential and respected voice in the AME Church.

As a minister whose career in the AME extended well into the 1920s, Johnson was quite familiar with the doctrinal issues at stake in the fundamentalist-modernist conflict. He was a stalwart defender of numerous key fundamentalist doctrines, including especially biblical inerrancy and the divinity of Christ. Modernist perspectives that necessarily denied such doctrines were in his view "vitally defective," being both injurious to man and dishonoring toward God.[12] So when Johnson preached his sermon titled "The Christian Ministry," he did so with the twofold aim of expounding a positive assessment of the role of the Christian ministry and of offering a negative evaluation of those who might seek to undermine it.

Johnson's text from 2 Corinthians 4:1–2 finds the Apostle Paul contrasting the purity of his ministry, as a commission received from God, against the deceitfulness of his Corinthian antagonists, whose attempts to exalt themselves above Christ's true apostles led them to boastfully call themselves "super-apostles": "Therefore seeing we have this ministry, as we have received mercy, we faint not; But have renounced the hidden things of dishonesty, not walking in craftiness, nor handling the word of God deceitfully; but by manifestation of the truth commending ourselves to every man's conscience in the sight of God" (KJV). Having read this text aloud and introduced its primary intent of contrasting the Apostle Paul against the wicked false teachers in Corinth, Johnson paraphrased the apostle's message for the current day and age: "We are ... not handling the Word of God deceitfully—not preaching an adulterated truth as a flexible gospel; not blind to the prejudices, or silent as to the vices, of those who hear us; but by manifestation of the truth, commending ourselves to every man's conscience in the sight of God."[13]

Here, again, any compromise with respect to central Christian doctrines amounted to an attack on the very gospel itself. Such compromise, which resulted in a "flexible gospel," was "deceitful," "adulterated," and those who took such a view, motivated by "eagerness to conciliate prejudice and disarm opposition," managed not only to "compromise ... the high tone of Christian teaching" but to present the gospel "only as one among many systems, which all men may accept, or reject at pleasure."

Though he failed to use the exact word, the picture he painted was clearly meant to elicit the image of modernist theological compromise on such key issues as those enumerated in *The Fundamentals*. In fact, Johnson directly contrasted these false teachers' gospel of compromise with the doctrinal pillars of traditional Christianity, including the central issues of substitutionary atonement and individual justification. Whereas the real Christian ministry was "Heaven-inspired and Heaven-sustained" to deal with the renewal of "the inner man," these modern teachers were perfectly willing to eviscerate gospel truths such as "the atonement," the "sinner's pardon," and the regenerating work of the Holy Spirit in favor of "the teaching of the political agitator [or] the philanthropic idealist" who "ignores . . . the doctrine of the fall." In modernist theology, he concluded, the old gospel "whose sound is always music and whose sight is always joy" was so dreadfully obscured as to make it "hardly to be recognized."[14]

At the same time, Johnson was concerned to make clear the positive duties of the true Christian ministry, built on the essential fundamental doctrines of the "old gospel." Modernist compromise on these core theological issues, he said, was driven by their conviction that the historical orthodoxy of ages past was unable to effectively address the evils and injustices facing modern society.[15] Modernists' ultimate infidelity was therefore born out of "their eagerness to conciliate prejudice and disarm opposition." But for Johnson this modernist approach seemed especially foolhardy, because the orthodox Christian ministry, armed with the age-old fundamental doctrines of the church historic, was not merely an institution relegated to the realm of otherworldly reflection, but was in fact an institution ordained by divine providence to have an active and effective role in the events of this world. The Christian ministry, Johnson intoned, "has a business with the world. Some people think it has not. It is the divinely appointed agency for the communication of God's will to man."[16]

Without question, this duty was otherworldly, or heavenly-focused, in certain crucial respects. As an agent charged with communicating the divine will to the world, the Christian minister was responsible first and foremost for preaching spiritual truths in order to save lost souls. The preacher ought to be an "ever-speaking witness of man's feebleness and of God's strength," and his message must be grounded in "the great truths of God's will and man's duty, of the atonement and the sinner's pardon, of the Spirit's work and the believer's growth." The business of the ministry "has to do with eternity," and the eternal aspect of the business of soul-saving and preaching the gospel thus superseded every other human institution.[17]

At the same time, however, Johnson's view of the ministry was not limited to the otherworldly. As he said in his paraphrase of the sermon text, "[We are] not blind to the prejudices, or silent as to the vices, of those who hear us." Contrary to those who saw theological compromise on essential Christian doctrines as the only way to effectively "conciliate prejudice" in the world, Johnson seemed to be saying, the Christian minister whose feet were firmly planted on the foundation of biblical and historical orthodoxy was able—was, indeed, duty bound—to identify and address the "prejudices" and "vices" of the world around him. Later on, as he approached the conclusion of the morning's message, Johnson opined on the minister's charge to appeal to men's consciences, once again reaffirming the dual application of the minister's charge: "His wont, his business, his sole business, is to bring out the world's conscience in answer to the truths of Divine revelation. . . . Not simply that people may escape hell, and reach heaven, but that through awakened conscience people may resolve on a holy life."[18]

The minister's duty, then, built upon the "great truths" of the "old gospel" which some modern thinkers were so eager to cast aside, was bound up in firstly pointing people toward reconciliation with God and eternal life, and secondly overcoming the vice, prejudice, and evil in the world by applying the truths of divine revelation to individual consciences. From this perspective, in fact, only a theological conservative committed to the fundamentals could effectively work to overcome prejudice and vice in the world, because the entire basis of such transformation was the power of the "Divine revelation" of scripture. In other words, according to Johnson, the fundamentalist was actually *better equipped* to speak to issues of vice and injustice in society than was the modernist—a notion entirely contrary to the modernist presupposition that Christianity's relevance to the modern world depended upon its willingness to embrace doctrinal adjustments and innovations.[19] Unwilling to concede the arena of prophetic social exhortation, Johnson posited that adherence to the Christian fundamentals, not divergence from them, was the only sure basis upon which ministers could offer any hope of lasting social change.[20]

In his exposition of 2 Corinthians 4:1–2, Johnson remained relatively vague on the types of "prejudices" against which the Christian ministry was to stand as a bulwark—though, his choice of the word "prejudice" in and of itself, given the context of an African American church in the age of Jim Crow, certainly lends implicit racial overtones to the oration. Elsewhere, however, he was pleased to expound in more detail on the social benefits of the old-time gospel of "[salvation] by Grace through faith," which like Christ himself "is the same yesterday, today, and forever." In a sermon tellingly titled "The Outlook," Johnson expressly considered the future of the black race in the twentieth-century United States by looking backward to the progress of the nineteenth century. Positing that "the dominant feature of a people's religion is the dominant feature of the life of the nation," Johnson proclaimed that the one dominating thought of the prior century was "emancipation." The unchanging gospel of a crucified and risen Christ had been applied in the foregoing decades to effect perhaps the most earth-shattering social change in the history of the United States—deliverance of African Americans from the yoke of literal slavery—and renewed applications of the same truth to new and different circumstances would define their future in the coming century as well. The "future of the negro" in the twentieth century, his "ability to hold his own . . . against the aggressions of his enemies in this country," would depend more upon the quality and overt application of his faith-formed character than upon anything else.[21]

While Johnson's encounters with modernist theology, at least in its formalized twentieth-century encapsulation, came toward the latter stages of his career, a fellow Methodist preacher in his region by the name of Isaac Reed Berry was coming of ministerial age during the height of the fundamentalist-modernist controversy. A native of Fodice, Texas, Berry made his way east in his early twenties with a thirst for higher education. After earning a bachelor's degree from Howard University under the tutelage of Dean Kelly Miller and subsequently training as one of very few black students at the Boston University School of Theology, Berry was ordained to the ministry in 1917. Over the course of several decades he pastored numerous churches in the upper South, including churches in Virginia and Maryland that fell within the very same district over which John Albert Johnson sat as presiding bishop during the 1920s.

Although Berry's pastoral career was just lifting off as Johnson's was entering its twilight, many of the same themes, theological commitments, and polemical thrusts against modernism were to be found in his sermons. If anything, Berry was perhaps more overt in his sermonic affirmations of fundamentalism and more aggressive in tone when addressing the dangers of modernist theologizing. For one thing, he was not shy about lauding and affirmatively quoting popular fundamentalist figures as he addressed his congregation. On the occasion of a sermon on John 3:17 centering on the topic of evangelism and conversion, Berry opened his discourse pointing to the example of Billy Sunday, the controversial professional baseball player turned fundamentalist revivalist, as an evangelistic model to emulate. Sunday was here affirmed as "America's greatest asset" and "one of the greatest soul winners since the days of the apostles," whose ministry ensured that "the moral history of this world will be forever changed." Once "a Christless Sabbath desecrating baseball player," he had been transformed into one of the preeminent instruments of God's salvific work in the world.[22]

Beyond citing approbatory anecdotes, Berry was also known to quote from his pulpit such major fundamentalist figures as North Carolina native A. C. Dixon, a fiery Baptist preacher who spoke and wrote aggressively against the social gospel, higher criticism, and all manner of modernist theology. In a sermon on the doctrine of hell, which was filled with both fundamentalist doctrinal affirmations and antimodernist condemnations, Berry invoked the words of the well-known fundamentalist: "It was A. C. Dixon who said, 'If we had more preaching on hell in the pulpit, we would have less practice of hell in the community.'"[23] Here, Berry was alluding to an article that Dixon penned for the *Watchman* in 1904 arguing passionately in favor of a constellation of fundamentalist positions that he perceived to be under attack, including the deity of Christ, the inerrancy of the Bible, supernatural regeneration, the virgin birth, and the dangerous infidelity of evolutionary theory.[24] The fact that Berry read, recalled, and quoted Dixon on this count illustrates a significant degree of doctrinal kinship, as well as a willingness to publicly associate himself with fundamentalism through his pulpit ministry.

But Berry was not simply quoting a person who happened to preach fundamentalist doctrines. In quoting Dixon, he was in fact drawing on one of the primary editors of *The Fundamentals*. Moreover, Berry's argumentation in this sermon at times bore striking resemblance to that found in the pages of *The Fundamentals*, making his reference to Dixon all the more conspicuous. Regarding Matthew 25:46—"And these will go away into eternal punishment, but the righteous into eternal life"— Berry argued for the perpetual nature of hell, because the same Greek word for "eternal" is applied as a modifier to both the punishment of the wicked and the life of the righteous:

> The Greek word for eternal is "aeonian." It comes from the noun "aion" from which we get our "aeon," which means "age, epoch, or a long period of time." . . . In the N.T. as well as in the Greek translation of the O.T. (the Septuagint) it is the one word that is used when the idea of "endless" is meant to be conveyed, and it must be so constructed unless the context, or the word it modifies, demands otherwise. Then, too, the same word being used in both the clauses of the verse under examination, it would appear that if the eternal punishment is not endless, neither is the eternal life.[25]

Notably, this is the same line of argumentation W. C. Procter takes in his examination of hell in volume three of *The Fundamentals*:

> Much has been made of the fact that the Greek word "*aionios*" (used by our Lord in Matt. 18:8 and 25:41, 46, and translated "everlasting" in the Authorized, and "eternal" in the Revised, Version) literally means "age-long." . . . The dilemma becomes acute in considering the words of our Lord recorded in Matt. 25:46, where precisely the same word is used concerning the duration of the reward of the righteous and the retribution of the wicked, for only by violent perversion and distortion can the same word in the same sentence possess a different signification. . . . The doctrines of heaven and hell seem to stand or fall together, for both . . . have the same word "everlasting" applied to their duration.[26]

This is enough to at least make one wonder whether Berry was an explicit consumer of *The Fundamentals*. In the course of just this single sermon, Berry demonstrated a familiarity with A. C. Dixon's writings, a readiness to quote and to approvingly cite fundamentalist exemplars, and a profoundly close parallel to *The Fundamentals* in doctrinal argumentation.

This sermon on "Hell" also illustrated another commonality between Berry and the likes of A. C. Dixon—his willingness to go on the offensive against modernist compromise. The "child of faith" would accept the doctrine of hell, unpalatable as it might seem to the human mind, because "God's word says there is a hell." Many modern people, relying on their own "cunningly devised speculations," may claim to have "outgrown this antiquated creed"—a cadre that included "new-thought theologians, dream-enamored poets, and sentimental preachers"—but they would do so in defiance of "anything they ever read in the Word of the living God." In reality, these modernist "sentimental preachers" were preaching "the devil's doctrine that hell is only a myth." Such liberal innovations, diverging as they did from the teachings of scripture and the longstanding historic faith of the church, were beastly ideas that were "spun always out of man's own brain like the web of a spider out of his own belly." Purveyors of these manmade ideas might be up to date on "modern psychology" or other "natural considerations," but Berry rested his case on the eternality and trustworthiness of the Bible: "I would rather be a little bit out of date than be out of harmony, even a little bit, with the abiding eternal Word of God."[27]

As these thrusts of the rhetorical sword demonstrate, Berry's preaching was often characterized by his emphasis on what he understood to be the nature of the Bible—its eternality, immutability, authority, sufficiency, veracity, and inspiration, among other qualities—and on the significance of these biblical qualities for true Christian faith and praxis. As a result, one especially prominent target of Berry's antimodernist polemical ire was the practice of higher biblical criticism, which he saw as a profound betrayal of the scriptures themselves and an enormous danger to his congregants' souls. This concern placed Berry squarely in line with the theological attitude reflected in *The Fundamentals* (completed, incidentally, just two years prior to Berry's ordination).[28] Chastising the modern church for its wanton lack of spiritual zeal and fervor, Berry thundered out his warning that "The church today is being rocked to sleep by Satan in the cradle of carnality, drugged by such opiates as annihilation, new theology, [and] higher criticism."²⁹ There seems to have been little ambiguity in Berry's stance regarding modernism's "new theology" and the higher critical approach to biblical scholarship.

On other occasions Berry went to even greater lengths to decry those who would reject the Bible as God's very word. In late 1923 or early 1924, as debate and invective with regard to fundamentalism and modernism whirled in the wider American Protestant landscape, Berry took to his pulpit to deliver a sermon entitled "An Attempt to Destroy God's World, Rejecting the Saving Word."³⁰ This particular morning Berry took his opening text from Isaiah 40:8 ("The word of God shall stand forever"), indicating the sermon's prevailing theme, but he spent a great deal of his time narrating, with his characteristic storyteller's flair, an entirely different text—the story of ungodly King Jehoiakim from Jeremiah 36. As the story goes, God commanded the prophet Jeremiah to write down his prophecies of judgment against Israel and Judah in order that they might be read and proclaimed publicly in the temple. However, once King Jehoiakim heard about this, he was so incensed at the imprecatory words of the prophet that he confiscated the scroll, and, as his scribe read it to him, the king cut the scroll to pieces with a knife and burned the scraps in his fire pot. "The guilty king would not tolerate such a Bible," Berry concluded. "Jehoiakim dared to set himself above the Word of God. He hated it because it showed forth the evil of his deeds and therefore he wished to have it destroyed."³¹

Having built up the congregation's perception of King Jehoiakim's crime as a particularly heinous and wicked affront to God, Berry deftly noted that even today "Jehoiakim's knife is still being used against the Bible." It rested most ominously in the hand of "the coarse infidel" who would seek to eviscerate the scriptures. Like Jehoiakim, Berry declared, "Higher criticism has dissected [the Bible] and put it through the fiercest fires. . . . Infidelity has attacked it with every possible kind of knife and fire, but it has kept multiplying and filling the world." In terms quite reminiscent of the language of *The Fundamentals*, Berry laid higher criticism and "infidelity" in parallel, complete with an imprecatory modern-day application of God's judgment on Jehoiakim: "'His dead body shall be cast out in the day to heat and in the night to the frost.' So shall perish in their wickedness all those that try to cut and burn the law of the Lord." Those who might seek to dissect the Bible would pass away, Berry proclaimed, but the "inspired" and "imperishable" Bible itself would always endure without fail.[32]

Berry returned to this theme in another sermon centered once again on an Old Testament narrative, titled "A Lost Bible Is Found." Drawing from the story in 2 Kings 22 of Josiah rediscovering the Book of the Law during his renovation of the temple, Berry aimed to convince his congregants of the various ways that the Bible was being "lost" in their day and age. The Bible, he said, is sometimes "lost" even among church-going people because of disuse, neglect, or wild misinterpretation. But the wiles of worldly scholarship and unbelief also conspired to bury the Bible and quench its light—a conspiracy most notably headed by the "confusion" spread by "extreme and contradictory criticism" of the Bible. This biblical criticism joined with "worldliness, infidelity, bigotry, sacerdotalism, [and] unbelieving and unreasonable scholarship" to represent the Bible as a collection of "arbitrary rules and regulations that change with climate and class, age and condition" rather than as the immutable and universally applicable "eternal laws of God's nature and of our own life." While such insidious forces aimed to "hide the Bible, bury it, keep it from doing its blessed work in the world," it was up to the believers within earshot of Berry's sermon to embrace the role of King Josiah, recover the Bible, and further God's work in the world.[33]

It is noteworthy that within his deprecatory litany of antichristian forces, which began with biblical criticism and ended with unbelieving scholarship, Berry also conspicuously included "bigotry," almost certainly because he saw any subversion of God's word as undermining God's commands for social equality, unity, and fraternity. From Berry's pulpit, texts that testified to the singular origin of mankind as God's special creation, such as Acts 17:26 ("[God] made of one blood all nations of men") and Psalm 133:1 ("Behold, how good and pleasant it is for brethren to dwell together in unity"), underscored the full humanity and equality of African Americans and amounted to a divine rebuke of the Jim Crow racial hierarchy.[34] If modernist higher critics eroded the trustworthy foundation upon which such a rebuke stood, then they were functionally upholding bigotry as well as denying a fundamental truth of the faith. In this respect, for Berry fundamentalist conviction and antimodernist polemic dovetailed with racial reality. Upholding the Bible against critical threats constituted a racial as well as a religious duty. Modernists might hold the Bible to be errant in its history and malleable in its commands, but Berry reassured his congregants that indeed "its doctrines are holy, its precepts binding, its histories true, and its decisions immutable." He even invoked the global historic tradition of the church by quoting the luminary fourth-century preacher John Chrysostom: "Here is the cause of all evils, our not knowing the Scripture." Higher critics were part of "the cause of all evils"—including "bigotry"—since they cast doubt on the authority and veracity of the scripture.[35]

Higher criticism was not, of course, Berry's only polemical target from the pulpit. If the issue of biblical inspiration was significant enough for Berry to place modernist doubters outside the Christian faith, then so too were the other fundamentals, including the atoning work of Christ on the cross. The centrality of Jesus's blood atonement in Berry's theological system provided him with reason both to denounce modernist infidelity in the starkest of terms and to apply the blood of Christ to the pressing racial injustices of his day. The doctrine of Christ's substitutionary atonement on the cross was "absolutely necessary for the atonement of man's sin and for the reconciliation of the sinner to God" and therefore constituted nothing less than "the cardinal doctrine" of the apostles' first-century preaching.[36] In a sermon-length exposition devoted to this single idea, he proclaimed that "the blood of Jesus Christ" is "God's one essential for salvation":

> Oh, I wish I had the power to write in letters of flame across the skies—"without the shedding of blood there is no remission of sins" for there is no hope of going to heaven without the shed blood of the Crucified Son of God. And the man who rejects the blood will have a fearful time when he meets God face to face. For if there is no remission without the shedding of blood, then the man who rejects the blood is hopelessly lost. We must go by the way of the atonement if we go to heaven. . . . Your only hope and my only hope, and the world's only hope lies in the fountain of Jesus' blood.[37]

Given the weight that Berry placed upon the necessity of Christ's shed blood, he considered those who denied the doctrine of substitutionary atonement to be tools of the devil, complicit in "Satan's masterpiece" of convincing men that the blood of Christ is nonessential. Satan's gospel "is a gospel of works and is being preached by a lot of salvation-by-character infidels today." Invoking Matthew 7:21-23, Berry made it clear that these "infidels" were people who explicitly claimed to be Christians while in fact preaching a false and damning gospel.[38] They might all be "splendid people" with a "splendid record of good works to their credit," but if they "drifted out to eternity without the blood of Jesus Christ" then they were really in the end nothing more than "the dupes of Satan."[39]

Tellingly, one of the personalities whom Berry placed in the shoes of the false believers of Matthew 7:23—that is, one to whom Jesus would say, "I never knew you"—was described as "a member of the Riverside Church," which was the Manhattan congregation of leading modernist spokesman and pastor Harry Emerson Fosdick. This leaves the compelling impression that Berry was not merely calling out a vague idea of liberalism, but was in fact pointing to the most famous of all modernist churches and modernist preachers of the era in his polemic. Indeed, it is difficult *not* to imagine that Berry had Fosdick specifically in mind when, barely a paragraph later, he intoned: "Some of our greatest preachers, so called, have taken the fire out of hell, the glory out of heaven, the blood out of the atonement, the inspiration out of the Bible, and God out of Christ. They have gone over to Satan, and they are his, bag and baggage." One would be hard-pressed to find a more pithy fundamentalist critique.[40]

But even so, Berry was not content for the Christian faith and the Christian life to simply halt at the doctrine of atonement or any of the fundamental doctrines. These doctrines formed the basis of the Christian faith and the foundation of the Christian's life in the world, and as such they entailed social applications centered on justice, equality, and fraternity. Taking a Christmas text from Luke 2:14—the angels' proclamation of Christ's birth—Berry tackled at length the subject of human brotherhood and the evils of racial, economic, and class inequality in a sermon titled "The Brotherhood of Man." In doing so, however, he bookended the sermon with multiple references to Christ's atonement as a propitiation (an atoning sacrifice that absorbs God's wrath), as if to position the entire discussion of social conscience within the larger frame of the fundamental doctrines surrounding Christ's person and work.[41] Setting up the concept of human social conscience within the context of the atonement, Berry opened the sermon by reading the text,

"Glory to God in the highest, and on earth peace and good will to men," and then proclaiming that "Christ came into the world not only to be a propitiation for the sins of men but also to establish and perfect the brotherhood of man."[42]

In order to begin addressing issues of systemic injustice—both racial and economic—Berry defined the "brotherhood of man" as having both individual and social components. This brotherhood not only exists "between man and man" but also "between the individual man and society," meaning that there is "an obligation resting alike upon the individual and society." Yet this ideal of human brotherhood was being stymied by the "inequitable distribution of wealth and the lack of equal opportunities for all." In identifying systemic inequities that demanded redress, Berry was by no means supporting an attitude of dependence or vocational indolence—indeed, in other contexts he lauded the inestimable value of individual diligence and hard work as "the key that has unlocked all the treasures throughout the centuries." But systemic imbalances in society had to be rectified so that true Christian charity was available to those who sincerely needed it and opportunities were equally available to all people regardless of class or social standing.[43]

This attitude of social concern also dovetailed with spiritual concerns for people's individual salvation, connecting it back to the sermon's bookended references to propitiation and atonement. Yes, Christ came into the world to become a propitiation for mankind's sin, and Berry's concern for saving souls remained evident throughout the whole sermon, but he also believed that meeting physical and social needs often served as important preparation for people to accept the message of Christ's propitiatory sacrifice. The Christian, therefore, should be looking to meet the needs of others (individuals and groups) in society as a way of reaching out with the message of Christ to meet their even greater spiritual need: "Brotherhood comprehends the physical needs first and then it looks to the hunger of the soul." Thus, although Berry held that "the grand object and the great duty of the gospel ministry . . . is to lift up the Savior by preaching before sin-sick men, who need salvation, who desire the forgiveness of God's grace . . . to lift him up in the greatness of his love to sinners, and in his all-sufficient power to save from sin, death, and hell," his conception of gospel ministry was not divorced from the physical and social needs of the surrounding world.

Meeting such needs was not the central purpose of the ministry, but it was a significant outworking of that ministry's function in the world. Ever with an eye toward personal salvation through faith in Christ, Berry's gospel had clear and undeniable social implications without becoming a "social gospel."[44]

As Berry's sermon on "The Brotherhood of Man" proceeded, he continued to expound the twin themes of spiritual and social needs in the context of systemic injustice. Berry argued that it would be impossible for the nation to instill in its children a "high and spiritual character" so long as "means of life are denied to any individual, class, or race to develop into robust manhood and womanhood." With this mention of race, he was able to pivot from inequality in general to racial inequality in particular. The fact that social inequality prevented oppressed communities from developing "robust manhood and womanhood" appears to speak to the dehumanization of African Americans by the era's racial codes. Race antagonism, he noted, was one of the clearest and most notable hindrances to the brotherhood of man.[45] And the solution he proposed involved challenging one of the most visceral elements of the Jim Crow racial hierarchy—the prohibition on racial intermarriage.[46] Recognizing that toppling this deeply institutionalized prejudice was a necessary step in order for black Americans to attain full civil equality and to be recognized as fully human in the eyes of the wider American society, Berry argued that "when wedlock is unrestricted except by moral law, individual taste and pleasure, the heart of the races will beat as one. When this is accomplished, one race will cease lauding it over and domineering any other race and the race antagonism will melt away like a frost on a bright spring morning before the glare of the rising sun." If this key element of his era's racial codes could be overcome, if the races were able to mix freely within marital and familial bonds, then human brotherhood would be closer to reality and the message of Christ would spread even more prolifically.[47]

Hence, Berry's commitment to fundamentalist doctrines such as the propitiatory atonement of Christ—which is the context in which he bookended this message—led him to address racism in ways that would have been unthinkable to many of his white fundamentalist counterparts, regardless of how closely they might have aligned on the specifics of their doctrine. The commitment to fundamentalist theology and to antimodernist polemics did not elicit an obsession with the afterlife to the exclusion of life in this world; on the contrary, for black ministers like Berry, fundamentalist doctrines appear to have undergirded a commitment to social interventions that challenged the prevailing halls of power.[48] In another sermon decrying the church for the "great social sin" of "segregating itself" and making certain types of people feel unwelcome, and at the same time expounding on the need for the church to rediscover its old convictions about the deity of Christ, his atoning death, the plan of salvation, repentance, regeneration, and justification, Berry summarized the intimate connection between his core, uncompromising doctrinal beliefs and his call for social action: "It is well, the two attributes go together. To ache for Christ means to love human beings, for Christ died for such."[49]

On yet another occasion Berry highlighted the widespread racial inequities of his day by drawing on the principle of Christian unity to make his point. The unity of the church, based on Christians' common redemption through Christ's shed blood, ought to pertain equally "on earth and in heaven." In heaven now, and ultimately at the Second Coming "when Christ shall come in His great majesty of power to judge the quick and the dead," then there will be "no class spirit," "no prejudice," "no racial discrimination," "no envy, jealousy, and selfishness," and "we will all have recourse to the joys that God has prepared." And so it ought to be here and now also, instead of the "destruction of homes, and disfranchisement and discriminations in most subtle, cruel, and hideous forms" that the "Negro suffers today."[50] Thus again and again, Berry's social message, including his *racial* message, stemmed from the very old-time doctrines that modernists had rejected. "We do not need a new theology, a new salvation, a new redeemer," he said. "Jesus Christ is not only drawing more men unto him than ever before, but is gloriously saving them and making them useful members of his church and society."[51] For Berry, the old theology held the remedy to spiritual *and* social ills.

Such hostility toward modernists' penchant for "new theology" manifested in Berry's treatment of other fundamental doctrines as well. In one sermon on the doctrine of prayer, Berry denounced modernism by name, identifying it as an enemy of the faithful biblical teaching on prayer. Prayer entailed "taking God at his word"—something that modernism's rejection of biblical inspiration precluded by default. "The modernist" was here lumped together with "the infidel," "the philosopher," and "the cynic" as faithless enemies of the word of God. "To the modernist," Berry declared, the biblical practice of prayer is "obsolete," whereas "to the believer" it is "irresistible and brings a crown of victory." This clear dichotomy between "modernist" and "believer" conveyed the unmistakable conviction that modernists were not real believers; in Berry's mind, modernists actually stood outside the bounds of the true Christian faith.[52]

In another sermon, this time on the deity of Christ, Berry likewise unloaded on the "false accusers" who would dare to deny such an important doctrine. The modernist idea that "Jesus Christ was good but he was not God" struck Berry as both blasphemous and incoherent. Anticipating the "liar-lunatic-lord" trilemma for which C. S. Lewis would later gain great acclaim, Berry argued that if Christ is not God then he was either "an unpardonable egotist or a hopeless lunatic," but he was most certainly not merely a good moral teacher.[53] To demonstrate Jesus' eternal divine nature, Berry pointed to Christ as the central revelation of the whole Bible, from Genesis to Revelation. Unfolding this expressly Christocentric interpretation in an extended poetic litany, one can almost hear Berry's rhythmic cadence roll off the page in a lyrical fashion that would not be out of place among many an African American preacher today, or even certain of today's Christian hip-hop artists.[54] In the process, Berry identified Christ in terms not only Messianic, redemptive, and salvific, but also explicitly divine:

> Jesus Christ is the heart of the Bible. He is the Shiloh of Genesis, the I Am of Exodus, the star and scepter of Numbers, the rock in Deuteronomy, the captain of the Lord of Hosts in Joshua, the redeemer in Job, He is David's Lord and shepherd, in the Song of Songs he is the beloved; in Isaiah he is the Wonderful Counselor, the Mighty God, the Everlasting Father, the Prince of Peace; in Jeremiah he is the Lord the righteous, in Daniel he is the Messiah, in Zachariah he is the branch, in Haggai he is the desire of nations, in Malachi he is the messenger of the covenant and the sun of righteousness, in the Gospels he is the Redeemer of the whole world, in the Revelation he is the Alpha and Omega.

Berry's recital was replete with divine titles and descriptions—from "the I Am of Exodus" to "David's Lord," from the prophets' "Mighty God" and "Lord the righteous" to Revelation's "Alpha and Omega." From this vantage, any correct reading of Scripture must start with the recognition that "Jesus Christ is the heart of the Bible" from beginning to end, a position that in turn requires recognition of his deity. Consequently, for Berry the divinity of Christ was not only a "fundamental" doctrine on its own terms, but it was also deeply connected to the larger tapestry of Scripture from Genesis to Revelation. This was no isolated theological trifle that could be compartmentalized or severed from the rest of Christianity; the Bible testified about a divine Christ, and in turn confessing Christ as divine was foundational for a true and faithful understanding of the rest of the Scripture. So crucial was this doctrine, Berry concluded, that those modernists and skeptics who reject Christ's deity also reject his saving grace—they once again "crucify him by denying him," meaning that on the day of judgment Jesus will likewise deny them, casting them into the darkness of eternal damnation. Issuing a similar proclamation in yet another sermon on the same topic, he declared in no uncertain terms that Christ's divinity was a sacrosanct pillar of the Christian faith: "It is the Godhead of Jesus that gives value and power to his mission and work. Deny him this crown, and he is reduced to the level of our humanity and the world is left without a redeemer that is mighty to save." To eliminate the divinity of Christ was to eliminate the very essence of Christianity itself, and its entire evangelistic call to salvation.[55]

This evangelistic call to trust and believe in the divine Christ once again provided Berry the opportunity to connect the "old" theology to issues of race. On one such evangelistic occasion he preached a message titled "Blessedness in Sight" based on Luke 10:23, a verse in which Jesus highlights his messianic status by privately telling his disciples, "Blessed are the eyes that see what you see." Berry began and ended his sermon by affixing this idea of "blessedness in sight" to the mission of Jesus. He opened the oration by describing the scene from Luke 2, when God granted Simeon the grace to lay eyes on "the Lord's Christ" before he died, pointing to the blessedness inherent in Jesus's mission to save sinners. He similarly ended with an overt evangelistic call, encouraging his hearers to consider whether their spiritual eyes had truly been opened to their need for Jesus: "Sinners today . . . are going down to hell as fast as time can move. They won't see. . . . Sinner, death is a mad dog seeking whom he may devour. Don't let him catch you, but run, run right into the arms of Jesus. I want to ask you one question—you think you see, but do you see your name written on the Lamb's Book of Life?" In between these evangelistic appeals, Berry ruminated on various ways that people in the world might be able to rightly "see" the world around them.[56]

Notably, Berry's reflections about the blessedness of "sight" included two specifically racial applications: the importance of books and of guns for "opening the eyes" of oppressed black people. On the significance of books for the African American community, he set the discussion initially in the context of slavery. Whereas God "gave us eyes to see," nevertheless "there is a class of citizens that do not want the other class to see" because "seeing sometimes is a dangerous thing. . . . In the days of slavery, it was dangerous for a slave to look in a book. If he did he was subjected to a severe punishment." Literacy had been withheld from slaves out of fear that it might cause them to resist their bondage, and so it was incumbent upon African Americans to pursue literacy now for the good of their race. Books "make you discontent and dissatisfied with your present state"; they "enable a man to improve his condition"; they "help a man to buy land and operate farms," to "own and control banks," to "cooperate with your fellow man for the good of the community," and to "improve your race." Reading books, then, was one method of empowering the black community to rise above the oppressive inequities that the surrounding Jim Crow society had foisted upon them. Indeed, it was the means of self-improvement both socially and spiritually: "If I wanted to know the history of my race and country, I would read books. If I wanted to know the road to heaven and the way to hell, I would read the books. Books will open your eyes and you will see."[57]

If reading books empowered the black community to open their eyes, then a much more literal form of such empowerment came via the firearm. While the power of guns to "force your will upon a reluctant mind and compel another to obey your behest" was not an unqualified good—indeed, it was in many senses "a dangerous thing"—nevertheless guns represented another means to "open your eyes" and to protect life and liberty. Turning his attention again to themes of slavery and emancipation, Berry noted that the Union would never have prevailed in the Civil War "if Lincoln had not armed the blacks." Not only that, but he also evoked the image of the most famous (and successful) slave revolution in the western hemisphere, the Haitian Revolution: "It was with the power of the gun that 2,000 French blacks fought the Battle of Choulevoi"—probably a reference to the Battle of Ravine-à-Couleuvres—and "it was the power of the gun that made Toussaint Louverture the idol of France. Guns are power." Both of these references emphasized the significance of an armed black populace for fighting back against brutalization and injustice, as well as the power that accompanied such resistance.[58]

Berry further lamented that "the negro youth of this country has not military training" and that society would not "send him to West Point or any other of our naval academies [because] he will become wise in the making and use of arms. He will come to see that guns are power." So in this formulation the progress of the race was tied up not only with the idea of an armed populace in general, but also the availability of black participation in the United States military. In this respect Berry's discourse resonates with elements of the New Negro movement—a cultural movement associated with the Harlem Renaissance that emphasized racial consciousness, self-organization, and responding to racial violence with armed self-defense. Indeed, as the New Negro movement emerged in the wake of World War I—just at the time, perhaps not so incidentally, that Isaac Reed Berry was beginning his pulpit ministry—African American veterans played a significant role in challenging white supremacy and embodying many of the ideals of the "New Negro." It is not entirely surprising, then, that Berry elevated black military service as a major avenue for African American progress. "Guns are," after all, "dangerous things to open man's eyes." That these calls for racial advancement through literacy and through armament came as sermon applications amid the evangelistic call for people to "open their eyes" to their spiritual need for the divine Christ illustrates again Berry's willingness to challenge the social and racial status quo, even as he simultaneously maintained a focus on the theologically conservative dictates and fundamentals of his faith.[59]

## "A Happy Blessed Companionship"

If preachers like John Albert Johnson and Isaac Reed Berry took to their pulpits to stridently propagate the core fundamentalist doctrines and overtly condemn modernist theology with polemical flair, their Baptist colleague Lacy Kirk Williams went a step further. Born to two former slaves in 1871, Williams spent his youth in the deep South countryside of Alabama and later Texas, where even as a young boy he played at being a preacher when he and his siblings amused themselves by "holding church" in the backyard of their local schoolhouse. From the very moment of his conversion at the age of thirteen, Williams's path to the ministry seemed to be set, for his salvation experience was accompanied by a dream of his local reverend setting a plow in young Lacey's hands in the midst of an open field and telling him "This is the gospel plow; I will show you how to use it." From an early age Williams aspired to transcend his humble origins and pursue an education in service of "the old-time religion."[60] By 1916 he had risen to a position of sufficient prominence as to be offered the pastorate of Chicago's massive Olivet Baptist Church, and in 1922 he was elected president of the National Baptist Convention (NBC), USA. It was from this position as the president of the NBC that Williams, in the immediate aftermath of the Scopes trial in 1925, decided to overtly adjudicate the bitter and pressing fundamentalist-modernist controversy, and in doing so he clearly, expressly, unequivocally declared that he stood firmly on the fundamentalist side of this great theological divide.[61]

In September 1925 Lacey Kirk Williams was in his third consecutive year serving as the president of the nation's largest black Baptist denomination. In his annual address to the convention Williams not only spent time, as one might expect, informing the convention representatives about the status and affairs of the denomination's various ministry apparatuses, such as the Mission Boards and the Sunday School Publishing Board, but he allocated a substantial portion of his address to adjudicating the urgent issue of fundamentalism and modernism. Just months after the conclusion of the highly publicized Scopes trial, which had thrust the topics of evolution and fundamentalism into the national media spotlight, Williams addressed the leaders of his convention and boldly denounced modernist religion and the closely related topic of evolutionary theory. Evolution, Williams declaimed, was defective on both epistemological and biblical grounds. Even on its own terms, evolution constituted a "fatal, paralyzing hypothesis" that "has no final word on the origin of the species"; it "does not pretend to account for the origin of matter and this world," which for Williams profoundly undercut its purported epistemological and explanatory power. Given that "evolutionists have no satisfactory explanation" for the origin of matter or the origin of life, Williams wondered aloud "how any person in the guise of true academic freedom or in the name of science, logic, religion or theology can advocate a cause so void of all the attributes ascribed to it." But even beyond the question of its own internal value, Williams confidently declared to the NBC that evolution failed the test of biblical scrutiny. To "accept the Biblical account of man's creation," as the president urged his convention to do, was to necessarily "discount the cruel philosophy that he is a creature of fate or a product of the 'survival of the fittest'"; to "believe in the doctrines of the fall of man and consequently the doctrine of Regeneration by the grace of God through Christ Jesus" was to reject the evolutionary narrative of human origins. On the grounds of both its unsustainable internal epistemological claims and its conflict with the external authority of scripture, Williams preached that evolution failed the test of truth.[62]

More than just evolution, the entire program of modernist religion was the focus of Williams's critical attention in this address. Invoking 1 Timothy 1:19, one of the central biblical texts on heresy and false teaching, Williams charged modernists with employing methods that "if not bravely and wisely combatted are calculated to make shipwreck of the faith of an untold number."[63] Just as Paul the Apostle, in charging his protégé Timothy to hold fast to sound doctrine, held up Hymenaeus and Alexander as examples of blasphemers who had "made shipwreck of their faith" and had consequently been "handed over to Satan," so Williams decried the modernist movement as a deceptive siren song intended to shipwreck the faith of unwary Christians.[64] Undermining both the faith of their proselytes and the definitional doctrines of the historic Christian faith itself, modernists "not only discard the inspiration of the scripture, but deny the Deity of Christ and likewise the doctrine of Salvation through his death and suffering. Thus believing, they offer an uncertain dynamic for life and a vague, unsatisfactory immortality, not based upon regeneration, a personal resurrection and a personal relationship to Christ."[65]

In contrast, Williams expressly identified himself—and urged his entire denomination to likewise identify—with the fundamentalists. On grounds biblical, historical, and epistemological, this most influential of black Baptist pastors proclaimed the superiority of the fundamentalist cause. To demonstrate biblical superiority, he invoked all "five fundamentals" in quick succession as examples of fundamentalism's praiseworthy devotion to scriptural teaching over against modernist infidelity:

> [Fundamentalists] accept the teachings of the scripture on the Virgin Birth, the Deity of Jesus Christ, his vicarious sufferings, and his bodily resurrection, his ascension and Second Coming. The Scriptures are to them pregnant with convincing and heart-moving truths. The differentiation, I think, between the Modernists and the Fundamentalists has been very clearly and fairly drawn, and we should not hesitate to take and announce our position. I therefore declare unto you that I believe that we should take our stand with those who believe in the full, sufficient authority of the Scriptures in matters of religion.[66]

Ultimately, then, Williams' endorsement of fundamentalism boiled down at its simplest to the central importance of maintaining a correct doctrine of scripture. Christ's deity, virgin birth, substitutionary atonement, physical resurrection, and second coming, essential as they were to the true Christian faith, all found their basis in the authoritative and inspired testimony of scripture itself. Compromise on the doctrine of scripture would ultimately lead to the abandonment of all these fundamental teachings. For Williams the choice was clear.

Atop this foundation of biblical certainty, Williams appealed to the subordinate but complementary authority of the church historic as evidence for the cause. If the fundamentalists were standing shoulder to shoulder with the theological giants of the past, those stalwart preachers and teachers whose powerful gospel proclamations continued to ring forth down through the halls of history, then their position was on even more solid ground. "Fundamentalists, it seems, keep very good company. They are with Moses and the prophets, Paul and Peter, with Spurgeon, Toliver, Morris and a numberless crowd. Standing with these, it is a happy blessed companionship." While Moses, the prophets, Paul, and Peter served as biblical church-historical exemplars, and Charles Spurgeon stood as a towering figure on the nineteenth-century English Baptist landscape, the references to "Toliver" and "Morris" evoked figures in the black National Baptist tradition with whom Williams shared personal connections. Elias C. Morris was his predecessor as the denomination's president, and evangelist I. Benjamin Toliver first organized Mt. Aria Baptist Church in Taylor, Texas, where Williams had once served as pastor.[67] The "happy blessed companionship" of the fundamentalists knew no color line, for it included faithful laborers from among the National Baptists side by side with Britain's "Prince of Preachers" and the very prophets and apostles themselves. Indeed, standing in solidarity with such towering figures of the past was a desirable and honorable position to occupy, and in fact to deviate from these old-time fundamental doctrines would be a show of arrogance and depredation to the legacy of these forebears. The fundamentalist faith, Williams declared, was "good enough for them and it is good enough for us."[68]

To this point much of Williams's anti-modernist polemic sounded quite like what one might have expected to hear from a white fundamentalist preacher. But beginning with his references to E. C. Morris and I. Benjamin Toliver as part of the "happy blessed companionship" of the fundamentalists, Williams executed a rhetorical turn that would likely never have passed the lips of his white fundamentalist counterparts. He judged modernism to be deficient not only on biblical grounds but also on racial grounds. The spirit of modernist theological innovation represented not only a break with historical luminaries like Charles Spurgeon but, even closer to home, it represented an attitude of disrespect toward the honored founders and leaders of the National Baptist denomination itself, and therefore an affront both to their theological legacy and to the racial progress for which they had fought and which God had providentially provided through their activities. Such people, Williams said, "built up this denomination. These pulpits are products of their labors, they are the answers and fruits of the progress of a people, grateful to God because of what He did for them."[69] The pulpits of the National Baptist churches—pulpits from which some ministers might be tempted to subvert the fundamentals in favor of the vogue of rationalistic modernism—owed their very existence to the biblical fidelity of these saints, whom God had honored by providing their race with the gift of progress. Moreover, the burden of pushing for *future* social and political progress was also here laid at the feet of the faithful church, as Williams envisioned the church as the proper and supreme avenue for pressing the United States government toward such needful goals as bolstering black public education funding and ensuring equal voting rights.[70] Yet all such social action of the church in service of the progress of the race—social service activities that Williams himself implemented as part of his ministry at Olivet Baptist in Chicago—would ultimately constitute nothing more than a "barren" ministry if detached from the "old time" gospel and the fundamental doctrines of the faith. The men who occupied the National Baptist pulpits were duty bound to "preach and contend for that gospel and doctrines that Christ stood for." Taking rather explicit aim at the social gospel, Williams further warned his fellow National Baptist pastors that preaching "social service alone" might result in "eloquent, pleasing addresses, orations or popular sermonettes," but would ultimately prove to be hollow and desolate; for any ministry to be "a heart-throbbing, soul-edifying and not a barren one, it must sound in no low, uncertain tones the gospel we are commanded to preach." For the African American community to continue making strides toward equality National Baptist churches and pastors had to engage in social service and activism, but this social action also had to be grounded in a ministry devoted to the fundamental doctrinal truths of the gospel.[71] Several years later in another context, Williams famously articulated this idea of the church's need for robust social programs to be paired with a robust spiritual gospel as "a religious program that will be passionately human, but no less divine."[72] This description in itself was, of course, an allusion to the doctrine of Christ's divinity and the hypostatic union of his "fully human" and "fully divine" natures—one of the very same "fundamentals" that his 1925 convention speech set out to defend as essential to the National Baptist pulpit ministry and the advancement of the race itself.[73]

As Williams's presidential address to the convention continued to link fidelity to the fundamentals with the racial and social significance of the NBC's heritage, he also connected the denomination's Baptist identity itself with the core fundamentalist convictions. These National Baptist pulpits were built upon Baptist doctrines and Baptist money, "and no man can honorably occupy them and at the same time use them to tarnish and discredit the vital heritage turned over to him, by predecessors who believed in the old time religion." Like other black fundamentalists, Williams rhetorically linked faithfulness to the doctrines of the "old time religion" with both past accomplishments and future hopes in the arena of racial equality; to undermine these old, time-tested doctrinal truths constituted not only a theological betrayal, but a denominational (and, thus, racial) one as well.[74] To "tarnish and discredit the vital heritage" bequeathed by the long line of black Baptist predecessors was tantamount, it appears, to making "shipwreck of the faith of an untold number" in accordance with the apostasy passage of 1 Timothy 1:19–20. In this way Williams underscored the urgency with which National Baptists must "bravely and wisely combat" modernist incursions into black Baptist life.[75]

This exhortation was also delivered in the context of Williams's holding up the NBC as the institution best positioned to rebut the racist claim that "Negroes are incapable of self-control" and his hailing black Baptists as "the only group of religionists who may illustrate that Negroes can live under popular government, enjoy its favors and rights, and share and help to carry its burdens and responsibilities."[76] If indeed National Baptists represented the best chance for African Americans to prove to the skeptical white majority their worthiness and fitness for self-government, and if fundamentalist doctrine represented the faithful historic identity of the convention and its founders, then, according to Williams, modernism represented a clear and present threat to the social advancement of the race itself. Thus the president of the convention connected the legitimate inclusion of African Americans as true participants in democratic self-government—a noble goal shared by members of the race across the theological spectrum—with the preservation and proliferation of those most important doctrines that defined the fundamentalist movement. The fact that a desire to validate African Americans as legitimate participants in the American democratic identity was by no means limited to black fundamentalists, theological conservatives, or even religionists in general makes Williams's connection between National Baptist identity, religious fundamentalism, and full participation in American identity all the more intriguing.[77]

Having laid the foundation of biblical fidelity and added to it the weight of historical constancy, Williams returned once again to the epistemological superiority of the fundamentalist perspective over against that of modernism and evolutionary theory. Earlier in his address Williams had dispensed with the charge that fundamentalists were antiscientific, explaining that, to the contrary, they accepted science in its truest role: as a useful yet fallible authority with limited explanatory power, subordinate to the infallible authority of divine revelation. Elaborating further as he capped his defense of fundamentalism, Williams observed:

> We cannot afford to give up God's true and tried word for that which confesses itself to be a doubtful guess and an obscure hypothesis. To lead men to the light and life, we need, and we have in the gospel, some certainties, some verities and some factors that begin where science and all else, except revelation, limps and gives no final word. On the problem of the origin of this cosmos, while evolution is silent and confesses it does not know, the Bible is clear and definite, its writer knew and said: 'In the beginning God created.' Evolution does not pretend to account for life—the Bible does.[78]

Where modernist skepticism provided no consequential answers for the ultimate questions of origin and meaning, the Bible spoke with authority. Where evolution offered merely "a doubtful guess and an obscure hypothesis" which "limps and gives no final word," God's own voice reverberating through his self-revelation promised "certainties," "verities," and "clear and definite" knowledge to lead men to "the light and life" of Christ's gospel. Where modernistic rationalism offered no firm footing upon which to ground epistemological claims at all, the fundamentalist position recognized "God's tried and true word" as the bedrock upon which questions of ultimate knowledge rest. And, of course, whereas modernism represented a betrayal of the faith historic and of the NBC's black forebears, the embrace of old-time fundamentalist doctrines offered, in Williams's analysis, the chance for black Americans to demonstrate their fitness for social inclusion and to continue to push for racial progress.

* * *

Contrary to the historiographical view that black ministers were far removed from the fundamentalist debates that raged in the first several decades of the twentieth century, we have seen that across denominational and geographic lines, theologically conservative black pastors readily stood before their congregations not only to teach the doctrines of fundamentalism but also to make pointed attacks on the liberal theology being propagated by encroaching modernists. Indeed, they were willing to use their authoritative position in the pulpit, as the very representatives of God before their congregations, to warn their flocks of the spiritual dangers and pitfalls that accompanied modernist infidelity. In these polemical attacks, black fundamentalist ministers sounded in many ways like their white counterparts. Fundamentalists on both sides of the color line instructed their hearers to remain steadfast and true to both the biblical testimony and the historic orthodoxy of the church, and they castigated modernist innovators as theological compromisers, agents of Satan, and the type of dangerous false teachers against whom the New Testament warns.

Where black fundamentalist preachers differed from their brethren on the other side of the racial divide was in their willingness to offer racial applications of their doctrines that challenged the sociopolitical status quo. Men such as Isaac Reed Berry, John Albert Johnson, and Lacey Kirk Williams connected fidelity to the fundamentals with the black race's hope of progress in this life (as well as their hope for the next), while also portraying modernists as working, wittingly or not, against the best interests of the African American community. It would never have crossed the mind of someone like Texas's famed fundamentalist leader J. Frank Norris, a well-known segregationist, to connect interracial marriage to the doctrines of atonement and justification, as Berry did. If anything, Norris would have seen such a proposal as an abhorrent betrayal of the God-ordained Jim Crow social order. Even white fundamentalists who were willing to partner with their black brethren on a somewhat equal basis—some of whom we will meet in the next chapter—typically opposed interracial marriage and would have undoubtedly balked at Berry's view in that regard. Differences in social worldviews and racial contexts may not have eliminated the bedrock theological commonalities, but they certainly did produce manifestations of fundamentalist religion that took on divergent hues on either side of the color line.

4

Religious Education and Interracial Cooperation

*The American Baptist Theological Seminary*

On October 4, 1936, in Princeton, Indiana, the white First Baptist Church, an avowedly fundamentalist congregation, welcomed a group of young black musicians into their Sunday evening service. As these young men performed, one of their number, Brother Chappelle, was invited to deliver a message before the church, which he did. It was met with great approval by Ford Porter, the church's outspoken fundamentalist minister, who especially appreciated Chappelle's "unhesitating" affirmation of "the whole Bible as the verbally inspired Word of God." Porter embraced the faith being preached by Brother Chappelle and his fellow musicians as essentially theologically accordant with the faith of his own fundamentalist congregation, especially when it came to such foundational issues as biblical inspiration. Moreover, this visit left Porter favorably disposed toward the school these young men represented. These were the Seminary Singers, traveling representatives of the American Baptist Theological Seminary (ABTS), a school in Nashville for training black Baptist clergy. The singers "make a good impression and are a good advertisement for [their] School," Porter concluded, thanks in large part to Brother Chappelle's affirmation of the seminary's fundamentalist view of biblical inspiration. The musicians left town with an open invitation to return to First Baptist, and the church's fundamentalist preacher was sufficiently impressed that he felt compelled to write a detailed letter of appreciation to a trustee of the school, expressing his firm support for the endeavor.[1]

As we have seen thus far, black fundamentalism was less institutionally rigid and less overtly separatist than its white counterpart.[2] While whites often gravitated toward fundamentalist-specific newspapers, networks, publishers, churches, and conferences—in many cases separate from, and sometimes even skeptical of, traditional denominational ties—black fundamentalists were less willing to abandon their traditional associations and denominational affiliations due, at least in part, to the urgent problems of smothering legal and social oppression that faced the entire black community on a daily basis. Yet even so, the formation and propagation of the black fundamentalist perspective was not wholly bereft of institutional support. Black theological schools, in particular, played a role in igniting and sustaining fundamentalism within the black ecclesiastical structure. Historian Albert G. Miller has argued that the development of African American Bible schools in the middle decades of the twentieth century was "crucial in the development of the larger black fundamentalist movement." Designed "to stop the influence of modernism and liberal biblical interpretation in the African American community," these educational institutions served "vital roles in the development of a fundamentalist worldview in the black community both before and after World War II."[3] In order to responsibly evaluate the basic contours of black fundamentalism—including the complex web of relationships that crossed racial lines on the basis of theological solidarity and crossed religious lines on the basis of racial solidarity—it is both helpful and needful to elicit some consideration of fundamentalism in the context of African American theological education.

One particularly noteworthy institution was the American Baptist Theological Seminary. Founded and funded as a joint project between the white Southern Baptist Convention (SBC) and the black National Baptist Convention (NBC), ABTS aimed to equip black clergy with a formal theological education on the basis of the common Baptist identity and convictions of these two major denominations. Although it was of course a segregated school, it nevertheless stands as a remarkable historical instance of interracial cooperation and fellowship in the Jim Crow South, based on both shared Baptist distinctives and, as we will see, common fundamentalist and anti-modernist convictions shared by Southern Baptists and numerous high-ranking denominational and institutional officials from the National Baptists during the 1920s and 1930s.[4]

In fact, in comparison with the several schools that Miller invokes to substantiate his argument, ABTS stands out as exceptional on at least two counts. First, it is easily the earliest of the group. Of those addressed by Miller, the earliest is the Southern Bible Institute, founded in Dallas in 1928; others include the Manhattan Bible Institute (1938), the Carver Bible Institute (1943), the Cedine Bible Camp and Institute (1946), the Fellowship Bible Institute (1953), and the Manna Bible Institute (1953).[5] In contrast, ABTS opened its doors in the fall of 1924, and was, in fact, the product of cooperative efforts between Southern Baptists and National Baptists that stretched back well into the prior decade. This locates the initial forays into the founding of the seminary in the early years of the fundamentalist movement—well before the flashpoint of the Scopes trial, and closer to the completion of *The Fundamentals* (1915) and Curtis Lee Laws's coining of the term "fundamentalism" (1920). As a result, the school's institutional records reflect that members of both Baptist bodies were well aware of the dangers posed to fundamentalist Christianity by modernist theological commitments.

The Nashville seminary is also distinct by virtue of the degree of African American initiative and control in its origins and proceedings. In his examination of fundamentalism in black Bible schools, Miller offers brief historical sketches of the Southern Bible Institute and the Carver Bible Institute, both of which were unilateral creations of white ministers seeking to address a perceived need in the black community. Moreover, the administration and faculty of both schools were, initially and for many years thereafter, overwhelmingly white.[6] These institutes might be considered examples of "interracial cooperation" in the sense that both white and black people were involved in the project, but they were involved in vastly different capacities. The fact that the student populations were black while the faculty, administration, and founding personalities were almost exclusively white suggests that the schools might well be classed as exercises in southern paternalism rather than as any sort of interracial partnership.

The American Baptist Theological Seminary, on the other hand, was an interracial cooperative endeavor from the outset. Not only was the need for black theological education recognized and acknowledged by both the white and black Baptist denominations, but the leadership and governance of the school was likewise shared between the two racial groups. Southern Baptists were granted a two-to-one ratio on the holding board, which controlled the school's property, while National Baptists enjoyed the same proportional advantage on the board of directors (lending the National Baptists an advantage in absolute numbers, since the board of directors was the larger of the two bodies). Furthermore, the faculty was predominantly composed of black instructors. In fact, the founding documents explicitly provided that the seminary's president would always come from the National Baptists. Far from a project predicated on the concept of white leaders showering their exalted knowledge down upon the theologically impoverished black masses, ABTS was indeed an interracial endeavor in which both black and white Baptists had financial, administrative, and institutional stakes. And while white participants in this venture did at times display varying shades of paternalistic thought, they also at times demonstrated a level of cooperation, concern, and fellowship across racial lines that was unusual among their peers.[7]

Given its unique character, then, it is surprising that the American Baptist Seminary has garnered relatively little attention in the historiographies of fundamentalism, Southern Baptists, or even National Baptists. Not only is it absent from Miller's examination of fundamentalism in black theological schools, it also earns only passing mention in such books as Paul Harvey's *Redeeming the South*, a monograph explicitly concerned with white and black Baptists in the South, and Lillian B. Horace's biography of Lacey Kirk Williams, the National Baptist president who oversaw the seminary's founding. Harvey seemingly dismisses the school as "small, underfunded, and conflicted by its place in a region that had never come to terms with black higher education" and sees it as an institution whose "ultimate authority for governance was to rest with whites"—a curious contention, given the school's administrative construction.[8] Horace, by contrast, briefly mentions it as a project with potential to "break down hostility" and "bring about a friendly relation between the racial groups."[9] Yet she, too, treats the seminary more as a historical footnote than as a unique object deserving of substantial inquiry.[10]

In reality, though, ABTS represents a fascinating historical convergence that can shed light on the various racial and religious commitments that characterized life and ministry for black fundamentalists during the interwar period. Though fundamentalism and the black community are rarely connected in the historiography of African American religion, the American Baptist Seminary project was marked at its inception by fundamentalist doctrine and antimodernist concerns.

Southern Baptists' initial participation in the venture, in fact, was largely contingent on the school's fidelity to the theologically conservative fundamentals of the Christian faith—a concern shared by numerous participating members of the NBC and reflected in the early adoption of a confession of faith that expressly adhered to, among other things, the five fundamentals.

The story of ABTS offers a compelling display of interracial cooperation and fellowship in the Jim Crow South on the basis of common religious identity—as Baptists and, for some, expressly as fundamentalists. At the same time, this joint educational venture also highlights the limits of such interracial cooperation in this historical context. For white Southern Baptists, even those who professed true concern and heartfelt love toward their black brethren, the culturally dominant belief in white superiority proved impossible to completely shake. For black National Baptist fundamentalists involved in directing ABTS, the joint venture with their white counterparts in zealous defense of the essentials of the faith existed side-by-side with a denominational willingness to include more modernistic thinkers in both membership and partnership due to their common racial identity and the pressing need for racial advancement. Just as earlier chapters have shown that black and white fundamentalists were largely united on essential doctrinal particulars, even as they differed with regard to social and political applications of their faith, ABTS offers a fascinating example of both trends—the unifying potential of shared religious convictions as well as the ever-present social divisions erected and buttressed along the color line by the nation's prevailing racial dogmas.

## "A Plan of Fraternal Cooperation": Inception and Founding

On the afternoon of Sunday September 14, 1924, just a matter of days before the American Baptist Theological Seminary was set to welcome its first class of students to campus, black and white Baptists gathered together to dedicate the school's first building. Just recently completed with funds from the Southern Baptists' "75 Million Campaign" (the predecessor to the SBC's now-longstanding Cooperative Program), it was, according to the local newspaper, "a handsome three-story brick structure with basement, affording space for offices, classrooms, auditorium and dormitory privileges, as well as furnace, kitchen and dining-room." To celebrate the opening of the new seminary, the afternoon's program involved participation from representatives of both the Southern Baptists, including I. J. Van Ness and O. L. Hailey, and the National Baptists, including J. H. Garnett and the denomination's president, Lacey Kirk Williams. In his dedication comments, Williams observed that the school represented hope for the amelioration of southern racial divisions, but it also illustrated the enormity of the gap between white and black southerners. Characterizing the seminary project itself as "a contribution to the reduction of the supply of lyncher's ropes, to the intellectual, civic, moral and spiritual development of the Negro race, and to a better understanding and fuller cooperation between the Negroes and the whites of America," he asserted that "nothing could be more representative of the better feeling between the whites and the blacks" than this cooperative task on behalf of black clerical education. But at the same time, Williams did not let his white partners entirely off the hook for the present state of southern affairs. While he noted that "white people have made several distinct contributions to the negro race," and that the newly dedicated seminary building was "the greatest contribution" that the South's white Baptists had made in this regard, he also "assured his white brethren that their debt to the black race had not yet been paid."[11] From the beginning, ABTS represented both a hopeful vision of racial confraternity and a reminder of the seemingly impregnable categories of race that structured southern society and reified racial inequality.

Although that September afternoon in 1924 marked the school's official opening, the real inception of the ABTS project stretched back more than a decade earlier, prior even to First World War. Sometime in the early 1910s, Sutton E. Griggs, who served at the time as the educational secretary of the NBC, first broached the idea of a joint venture with white Southern Baptists to found a National Baptist seminary for the training of black Baptist clergy. Griggs quickly found kindred spirits among the Southern Baptists, including Edgar Young Mullins and Orren Luico Hailey, and at the May 1913 meeting of the SBC Dr. Mullins introduced a resolution pledging the denomination's support for the enterprise and approving a joint Southern and National Baptist committee to further explore the feasibility of establishing such a seminary.[12] By

Figure 4.1. Griggs Hall, the seminary's first building, as seen in the school's 1925 catalogue. Image reproduced courtesy of the Southern Baptist Historical Library and Archives, Nashville, Tennessee.

September of that year, the new joint committee was declaring it "exceedingly desirable and expedient" to build "a general seminary for the training of the Negro preachers of the gospel" at the behest of and under the auspices of the NBC, in conjunction with the "practical and financial cooperation of other organizations of Baptists who may indicate a desire to share in this important work."[13]

As promising a start as this appeared to be, activity on the seminary ground to a halt between 1915 and 1919 partly on account of World War I, but also because of a looming divide between two factions within the NBC.[14] A dispute over control of the National Baptist Publishing House ultimately split the denomination into two distinct National Baptist bodies—one unincorporated and one incorporated—the latter of which continued in cooperative fellowship with the Southern Baptists from 1919 onward.[15] In 1914, prior to the project's temporary stay, the joint committee had undertaken to settle on a location for the seminary, ultimately coming down to a decision between Memphis and Nashville. Though the committee initially settled on Memphis, the Memphis delegation's failure to make good on their financial promises prompted A. M. Townsend and the Negro Baptist Ministers' Conference of Nashville to petition for reconsideration. Weighing in the Nashville contingent's favor was its ability to follow through on its $25,000 proposition, thanks to the backing of both the city's Negro Board of Trade and Nashville's white businessmen, who were represented by the Commercial Club. Nashville, promised the black Baptist ministers in early 1915, was eager to house the seminary and to ensure its success because it would represent a significant landmark in the history of southern race relations. In this vein the Nashville ministers described the proposed seminary as "the first effort made by our White brethren of the South toward the education of our Negro Ministry."[16] Once the seminary project was reignited following the National Baptist split, the question of location was revisited, and by 1920 Nashville was at last the committee's city of choice.[17]

As the joint committee renewed its work, the question of the physical setting was not the only pressing issue. Given the multiple racial as well as denominational interests vested in the project, any forward movement in the work required that the joint committee first clearly elucidate a set of principles for managing, administering, and governing the institution. By 1922 the Southern and National Baptists had agreed upon an administrative structure that would later be formally encapsulated in the school's bylaws. Oversight of the seminary would be split between two governing bodies, each with the responsibility to elect its own officers. The holding board, consisting of twelve members with an eight-to-four advantage for the Southern Baptists, would hold ownership of the institution's property and lease the property to the seminary annually for a nominal sum. The board of directors, composed of thirty-six members and a two-to-one proportional advantage for the National Baptists, was to have complete direction over the functioning and activities of the seminary itself. In addition, the president of the board of directors and the president of the seminary were both to be National Baptists, while a Southern Baptist was to hold the position of general secretary.[18]

Although the ultimate governing structure of the institution did not necessarily reflect the NBC's original desire for total control over the seminary, the distribution of board memberships and administrative offices gave black Baptists substantial power over the operation and direction of the school.[19] Not only did National Baptists enjoy a two-thirds majority on the board of directors, which along with the presidency of the institution gave them the clear majority in directing the operating affairs of the school, but they also held the advantage in terms of total number of board seats across the two governing bodies, twenty-eight to twenty.[20]

Moreover, the significant African American influence inherent in this governing structure contrasts markedly contrasts with that of other institutions for black fundamentalist education in the same era. Consider, for example, the Southern Bible Institute (originally the Dallas Colored Bible Institute), founded by Edmund H. Ironside, a white seminary student at Evangelical Theological College (now Dallas Theological Seminary). Ironside started the institution as a result of conversations with black preachers in Dallas who desired theological education, and he served as the school's president for the first fourteen years of its existence, thus setting a precedent of white presidential leadership that would remain intact well into the twenty-first century.[21] The Carver Bible Institute in Atlanta was likewise founded and largely controlled by a white graduate of Moody Bible Institute, Talmadge Payne.[22] In contrast, ABTS emerged from an interracial cooperative effort between two major denominations, initiated by a major National Baptist leader, and boasted a governing structure that was majority African American.

The unusual nature of the interracial cooperation surrounding ABTS might be seen even in the small fact that the board of directors' minutes record that black ministers often led the opening and closing prayers—an experience that was by no means typical for racial minorities in "mixed" settings. For example, a Mexican American minister who had been trained in a Presbyterian seminary during the interwar period lamented that "at Synod meetings a Mexican American has never directed a study group, said a prayer, or anything."[23] Although the experiences of Mexican Americans and African Americans in this period are obviously not identical, and the denominational distinctions between Baptists and Presbyterians should not be discounted, this contrast does speak to the desire for full interracial partnership on the part of the founders of the American Baptist Theological Seminary.

Participants from both sides of the color line saw the school's administrative structure as a unique opportunity for fellowship that augured great hopes for the future. The importance of not only working together across racial lines, but also *praying* together, was evident to Eugene Perry Alldredge, one of the leading Southern Baptist advocates for this denominational joint venture. As the school approached its tenth anniversary in 1934, Alldredge spoke of being deeply encouraged at "the actual experience of a growing fellowship and spirit of cooperation" between white and black Baptists, which was possible only because "the two groups have served together, suffered together, hoped together and prayed together for the Seminary."[24] What had begun as a hypothetical possibility for deeper fellowship between the racial groups was, in Alldredge's eyes, being realized by virtue of the "actual experience" of common work, common goals, and common prayer on behalf of ABTS. The longtime dean of the seminary, National Baptist James H. Garnett, went further to say that the school was "evidently the dictate of Providence" because "nothing else just like it has ever been undertaken before."[25] Like Alldredge, Garnett celebrated "the great advantage that has, and will result from the contact which the operation of this Seminary has brought about between the White and Colored Baptists of the South"—a project for which he was "willing to make any reasonable sacrifice."[26]

With this unusual administrative structure in place, ABTS was from the start both a testament to a remarkable willingness to promote fellowship across racial lines and a deliberate (albeit limited) theological challenge to the idea of absolutely inviolable racial barriers. Both black and white members of the joint commission recognized in their 1921 report to the Southern and National Baptist Conventions not only the historical import of this partnership, but also the expressly theological moorings of the project itself. The very basis of this endeavor, they noted, was grounded in the doctrinal imperatives of Christian love and the shared brotherhood of all those who partake in the gospel of Christ. The fact that 3 million white Baptists and 3 million black Baptists could "unite in an enterprise which has as its sole objective the training of colored men for the ministry of Jesus Christ" represented "really a notable event . . . prophetic of better relationships between the races." Moreover, the institution itself would stand as "a monument expressive of the Christian fellowship which exists between the Southern Baptist Convention and the National Baptist Convention" and through which "the two races will be more closely bound together in loving devotion to our risen Lord." The committee further reported that at a time "when so many evil-minded persons representing both races, are endeavoring to intensify racial antagonism . . . this commission is made up of those, both white and colored, who seek to incarnate the constraining love of Christ." Thus, as reported to both conventions, this interracial endeavor was not only an important cultural landmark, but it was in fact understood to be an essentially theological engagement, necessitated and driven by the gospel. Even more specifically, it was driven by a fundamentalist understanding of theological doctrines: the literal atonement through Christ's death meant that "the racial partitions which separated humanity were broken down," and the literal physical resurrection of Christ was the basis for the increasing "Christian fellowship which exists" between white Southern Baptists and black National Baptists.[27] Yet even the best intentioned of human enterprises cannot fully transcend its cultural context, and from its conception ABTS was no exception on either side of the partnership. If the seminary project was in some respects a step toward better race relations, it was also a reminder of the persistence of racial dividing lines in American life.

From the Southern Baptist position, perhaps no single person better represented the spirit of Christian fellowship and cooperation than Orren L. Hailey—and certainly no white man was more indelibly associated with the seminary in its early years. In fact, Hailey himself provides a compelling example of the juxtaposition between an unusual openness to interracial fellowship and the latent cultural sense of stark racial differentiation. The son of an antislavery southerner, young Orren Hailey absorbed from his father a sense of compassion for the plight of African Americans in the South before, during, and after the Civil War, as well as, in the words of one lifelong acquaintance, "an inveterate adherence to what [he] believed was right, with no consideration of self-interest." Having long aspired to help establish a seminary for black theological education, Hailey devoted much of the last two decades of his life to the service of ABTS, both as a member of the joint commission and then as the institution's general secretary—a job that cost Hailey an enormous amount of time and energy traveling the country, visiting churches, raising awareness, and procuring funding for the school.[28]

Hailey's niece later recalled the solemnity and reverence with which her uncle faced the likely prospect of being appointed to the position of general secretary, even to the point of refusing his wife's heart-wrenching plea to turn down the appointment, because he considered the opportunity "a call from God" on his life. Hailey understood that the position would require a man of great conviction, strength, and resolve, because the undertaking guaranteed that all of "the southern traditions and prejudices" would be aligned against him and his work.[29] His time working (unsuccessfully) to resolve the National Baptist schism in the mid-1910s had convinced Hailey that a great many Southern Baptists firmly rejected any endeavor intended to help black southerners, meaning that his work for ABTS would involve not only administration and fundraising, but also the overwhelming task of challenging and overcoming the deeply entrenched racial perspectives embedded in the hearts and minds of multitudinous white Southern Baptists.[30] In that regard, Hailey certainly succeeded with his own wife, who in looking back upon her desire to dissuade her husband from the work of the seminary later wondered, "How could I have been so prejudiced and so deceived in my attitude toward the Negro?"[31]

Indeed, Hailey's tireless promotion of the seminary among both white and black churches across the country earned him respect from his National Baptist colleagues as well. In a 1928 letter to the ABTS board of directors, NBC president Lacey Kirk Williams praised Hailey's "heroic and selfless service" to the school.[32] In like fashion, upon Hailey's death in 1934, the seminary's longtime dean James H. Garnett offered a tribute in the *National Baptist Voice*, lauding the secretary's "invaluable mission," appointed by divine providence, of "bridging the chasm" between the races in the South and creating "deeper interest and greater sympathy on the part of the white Baptists for the needs of the colored Baptists."[33] Yet even as he clearly displayed racial views that were, in some respects, well in advance of many of his Southern Baptist contemporaries, Hailey also showed that the social and cultural milieu of his age was difficult to escape entirely. Prior to the formal establishment of the seminary, he expressed doubts as to whether "some one of the Negro race" was "capable of assuming the duties" of the institution's presidency without prior training from white Southern Baptists.[34] Such an evaluation may have been grounded partly in a simple recognition of the real educational disparity between the white and black communities, but it also represented an articulation of one of the era's most common racist stereotypes—the presumption of white superiority in matters of the mind.[35]

This dissonance is likewise reflected in a promotional article in which Hailey intended to convey to the public the principles upon which the school was founded. The article emphasized, on the one hand, a spirit of mutual cooperation and a mutual desire that black Baptists should have significant freedom in running the institution. The goal of the seminary was to "provide for the largest amount of freedom on the part of the Negro brethren in the conduct and support of the seminary" through the "cordial and fraternal relation" between the two denominations. At the same time, however, Hailey pointed out that Southern Baptist presence on the governing boards, including a Southern Baptist majority on the holding board, guaranteed that the "white friends should have the assurance that their liberality would be administered under the combined counsel of both peoples" and that therefore no essential Southern Baptist convictions would be violated.[36] Obviously, part of that assurance had to do with issues of doctrinal fidelity—including faithfulness to certain fundamentalist perspectives, as will become clear later in this chapter. But apart from these doctrinal concerns, it is no stretch to imagine that issues of cultural importance to white southerners, such as institutional segregation, were also motivations (even if below the surface) in the Southern Baptist involvement and support. After all, neither Hailey nor any of his compatriots appear to have so much as considered the idea of integrating the extant white Baptist seminaries after which ABTS was modeled.[37] Moreover, the assurance that the school would include significant white administrative input was placed in counterpoint to the National Baptists' administrative freedom to "call into play all their native powers"—a likely reference to the common perception that African Americans were "naturally religious" whereas whites were more "naturally" intellectual.[38] In effect, then, the article subtly implied that, while the black leaders of the school would employ their superior affinity for emotional religious connection, the whites would be there to ensure that the intellectual and strictly doctrinal trajectory of the school remained in proper alignment. So with seminary preparations now in full swing, the color line was indeed being crossed in terms of interdenominational cooperation and even interracial fellowship on the basis of a common religious identity, but underlying assumptions about inherent racial distinctions and the propriety of segregated institutions were too deeply ingrained in the cultural mindset to brook any real question.

Such mixed attitudes were not the sole domain of white Southern Baptists. National Baptists recognized the significance of this project in the context of the Jim Crow South. As noted earlier, the Negro

Baptist Ministers' Conference of Nashville characterized the project as "the first effort made by our White brethren of the South toward the education of our Negro Ministry," grounding their enthusiastic support for the seminary at least partly in its unique character as a cooperative venture designed to offer white support while leaving substantial control in the hands of black leaders.[39] Likewise, the 1921 joint commission report reflected the hopes of the black Baptist participants as much as the white participants that ABTS would represent a social and theological bridge to bring the races into closer fellowship.[40] Yet at the same time National Baptist leaders also explicitly supported the seminary as a segregated institution on the basis of either their understanding of the distinctive ecclesiastical challenges facing black pastors, or their acceptance of prevailing theories of racial distinction, or both. This was, after all, an era heavily influenced by racial uplift ideology, which often connected racial advancement with a sense of class distinction embodied by certain tenets of bourgeois respectability such as self-help and temperance, as well as the prevailing cultural expectations regarding propriety in recreational activities such as music and dance. In many cases this uplift perspective served to reify the idea that the black masses, in contrast to the elite, constituted a racially distinct "Negro problem." Thus, even as the seminary's mission of educational improvement and uplift was seen as a necessary step toward racial advancement and respectability, it still could not entirely decouple from the theories of racial difference that underpinned a segregated social order.[41]

While both the 1913 and 1921 reports of the joint commission strongly implied the need for ABTS to exist as a black seminary in order to address the particular social circumstances facing black clergy, a letter from Sutton E. Griggs to the SBC in 1920 suggests that a concurrent sense of indelible racial differences, influenced in part by the day's scientific theories of race, affected the National Baptist founders of the seminary as well as their white Southern Baptist counterparts.[42] Writing to thank Southern Baptists for their support of black education, Griggs posited that "the human family has been divided into various races" and that nature had assigned "each racial group its special task even as she has done the cells of the human body." Invoking the bloody specter of World War I, Griggs argued that the German threat of "enforced amalgamation" was defeated only by "the attachment of men to their respective races.... French *enthusiasm* and British *persistence* [overcame] German *organization*. If there had been a fusion of the English and the French, French enthusiasm might have been swamped by British coldness, and British persistence might have given way to French volatility." This violent example testified to "the possibilities of evil bound up in the question of race adjustment"—evils that had recently become evident even in Chicago, the "great city of the liberal west," in the form of race riots.[43]

For Griggs the solution to the problem of "race adjustment," at least for the distinct white and black races in the United States, was black Christian education. While the black populace as a whole during the interwar period was becoming increasingly college educated, the same did not hold true for the clergy.[44] In Griggs's estimation this constituted an unsettling trend, for he believed that the alleviation of racial tensions required an educated black ministry that could equip the African American community to "use their consecrated lives and their trained powers to induce a spirit of love in the hearts of all men, knowing that from such a spirit there can come forth no unjust laws, nor unjust administration of laws."[45] With an eye toward this goal, Griggs approached the SBC to "express our warm appreciation of the interest you are manifesting in our education" and to promise that "the educated Christian negroes will not disappoint their sponsors." This investment in black theological education would provide for the ultimate goal of both races living "in peace and justice by the side of each other"—side by side but, as with the cells of a body, nevertheless distinct and separate.[46]

Though Griggs did not countenance the idea that the black race was inherently inferior, his affirmation of the idea that blacks were inherently different and separate does seem to accord, at least in part, with the scientific theories of racial differentiation common to the cultural milieu of his era. Nor was Griggs unique among black ministers on this count. Bishop L. W. Kyles of North Carolina, in addressing the 1924 AME Zion General Conference, made similar comments on the topic of blacks' constitutional rights of citizenship: "The position we take on this subject is not based upon any desire on our part for the amalgamation of the races. We are content to follow the divergent trend of the races in things purely racial.... We are willing to develop our distinct racial characteristics and to shape our character after the standards of Christianity.... Our contention is based upon the desire for the full enjoyment of all the rights of citizenship guaranteed by the Constitution."[47] Or to take another example from the Baptist ranks, National Baptist minister E. W. D. Isaac, a trustee of ABTS, explained to a Southern Baptist correspondent that the seminary was a crucial step toward "a more competent and more thoroughly consecrated ministry" that could properly "teach our people . . . the Christian view of conduct, character and destiny"; such a task was necessary in part because there were "strong forces at work" in the South for the "wicked purpose" of "disturbing the peaceful relations that exist between the white and black people of the South."[48] From this perspective blacks needed their own seminary not only because they faced a unique set of social circumstances, but also because the races were naturally distinct—a point with which members of the white Baptist convention agreed.

Hence, while ABTS represented a landmark effort in Baptist interracial cooperation and fellowship, it also demonstrated that any such effort was simultaneously circumscribed by cultural assumptions about race that were difficult for either side to jettison. This juxtaposition made the seminary a compelling mixture of cultural progressivism and cultural conservatism on the issue of race, even while it was an institution marked significantly, in its early stages, by a commitment to doctrinal fundamentalism.

## Doctrines and Disputes

Having explored the circumstances surrounding the founding of American Baptist Theological Seminary, including both racial and (to some degree) theological perspectives characterizing both sides in the decade leading up to the school's opening, the question remains as to the theological character of its teaching and administration—that is, whether it can really be characterized as a "fundamentalist" institution. An examination of the seminary's official doctrines as well as some of the theological controversies and disputes that arose over the first two decades of its existence will demonstrate that it was, both in institutional leadership and in denominational administration from both racial groups, an institution in its early years dedicated to doctrinal fundamentalism and opposed to theological modernism.

Figure 4.2. Beyond the classroom, the grill and bookstore afforded ABTS students the opportunity to socialize and bond with their confreres. Image reproduced courtesy of the Southern Baptist Historical Library and Archives, Nashville, Tennessee.

Shortly before ABTS opened its doors for the first time in October 1924, the board of directors officially approved the school's "Confession of Faith," a document intended to set the theological guardrails within which the institution would function. The chain of events leading to the adoption of the confession began in 1919, when Southern Baptists received the alarming news that the National Baptists had joined hands with the Interchurch World Movement, a liberal ecumenical organization, as part of an enlarged denominational fundraising campaign. O. L. Hailey, delivering the report of the seminary commission to the 1920 SBC annual meeting, sought to alleviate the concerns of his Southern Baptist brethren by noting that the National Baptist leaders "assure us that this arrangement does not call for any change in either their doctrines, or polity, nor any exchange of finances, further than a return to the Interchurch World Movement such money as was advanced them to carry out their enlarged undertaking."[49] Just two years later, however, the National Baptists further alarmed their Southern Baptist partners by joining with the Federal Council of Churches—a move that caused many Southern Baptists to question the propriety of their involvement in the seminary project, given the council's liberal tendencies. Hence, in April of 1924 O. L. Hailey told the seminary's board of directors that the SBC would continue this joint effort to build and launch ABTS on one condition: "that the Seminary should work out and adopt a clear-cut Confession of Faith which would be approved by both Conventions represented on the Board of Directors and would be signed by all presidents and all teachers of the Seminary."[50] Such a statement would serve as a bulwark against potential liberal or modernist incursions. These concerns were likewise shared by Eugene Perry Alldredge, whom historian Nathan Finn identifies as not only a Southern Baptist fundamentalist, but also an outspoken critic of the Federal Council of Churches. As a steadfast supporter of the ABTS project, Alldredge was appointed to chair the joint committee to draft the school's confession, ensuring that these fears and concerns would be accounted for in the seminary's official doctrinal statement.[51]

Unanimously adopted by the board in September 1924, the school's confession affirmed each of the "five fundamentals" within the first three articles. It also explicitly denied evolution and forthrightly recognized the personality of Satan, the reality of heaven and hell, and the literal resurrection of all men on judgment day.[52] Alldredge would later report that the seminary's confession was modeled largely upon the *Articles of Religious Belief* of the Baptist Bible Institute of New Orleans (later New Orleans Baptist Theological Seminary) and was crafted so that ABTS "never can have a modernistic teacher."[53] The *Articles of Religious Belief* had been composed by the Baptist Bible Institute's first president, Byron Hoover DeMent, and adopted at the school's inception in 1917–1918, just a few years before Alldredge and his committee embarked on their mission to craft a statement of faith for ABTS in 1924.[54] Although Alldredge and his committee did not simply copy the *Articles* wholesale—the ABTS confession contained four more articles, and broke up the doctrinal delineations somewhat differently, for example—they nevertheless did adopt several of the New Orleans articles almost word for word, with some slight modifications. For instance, the ABTS article on "The Depravity of Men" repeated everything in the New Orleans document's corresponding article, but after affirming that man was "created innocent," ABTS added further clarification to bolster creationist and anti-evolution sentiments by proclaiming that "man came into this world by direct creation of God and not by evolution." In other cases, deviations from the New Orleans statement offered explicit denials and condemnations of Catholicism. The ABTS article on "The Authority of the Scriptures" asserted with its predecessor that "these Scriptures do not require the interpretation of any church, or council," before listing two new additions: "[or] priesthood or pope." The confession's article on the Holy Spirit likewise borrowed significantly from the New Orleans document, but added the clear antipapal claim that the Spirit "is Christ's only Vicar on this earth." And on the issue of ecclesiology, ABTS inserted affirmations that the true church "has Christ and not the pope . . . as its Head," that its officers are "pastors . . . and deacons, and not priests or prelates," and that "it has for its teacher and guide the true vicar of Christ, even the Holy Spirit."[55] Such additions and alterations, in Alldredge's estimation, "clarified the language so that there could be no misunderstanding" and made the ABTS confession "the clearest, most comprehensive and most Baptistic statement of our faith governing any institution today."[56]

At the same time as ABTS was producing its document, Southern Baptists were also crafting the first *Baptist Faith and Message*, which the convention adopted in 1925. It should come as no surprise, then, that the ABTS confession was highly congruent with the 1925 Southern Baptist confession, which the SBC officially characterized as "a reaffirmation of Christian fundamentals" occasioned by "the prevalence of naturalism in the modern teaching and preaching of religion." In fact, when it came to the issue of evolution, the ABTS confession was even more expressly in line with the SBC's 1925 Committee on Baptist Faith and Message than it was with the earlier New Orleans articles, considering that the Southern Baptist denominational committee went out of its way to explain that "no paragraph, sentence or word in our Statement of Faith and Message can truly be cited as an endorsement of Evolution" and registered Southern Baptists' "protest against the imposition of this [evolutionary] theory upon the minds of our children in denominational, or public schools." Likewise on topics of the Bible's divine inspiration, the divinity of Christ, the virgin birth, the atonement, the literal resurrection of Jesus, and a host of other doctrines, these documents aligned exceptionally closely and reflected a variety of underlying fundamentalist theological concerns.[57]

Meanwhile, the experiences of other Baptist groups demonstrated that such confessionalism was no foregone conclusion, making the official doctrinal statements of ABTS and the SBC all the more notable. As both the seminary and the Southern Baptists were formulating their confessions of faith, fundamentalists in yet another Baptist denomination, the (white) Northern Baptists, were also militating for their convention to adopt a fundamentalist-approved confession in order to safeguard "denominational agencies . . . from the activities and influence of the agents of modernism and rationalism." The proposal, however, was overwhelmingly voted down at the Northern Baptists' 1924 convention meeting, where the denomination affirmed that such a statement "shall never be made a test of faith or service."[58] The Northern Baptist refusal to pass a fundamentalist confession of faith shows that this sort of confessional activity was not merely a matter of course. Understood in this context, both the seminary's 1924 statement and the SBC's 1925 *Baptist Faith and Message* illustrate a particular concern for upholding conservative theological positions and a warmth toward fundamentalist-approved confessional platforms that not all Baptist bodies shared.

Yet even as both documents reflected fundamentalist doctrinal commitments, the ABTS confession of faith and the SBC's *Baptist Faith and Message* were far from entirely identical, and not all of their differences were merely superficial. One point of distinction is especially relevant: the seminary's confession explicitly mentioned race in its article on evangelism, affirming that the gospel applies equally to all people "without regard to race or color or creed," while the *Baptist Faith and Message* spoke more vaguely of the Christian's duty to "extend the gospel to the ends of the earth." Such a divergence illustrates that African Americans' racial concerns and the participation of black Baptists in the process of crafting the ABTS statement shaped how Baptist theology was expressed in an African American educational context. Thus, what was for these black Baptists an obvious and pressing element of true Baptist faith and practice was something to which their white counterparts were, to varying degrees, willfully blinded on account of their suffusion and participation in the prevailing racist mores of the Jim Crow South. With respect to common fundamentalist theological expressions and concerns, however, the two confessions were of a piece, and it is no large stretch to see the fundamentalist concerns that motivated the 1925 *Baptist Faith and Message* as being similarly instrumental to the creation of the first ABTS confessional document under the direction of E. P. Alldredge.⁵⁹

The conservative bent of the seminary's confession was not solely a function of Southern Baptist influence. While the National Baptist Convention was by no means a categorically fundamentalist denomination, there were notable fundamentalist theological impulses within the convention, even among some of the most influential leadership. For example, the denomination's deeply respected president, Lacey Kirk Williams, exhorted all of the convention delegates in 1925 to side with the fundamentalists, proclaiming that modernism must be "bravely and wisely combatted" by churchmen lest it "make shipwreck of the faith of an untold number."⁶⁰ Williams himself was closely involved with the founding of ABTS. He was named in the school's charter as one of the original members of the board of directors, and in the year leading up to the school's opening he participated in numerous committees, including the Committee on Permanent Organization, the Committee on Finance, and the Committee on Incorporation.⁶¹ Similarly, Lewis Garnett Jordan—who was involved in recruiting for ABTS and served the convention as the general secretary of the Foreign Mission Board, the denominational historian, and the general missionary—represented a commitment to doctrinal fundamentalism within National Baptist leadership. Seeking to acquire several thousand copies of the SBC's *Baptist Faith and Message* to distribute at his convention, Jordan lauded the document as a noble repudiation of "unsound views of the Bible," a confessional standard that rightly embraced the "Christian fundamentals," and a needful remedy to the widespread naturalism infecting so much of "modern" religion. In the process he lamented the many religious schools teaching doctrinal "infidelity," and even felt justified in categorizing them as merely "so-called Christian schools." Recognizing that many National Baptist pastors came from such schools, Jordan solemnly warned that the "conflicting doctrines" of modernist sensibilities "must finally bring discord."⁶²

Certain fundamentalist sensibilities were also reflected in some of the school's efforts at outreach and advertisement, such as the work of the seminary's traveling musical group known as the Seminary Singers. Operating throughout much of the 1930s (at least as early as 1933 and continuing at least through 1937), the Seminary Singers were authorized "to travel over the country, advertise the seminary, and give concerts and special programs of spiritual songs and entertainments for churches and church organizations, both white and colored." In addition to their task of recruiting and raising general awareness for the seminary, they also served as a modest fundraising arm, sending 25 percent of their collections directly to the seminary. The singers' efforts were particularly aimed at "our Baptist churches, both white and colored" in hopes that Baptist solidarity might motivate these churches across the racial spectrum to "know these boys, hear them sing, give them generous free-will offerings for their services, and speed them onward in the good work which they are doing." E. P. Alldredge characterized them as "high-minded, talented and worthy Christian boys" who "represent a worthy cause and render a splendid service to all churches where they give their concerts," while the seminary's dean, J. H. Garnett, singled them out as one of the "high points" of the 1936–1937 academic year due to their "splendid work" of visiting "many sections of the country . . . in the advertisement of the Seminary."[63]

At times, seminary leaders received letters of thanks from particularly enthusiastic pastors who had encountered the Seminary Singers, some of which alluded to the doctrinal messages represented by the singers. One pastor from Greencastle, Indiana, for instance, praised the singers as "very faithful and representative personnel" before offering his blessings and prayers for ABTS on the basis that "we are all brothers when we have been born again through faith in the Lord Jesus Christ as our atoning sacrifice."[64] At the very least, this indicates a serious concern for the doctrine of substitutionary atonement on the part of this pastor, suggesting that the singers likely satisfied his queries on this issue. Even more straightforward is a letter from Ford Porter of Princeton, Indiana, whose First Baptist Church not only strongly affirmed "the verbal inspiration of the Scriptures and the other great fundamental Christian doctrines," but also withdrew its support from nonfundamentalist Baptist missionaries in 1934 in favor of supporting independent missionaries who "did hold to the fundamentals of the faith."[65] The fact that the Seminary Singers were welcomed into this separatist fundamentalist church for a Sunday night service—to perform music and to deliver "a very helpful and interesting message"—indicates that Porter felt relatively comfortable with their theological credentials. Not only did the singers make "a good impression" as advertisers for the school, but Porter was especially excited to hear their message that "the School stood unhesitatingly on the whole Bible as the verbally inspired Word of God."[66] At a minimum, then, the central fundamental doctrine of plenary verbal inspiration was explicitly affirmed as part of the singers' "very helpful and interesting message" to this church—and considering Porter's professed warmth toward the singers and his standing offer for them to return to his church in the future, it is fair to wonder whether perhaps even more fundamentalist bellwethers popped up in the course of their messages.

The example of the Seminary Singers, in addition to those of L. K. Williams and L. G. Jordan, goes to show that the fundamentalist doctrine of the seminary's confession of faith was not merely something external being forced upon the school by concerned Southern Baptists. While Southern Baptists did indeed have a vested interest in the matter, the fundamentalist bent of the seminary's confession also reflected the theological commitments that characterized certain significant elements *within* the NBC, including some major figures who were closely involved and invested in the seminary project. At the same time, however, National Baptists seem to have been somewhat more theologically diverse than their Southern Baptist brethren, as well as being more willing to accommodate a wider theological latitude within the convention and in external partnerships. A notable counterpoint to L. K. Williams's dire warnings about the dangers of modernistic teaching, for instance, was National Baptists' willingness under his tenure to associate with organizations such as the Interchurch World Movement and the Federal Council of Churches, regarding which the SBC was suspicious. Moreover, the membership of the NBC included those with more theologically liberal or progressive outlooks sitting side by side with the theological fundamentalism espoused by the likes of L. K. Williams and L. G. Jordan. For example, Mary Beth Swetnam Mathews has convincingly demonstrated that the *National Baptist Voice* was among the more friendly black denominational publications toward theological liberalism.[67]

Such conflicting views on issues of doctrine eventually manifested in theological controversies surrounding ABTS. Indeed, not only did the disputes demonstrate the avowedly fundamentalist underpinnings of the school—eliciting along the way affirmations of the seminary's fundamentalism from both Southern Baptist and National Baptist sources—

but consistent with Mathews's findings, individuals associated with the *National Baptist Voice* were often the ones seeking to push the school in a more modernistic direction.

For his part, NBC president Lacey Kirk Williams was expressing concerns about the editorial direction of the *Voice* at least as early as 1930. In a letter to Eugene Perry Alldredge—the chairman of the Southern Baptist commission on ABTS and, after O. L. Hailey, perhaps the foremost white advocate of the seminary—Williams requested advice on "the scope and place of the Denominational paper, that is, one of the Baptist Denomination." Evidently vexed by liberalizing tendencies at the Voice, Williams admitted that delineating the precise role of the denomination's newspaper "has been and is today ... a very difficult problem" in National Baptist circles, and his concern was to determine "how far and wide it may open its columns to articles that might be considered incendiary and in opposition to the expressed policy of the Denomination."[68] Notably, Williams's appeal to Alldredge for advice came in the same year that the *Voice* welcomed Dr. Russell C. Barbour as its new editor—an erudite man with a theologically progressive bent, an openness to the social gospel, and a fondness for modernist exemplar Harry Emerson Fosdick.[69]

R. C. Barbour's editorship of the *Voice* also seemed to agitate at least one of the stalwarts of the ABTS faculty and administration: Dean James H. Garnett. A Civil War veteran, Garnett had been born into slavery in 1847 and joined the Union Army as it advanced through the South.[70] As such, he was one of the seminary's eldest statesmen, and his labors on behalf of the school commanded admiration from all corners. Garnett had been on the seminary's faculty since it first opened its doors in 1924 and had served as the school's dean since 1927, making him the longest-tenured educator and among the most respected personalities associated with the institution.[71] He was also wholeheartedly devoted to the seminary's success through his academic service and his administrative responsibilities, and even literally got his hands dirty by personally effecting building repairs on the campus.[72] In fact, for several years beginning in 1934, Garnett was one of only two men left to shoulder the entire teaching and administrative workload at ABTS. Calling Garnett's work "heroic," E. P. Alldredge questioned whether "any Negro school in America was ever blessed with a greater dean and teacher than J. H. Garnett."[73]

So in February of 1936, after twelve years of service at the seminary and nearly a decade as its dean, the octogenarian Garnett felt compelled to push back against the modernism he felt encroaching on the school from the direction of R. C. Barbour and the *National Baptist Voice*. Spurred in part by one of Barbour's recent editorials, Garnett took to the floor at the NBC's Southeastern Regional Meeting in Columbia, South Carolina, in front of an audience that included National Baptist president L. K. Williams, chairman of the ABTS board of directors A. M. Townsend, and numerous other denominational officials. When he rose to address the convention's delegates, one can imagine Garnett inspiring a quiet attentiveness as the audience prepared to hear the words of this respected elder statesman on the topic of the denomination's lone seminary. Garnett began his address, unsurprisingly, by lauding the seminary's accomplishments, calling it "a work of providence" and "the finest opportunity for cooperation of the two races in the mission work that has ever been worked out in the South Land." Framed in this way, the school took on not only religious and spiritual significance as God's direct provision for black clerical education, but also racial significance as a crucial intermediate step toward ameliorating the racial tensions and divisions that had so long characterized the American South. With this affirmation of the religious and racial significance of the seminary established, Garnett proceeded to take direct aim at Russell Barbour for his attempt to undermine the foundational theological character of the seminary. Editor Barbour had recently proclaimed that "our great Theological Seminaries are liberal and modernistic in thought" and that unless ABTS was developed after that modernistic pattern "the School will become a joke." Taking the rhetorical posture of reminding Barbour of something that he should already have known, Garnett offered his rejoinder: "We wish to remind Dr. Barbour that the American Baptist Theological Seminary will never pattern after the modernistic teaching of the University of Chicago, nor any modernistic teaching. But, it will feel safe in following the teaching of the Southern Baptist Theological Seminary [SBTS] at Louisville, Kentucky."[74]

By invoking the pattern of SBTS Garnett was openly hitching his school's direction to an institution that, according to Baptist historian Gregory Wills, not only "had the trust of fundamentalist leaders" but whose graduates "in fact filled the front ranks of the fundamentalist

Figure 4.3. Longtime dean of ABTS James H. Garnett (left) visiting with a fellow Civil War veteran as they prepare to attend the 75th anniversary celebration of the Battle of Gettysburg. Image reproduced courtesy of the Southern Baptist Historical Library and Archives, Nashville, Tennessee.

leadership."[75] In these few words, then, Garnett offered both a positive affirmation of fundamentalist doctrine and an explicit repudiation of modernism, indicating the seminary's commitment to a theologically fundamentalist stance under his administration. His statement here also mirrored a similar expectation expressed two years prior by E. P. Alldredge, himself a fundamentalist, that "we may hope to see our Negro Baptist brethren with a great school . . . which will rival in service and in glory our own great Southern Baptist Seminary in Louisville, Kentucky!"[76] Associating ABTS with the model of the Southern Baptists' flagship seminary carried a certain theological tilt toward fundamentalism—both by Garnett and Alldredge. As Garnett brought his convention address to a close, he had just made clear this connection with SBTS and also rebuked R. C. Barbour's "modernistic" ideal for the seminary. His concluding statement, then, offered what might well be seen as a subtle reminder to Barbour and his "modernist" allies that Garnett's perspective *was* the institution's perspective: "The approaching commencement will close the twelfth year of the operation of the ABT Seminary. And, this will close my twelfth year in active service with this seminary."[77] Garnett's tenure at ABTS was coextensive with the school's existence, and his longtime position as dean gave him substantial control over the seminary's operations, lending a weight to his rebuke that few others could have matched.

Garnett's pointed response to Barbour's explicit efforts to liberalize the seminary may also shed light on a biting editorial that Barbour had published in the *National Baptist Voice* two years earlier, expressing outrage over being denied the chairmanship of the school's board

Figure 4.4. ABTS faculty and students posing together outside Griggs Hall during the 1937–1938 school year. Image reproduced courtesy of the Southern Baptist Historical Library and Archives, Nashville, Tennessee.

of directors. Barbour had lost to A. M. Townsend in what the editorial described as "a surprise attack which came at a time when the leaders of our Convention are working together as never before, with no thought of ambitious rivalries."[78] Given Barbour's express desire to model the school after the theologically liberal style of the University of Chicago, his indignation over being denied the chairmanship seems likely to have been related to his goal of setting the school in a new, more modernistic direction. Moreover, his sentiment that this turn of events would undermine the cooperation of NBC leaders who were "working together as never before" might also be taken to indicate dividing lines within the convention between the more fundamentalist-leaning members (such as Garnett, L. G. Jordan, and L. K. Williams) and the more modernist faction. Despite this division, neither side seems to have called for strict separation or for a denominational split, as was common among white fundamentalists of the day. Still, such conflicts and divisions weighed on the mind of the seminary's longtime dean. Within weeks of R. C. Barbour's failed bid for the chairmanship and subsequent editorial blast in the pages of the *Voice*, Garnett penned a letter to E. P. Alldredge expressing his "hope that the White Baptists will not relinquish their interest in this undertaking by the short sightedness of a few radicals among the Negro Baptists." Garnett saw a "great advantage" in the multiracial fellowship that the seminary's operations had occasioned "between the White and Colored Baptists of the South"—an advantage that, according to Garnett, had been realized to a significant degree during the first decade of the school's operation and that promised even greater yields in the future.[79] Fearing a modernist threat both to the future of the seminary and to the denomination's working relationship with the SBC, Garnett considered positions like Barbour's to be dangerously shortsighted and foolhardy.

Conflict with the *National Baptist Voice* continued to simmer when several years later J. Pius Barbour succeeded his brother as the paper's editor. There, he reiterated his brother's former critique of the seminary and lamented the fact that men trained in "the Historical approach"—who constituted "the vast majority of qualified Negroes" and who also happened to be "trained in the Northern schools"—felt unwelcome at ABTS.[80] The "Historical approach" almost certainly refers to the historical-critical or higher-critical methodology of biblical interpretation—a modernist staple that was roundly perceived by fundamentalists as fatally undermining the inspired and inerrant nature of the Bible. E. P. Alldredge, as the chairman of the Southern Baptists' commission on ABTS, quickly fired back at J. Pius Barbour, excoriating the editor's desire to allow "learned infidels" to inject their "poisonous infidelities" into the bloodstream of the seminary and make "infidels out of our Seminary students." This was a "scheme" on Barbour's part to allow "modernistic teachers to sow infidelity in the minds and hearts of the Seminary students." Alldredge pointed back to the seminary's confession of faith, arguing that ABTS could never "tolerate any man as teacher who could not and did not whole-heartedly accept this fundamental statement," because the school's confessional statement represented, in the words of the book of Jude, "the faith once for all delivered to the saints." *Of course* modernistic historical-critical proponents would feel uncomfortable at ABTS, Alldredge implied—that was the point. To tolerate any faculty member who would depart from the seminary's confessional standard would be tantamount to surrendering the integrity of the school's gospel message and compromising the seminary's mission "to teach the religion of the Lord Jesus Christ."[81]

In response J. Pius Barbour staked his own claim to orthodoxy, saying that he "believ[ed] in such doctrines as the Divinity of Christ and The Virgin Birth," even as he favored "the historical approach."[82] His affirmation of Christ's divinity and miraculous birth seem to place Barbour in a sort of interstitial space between modernist and fundamentalist poles—warm to higher biblical criticism and the more liberal methods of certain northern seminaries, but still attached to certain supernaturalist doctrines. Yet for someone like Alldredge, with a deep concern for preserving the fundamentalist character of the seminary, this still represented a form of modernism too dangerous to tolerate and too insidious to ignore. In this regard, it is notable that even as Barbour wrote to Alldredge in his own defense, affirming the deity of Christ and the virgin birth, he also conspicuously omitted any mention of biblical inerrancy or inspiration, which was the animating theological concern of fundamentalists with respect to historical-critical methodology.

Meanwhile, Alldredge brought this matter to the attention of National Baptist president D. V. Jemison, whose response again demonstrated the ambiguous tension that existed within the denomination on the question of fundamentalism and doctrinal diversity. Initially expressing surprise at Barbour's attacks on ABTS, Jemison affirmed his own and the denomination's fundamentalist character:

> We are fundamentalists and will not tolerate any modernistic teaching in the Seminary nor support a modernistic as editor of our National Baptist Voice. . . . We will not stand for any one of our Convention who is not a fundamentalist and whose writings are not conducive to fundamentalism. . . . Our president is a fundamentalist and of course the teachers who teach in our Seminary and Training School will necessary [sic] be fundamental.[83]

This is a sweeping, if also extremely generic, affirmation of fundamentalism and repudiation of modernism from the president of the NBC—albeit in an attempt to mollify an agitated fundamentalist Southern Baptist. Just three weeks later, however, Jemison moderated his tone. Assuring Alldredge that he had requested Barbour to "change his course" lest Jemison would "have to make some changes relative to the publication of the National Baptist Voice," Jemison also expressed his desire for Barbour to remain in his editorial position at the *Voice*, cautioning Alldredge not to prolong this dispute because it would "destroy the usefulness of Dr. Barbour" in promoting the seminary.[84] In the president's view, Barbour's utility to the goal of racial progress represented by ABTS outweighed both his promotion of historical-critical biblical methodology and whatever perceived threat such a theological position posed (in the minds of men such as Alldredge and J. H. Garnett) to the spiritual mission of the seminary—considerations that would have unquestionably been deal-breakers in white fundamentalist institutions.

This particular spat with J. Pius Barbour continued to cause problems for Alldredge as he persisted in his quest to raise funds and support for the seminary among his fellow Southern Baptists. Well over a year after the initial exchange with Barbour, Alldredge penned a letter to white Baptist evangelist A. D. Muse to assuage concerns about modernism infiltrating the school. Muse had recently become aware of Barbour's theological sentiments and published what was evidently an expose-style article on the topic titled "Cat out of the Bag," which also cast a shadow of suspicion on the SBC's participation in this joint endeavor with the National Baptists. Alldredge expressed deep concern that Muse's characterization of the situation "does the Negro seminary great injustice and great harm." Muse's assumption that "the modernistic editor of *The Baptist Voice* speaks for our seminary" could not be further from the truth. On the contrary, while it was the case that "Dr. Pius Barbour . . . is a modernist, educated at Crozier," Alldredge sought to assure Muse that Barbour's influence was limited: "He speaks for the small but powerful group of modernists in the National (Negro) Baptist Convention, and for no one else." In fact Alldredge took this occasion to explicitly frame the National Baptist denomination and the seminary project within his own fundamentalist paradigm: "[Barbour's] denomination is overwhelmingly against his position—I mean the vast majority of the Negro Baptist ministers and people are *as fundamental in their beliefs as you and I are.*"

As a way of further alleviating Muse's concerns, Alldredge turned to the seminary's confession of faith as an imprimatur of the institution's fundamentalist orthodoxy. The school's operations were grounded in "the strongest, most orthodox creed of any institution among Southern Baptists, barring none." Not only was it "the clearest, most comprehensive and most Baptistic statement of our faith governing any institution today," but it had the added virtue of being constructed by a joint committee of both black and white members and affirmed by the seminary's interracial governing body. This seems to have been a point of emphasis for Alldredge, a piece of evidence harnessed to support his claim that the National Baptists possessed innate fundamentalist convictions and were "overwhelmingly opposed" to Barbour's modernism. After all (the logic seemed to go), if the confession was a joint effort, then it naturally followed that this confessional standard was not merely forced onto the National Baptists from the outside, but rather that the NBC was itself rooted in fundamentalist convictions and that therefore black Baptists could be trusted (alongside white Southern Baptists) to safeguard the seminary against modernist incursions. Since the confession was "agreed to by the Negro brethren and the whites before any students were asked to come here," it was thus "made a part of the contract between the two conventions" and ensured that "this seminary never can have a modernistic teacher." Despite Barbour's desire to "bring in some teachers here who held to his peculiar school of thought" (which amounted to modernist "infidelity"), Alldredge concluded with confidence that the confession guaranteed that ABTS "is safer today than either one of our white seminaries." As it turned out, Alldredge's confidence on this score was misplaced; by the end of the 1940s, signing the school's confession was evidently no longer being enforced as a faculty requirement.[85]

Concerns about modernistic intrusions were not limited to the seminary proper, but extended also to the auxiliary Women's Training School. By the early 1940s, the Southern Baptist Women's Missionary Union (WMU) had begun to express apprehensions about the school harboring teachers with modernist views and assigning "textbooks that are distinctly modernistic . . . not for graduate students who would know how to receive the teachings of these books, but . . . young women who are decidedly immature in their thinking and reading and studies." If these errors were not corrected, the WMU vowed, "all further help and moral support will be withdrawn from the school."[86] Ultimately, E. P. Alldredge happily reported to a concerned Southern Baptist woman that "we have removed several of these rationalistic and modernistic text-books, also some of the teachers, and one dean, and we have secured an order from the Board of Directors that both the text-books and the teachers should be sound in their views." This victory concluded a "three year fight to bring this Training School back in line with our Negro Seminary and with orthodox methods and orthodox teachers." When the issue came to the attention of the board, it "took its stand with the Seminary—which from the first has been rock-ribbed orthodox Baptist."[87] Not only does this evaluation reinforce J. H. Garnett's assessment of the seminary as essentially antimodernist in its early character, but the fact that the NBC-majority board made these changes indicates once again that the resolution was not merely an instance of Southern Baptists imposing a standard from without, but was also a reflection of fundamentalist and antimodernist convictions on the part of some of the National Baptist administrators. At the same time, it was the NBC's partnership with the International Council of Religious Education that brought these textbooks to the training school in the first place, illustrating that even though many National Baptists may have been conservative or even "fundamentalist" in their doctrine, as a denominational body they were much more comfortable with having various nonfundamentalist associations than were their white counterparts.

Hot on the heels of this resolution, and seemingly in response to the ever-looming modernist threat, Alldredge made a remarkable proposal. In a letter to Ryland Knight, a member of the SBC's Home Mission Board and an original member of the ABTS board of directors, Alldredge proposed that the white Southern Baptist seminaries begin to admit black graduate students from ABTS. Acknowledging that this would require "some adjustments and readjustments in the operation of our three white seminaries," he argued for the proposition on three counts. First, it would help ABTS attract and retain students at a time when enrollment was at a low ebb. Second, it would "constitute a step toward further fellowship and comradeship between the two great Baptist racial groups." And third, it would allow the most talented black men "a chance to get the highest and best training in the nation without the necessity of wading through the rationalism and paganism of some of the higher institutions of learning in other sections of the nation."[88] Alldredge's concern about "rationalism and paganism" in this context can hardly be read as anything other than a worry about modernistic influences, revealing that his push for the acceptance of black students into white seminaries was driven by the imperative to propagate a doctrinal fundamentalist worldview among southern black clergy. Given that ABTS represented, in the words of seminary president J. M. Nabrit in the late 1930s, "the ideals of the South, separate in race, united in Christ," Alldredge's overture toward blurring the line of institutionalized segregation indeed qualifies as remarkable.[89] Just a year later, Alldredge's suggestion indeed came to fruition. In a letter to his National Baptist colleague and chairman of the ABTS board of directors A. M. Townsend, Alldredge observed with frustration that so many of the "Negro Baptist students" of the South continued to matriculate at northern white seminaries rather than at the Nashville seminary. If such students were determined to attend white schools in lieu of ABTS, he wrote with a measure of exasperation, then National Baptists should request that all of the SBC's "white seminaries admit colored Baptist students to the senior classes—as the Southern Baptist Seminary at Louisville is doing this year."[90] The fear that modernism would take hold among black Baptists was substantial enough to drive even some Southern Baptists to explore options that would violate the institutionalized racial segregation of the South.

Figures 4.5 and 4.6. Chairman of the ABTS board of directors Arthur Melvin Townsend and longtime Southern Baptist leader Eugene Perry Alldredge take part in the inauguration of President Ralph W. Riley (1945). Images reproduced courtesy of the Southern Baptist Historical Library and Archives, Nashville, Tennessee.

Such a desire to protect black churches from external threats that might undermine a fundamentalist perspective was in fact an animating motivator for ABTS agents of both races—and the threats at times extended beyond the confines of modernist theology. The menace of communism, for example, weighed on many fundamentalists' minds in concert with their fears of modernism. The topic received a chapter in *The Fundamentals*, and such leading fundamentalist voices as William Bell Riley and A. C. Gaebelein publicly contended that modernism posed a threat to both Christianity and democracy and would lead society down the ruinous path toward atheism and communism.[91] These same fears found expression within the ranks of ABTS's leaders and supporters, as well. In July 1937 seminary president James M. Nabrit identified the two great modern-day foes confronting black ministers: firstly "the rise of Communism," which threatened to "turn the religious faith of the Negro into ashes," and secondly the "rise of liberalism in religion," which sought to eliminate "old-fashioned regeneration" and replace it with bare moralism. Against such existential threats, Nabrit maintained, the seminary was duty bound to stand fast.[92]

Likewise, in an article for the *Christian Index* and reprinted in the *National Baptist Voice*, Ryland Knight urged his fellow Southern Baptists to give greater financial support to ABTS on the grounds that without solid conservative theological education, black clergy and laity alike would be "easy prey" for influences "subversive of American ideals," such as communism. Knight further invoked the exhortations of two prominent black leaders to press home his point. The words of Joseph J. Rhoads—the president of Bishop College, a historically black college in Marshall, Texas—reaffirmed Knight's view of the threat facing the black community and the black church: "Communism is making a subtle but attractive bid for a Negro following. There are two fertile and fatal fields for its propagation, namely, a mis-educated Negro ministry, and a religiously ignorant majority of the race." Knight also appealed to the example of National Baptist president Lacey Kirk Williams, who had warned his convention that "If [the religious inclination of the race] is not turned in the right direction, secular and often radical agencies will convert it into a weakness and capitalize it in the wrong direction.... There is a danger that our young people will follow red-eyed radicals rather than religious leadership." For Knight, these warnings from black leaders about the dangers of communism infiltrating the black community only magnified the grave importance of Southern Baptists' financial support for ABTS.[93] Thus the religious dangers represented by the encroachments of theological liberalism were perceived by ABTS partisans of both races to run parallel to the sociopolitical danger of communism, and conservative clerical education was the necessary solution to both problems.

In much the same way, the imperative of this type of black clerical education was at times driven by the threat of Catholicism—another common antagonist in the minds of many fundamentalists.[94] Recycling the old stereotype of blacks as "naturally religious" but intellectually inferior, white fundamentalists such as Curtis Lee Laws understood Catholicism to have a marked appeal to the "average uncultured Negro" because its worship was "calculated to work on the credulity of one who is naturally superstitious." Hence, the threat it posed "compels us to provide an educated colored Baptist ministry."[95] A booklet by the SBC's Home Mission Board similarly saw Catholics as "making a bid for [the Negro] on the basis of equal treatment," but here the argument was that this should impel Southern Baptists to "cultivate a more interracial mind and cooperate more fully to attack the deep social and cultural wrongs of our denominational kindred"—a prospect which naturally included support for "the American Baptist Theological Seminary located at Nashville."[96]

E. P. Alldredge also fretted over the southern expansion of external religious bodies, including both Catholics and the Federal Council of Churches, on the basis of their racial programs. With such threats on the horizon, Alldredge concluded that the only way to combat these encroachments was for Southern Baptists to "work out and follow out a worthy program of racial readjustment with their colored brethren in the South."[97] This sort of suspicion of Catholic intrusion was also expressed by a former student of ABTS, Illie E. Malry, who had once been a member of the Seminary Singers.[98] After leaving the school and settling in Chicago, Malry wrote to Alldredge expressing his worry that "so many of our people are being taught and led into CATHOLICISM." In light of this concern, his hope was that the seminary "may continue to be an uplift to humanity" by providing Christian training to combat Catholic efforts among African Americans.[99] Mallry's testimony illustrates from a student's perspective the same idea that was present in the minds of numerous leaders and administrators across the color line: the seminary's significance lay in producing black ministers well versed in the fundamentals of Christianity, who could in turn provide a bulwark for their communities against whatever insinuating threats might come against such a theologically conservative faith—from liberal modernism, to Roman Catholicism, to godless communism.

\* \* \*

Founded and funded on the basis of a unique type of southern interracial cooperation, yet nevertheless beholden to concepts of racial differentiation and institutional segregation, the American Baptist Theological Seminary displayed at once the unifying potential of common religious identity and the entrenched limitations of any such unity due to prevailing cultural dogmas. The conflicts and controversies of the school's first decades illuminate the complex set of allegiances that tugged at National Baptist fundamentalists, as they earnestly sought to "contend for the faith" without denying denominational or ecclesiastical fellowship to their opponents. Alignment with white fundamentalists on matters of doctrine, even in opposition to members of their own denominational body, was no sufficient reason to fully separate from fellow National Baptists who were also co-laborers for the cause of racial progress. And on the other end of the racial spectrum, ABTS illustrated for its Southern Baptist supporters a similarly complex relationship between southern racial precepts and fundamentalist impulses. For major white supporters of the school, paternalistic attitudes and general segregationist dogma coexisted alongside a mounting pressure to help support the fundamentalist convictions that persisted within portions of the southern African American community—and while this tension caused at least some white Baptists such as E. P. Alldredge to consider southern race relations in a somewhat new light, it also demonstrated that the era's racial dividing walls would not be easily overcome.

5

Contested Identities

*Fundamentalism, Race, and Americanism*

On the Sunday morning of July 5, 1931, black Methodist reverend Isaac Reed Berry took to the pulpit in his West Virginia church to address his congregation and, on this particular morning, to reflect on God and country. Independence Day celebrations had come and gone that weekend, providing an ideal moment to use congregants' still-heightened patriotic sentiments as a springboard to launch a discussion of religion's role in the great American experiment. This was a nation, he proclaimed, founded on Christian devotion, a devotion that had yielded multitudinous providential blessings. As the sermon gathered momentum, American civil liberty and Christian spiritual liberty no longer remained discrete categories, but blended together in a potent religious-patriotic cocktail: "In the faith of our fathers, the name that is above every name was carved on the cornerstone of our liberties three centuries ago.... Let [America] remember that the blood of the divine Son of God has bought the freedom that we have today." But his version of Christian nationalism entailed elements of specifically racial import as well. Given the ills of the day, which in the context of the Great Depression and Prohibition included predatory profiteering and bootlegging, but also encompassed societal injustices that were devastatingly particular to the black community—lynching and the social fallout of American slavery—Berry claimed that only a wholesale return to this religion steeped in "the blood of the divine Son of God" could safeguard the nation. Not even "the most astute statecraft" could ameliorate these evils. The only solution was for America to rediscover that its liberties and freedoms—the inalienable rights that justice demanded apply equally to blacks and whites alike—were rooted in the historic Christian faith.[1] This black gospel preacher, a staunch defender of fundamentalist doctrine, found it entirely plausible to connect the divinity of Christ, civil liberty, racial justice, and American identity. For Berry fundamental doctrines such as Christ's deity and atonement were not relegated to the realm of pedantic theologizing, but carried sweeping implications for defining identity on personal, spiritual, racial, and even national levels.

Amid the many controversies attending the fundamentalist-modernist conflict, passionate conversations unfolded within the African American community not only attempting to adjudicate the issue of Protestant fundamentalism per se, but also centering on questions of identity. How did the fundamentalist's religious identity square with a black racial identity? Were fundamentalist convictions compatible with (or even essential to) being an African American, or did fundamentalism represent a betrayal of the race? The very fact that some black clergy and laymen overtly adopted the "fundamentalist" mantle set the table for debates within the black community about whether such theological commitments constituted a help or a hindrance in the race's quest for social progress and cultural advancement. In a social-historical context that more or less dictated the ubiquity of racial identity as a defining characteristic for African Americans, fundamentalism was far from an esoteric issue confined to the arenas of theological debate and philosophical speculation. As we saw earlier, this was evident at American Baptist Theological Seminary (ABTS), as the institution was envisioned as a means of uplift and legitimization for the black community—a vision that suffused even the conflict between J. H. Garnett and R. C. Barbour over modernist theology and the future direction of the school. Debates over fundamentalism and its relative impact on the race as a whole, in fact, stretched beyond seminary classrooms and theological publications, engaging voices from across the theological spectrum, and even those without much religious inclination at all. Even if fundamentalism per se did not hold any particular interest for all such commentators, racial progress certainly did, and so fundamentalism was treated not only as a religious issue, but also as a racial issue.

In many civil rights contexts during this era and during the "long civil rights movement" as a whole, African American activists often emphasized nationalist themes of American democracy, American identity, and black people's rights to fully participate in the American experiment.[2] So as discourses about fundamentalism's utility to the black community sometimes centered on theological issues such as biblical literalism and divine creation or on social issues such as intellectual credibility, themes of American identity, ideals, and citizenship also inevitably crept into the conversation.[3] Even as black fundamentalists promoted doctrinal conservatism via the pulpit or the pen, they concomitantly staked their claim to legitimacy as partakers in the American experiment by lauding not only a theological continuity with "old-time religion" but also a degree of historical continuity with America's supposed identity as a historically "Christian people." In doing so, they embraced and articulated ideas of Christian nationalism in various ways and to various degrees. Rhetorically connecting their fundamentalist faith with such American ideals as emancipation, liberty, and democracy, these conservative religionists offered visions of a religiously inflected Americanism, and at times a reciprocal patriotically inflected Christianity, which promised hope for both the propagation of true religion and the advancement of their race. They sought to articulate a theologically conservative fundamentalism that was shaped by and responsive to their racial context, racial identity, and progressive desire to challenge the oppressive status quo.

At the same time, others in the black community were skeptical of or even outright hostile to fundamentalist religion, convinced that such "backward" thinking amounted to an albatross around the neck of the African American people as they fought for a fully realized American citizenship. As such opponents voiced their criticism, particularly in print media, they cast fundamentalists as out of step with other preeminent American ideals such as free thinking, free expression, and religious toleration. Reliance on any sort of exclusive fundamentalist identity, from this point of view, was profoundly unhelpful to the black community because the "intolerant" perspectives of both religious and racial dogmatism were considered to go hand in hand; in the words of one editorialist, racial prejudice and fundamentalists' religious intolerance "sleep in the same bed and are all but indistinguishable."[4] For these critics, fundamentalism was not to be associated with the desirable aspects of American heritage and American identity, but rather with the small-minded intolerance represented by antebellum slaveholders and the United States' history of racism. So, while both the pro- and anti-fundamentalist sides of the debate actively sought racial advancement for African Americans, they did so from markedly different perspectives regarding American identity and the social value of dogmatic Christian fundamentalism.

Fundamentalism: Religion of Racial Progress or Racial Regress?

As black fundamentalists argued for the utility of their faith, they often tied it to historical instances of racial progress. Recall, for example, the June 1925 editorial entitled "Our Group Are Fundamentalists in Religion," which appeared in the *Norfolk Journal and Guide* during the immediate buildup to the Scopes trial. Expanding on the title's straightforward thesis statement, the editorialist claimed, "Yes, the Afro-American people are Fundamentalists, and they can give a reason for the faith that is in them by pointing to what they have become in this free Nation from what they began in the days of the Colonies." The fundamentalist religion of the African American people, which here included "accept[ing] the Bible as our sufficient guide," was in fact "the same simple faith that a majority of the Christian people of the United States have." This simple religious faith, the author opined, "is sufficient for all of our National and personal requirements." Evidence for the utility and sufficiency of such a fundamentalist faith was immediately located in the national experience of the African American people: "It has brought us thus far, and the belief is general that it is sufficient to carry us further in the enlargement of higher and better things in human life and living. We have seen so many radical changes to our advantage in the gradual evolution of the past half century, and we are seeing so much of the like sort from day to day that we see no good and sufficient reason to waver in the Faith or stumble in the Promises."[5] For this editorialist, the attractiveness and necessity of fundamentalist religion was based not simply on a sentimental sense of connectivity with the community's traditional "old-time religion." Fundamentalism also served as the religious bedrock for the community's corporate survival during the era of slavery and its corporate advancement during the decades following emancipation. It was, in this respect, conceived as a *driver* of racial progress.[6]

Moreover, the author's overt connection between fundamentalist religious identity and black racial identity allowed him to connect the African American community as a whole with the Christian heritage—or as he put it, "the majority of the Christian people"—of the United States. By doing so he rhetorically positioned blacks as historical partakers in the "Christian American" identity—partakers who were therefore due the full benefits of freedom and liberty accorded to other participants in the American experiment. African Americans, he claimed, could justify their religious fundamentalism by "pointing to what they have become in this *free* Nation from what they began in the days of the Colonies." Not only that, but for him the connection between fundamentalist religion and African American identity was so tightly knit that if blacks were to "waver and stumble, as so many are doing, in denying the faith and running after false gods," the inevitable result would be that "we shall prove false to ourselves." In other words, abandoning the old faith in favor of new religious ideas and innovations would constitute a betrayal of their racial as well as religious heritage. This simple faith, then, according to the editorialist, intricately connected the religious, racial, and national identities of African Americans. Such a fundamentalist faith, as an essential part of the African American heritage, allowed black people to participate in the *freedom* that accompanied American identity and citizenship—a participation that was rhetorically justified by the advancement that the race had experienced since "the days of the colonies." The arc of US history bent toward freedom, and the United States' identity as a Christian nation and a Christian people (associated here specifically with fundamentalism) played a major part in setting and implementing that long-term trajectory.

The issues of slavery and emancipation, in particular, became points of argumentation for both sides in the contestation over fundamentalism. African Methodist Episcopal (AME) minister John Albert Johnson once again entered into this conversation. As we have seen earlier, Johnson's ministry, which extended into the late 1920s, was replete with examples of his express affirmation of the central fundamentalist theological positions, as well as overt polemics warning his flock of the dangers of modernist theology. This time Johnson joined the fray by connecting the old-time faith of the fathers with the destruction of American slavery and the hope for future racial advancement. In his pulpit ministry Johnson was prone to cast faith as the "dominant feature" of civilization. In one sermon reflecting on Matthew 6:33, for example, he proclaimed that Jesus' instruction "Seek ye first the kingdom of God and His righteousness" plainly indicated that "it was most important to know the main factor in civilization, that faith as distinguished from specialized, secularized reason, or intellect was the main factor—the initial, essential, dominant element in civilization." On another occasion he applied this idea more specifically to the United States and to the experience of the black community. Since "the dominant feature of a people's religion is the dominant feature of the life of the nation," Johnson asked in his sermon, what was "the one dominating thought of the Nineteenth Century? In a word—'Emancipation.' And where did it find it? In its religion." The emancipation of African American slaves was "the application of truth" necessitated by the particular "conditions of life" in the country at the time, but it was firmly and ultimately grounded in the unchanging and unchangeable orthodox gospel message that "men in all ages need the Cross, for pardon, cleansing, renewal, hope and inspiration ... [and] must be saved by Grace through faith." This message of religious truth, "like Christ Himself is the same yesterday, today, and forever."[7] Thus, Johnson visualized a remarkable constellation connecting his own fundamentalist perspective on the unalterable nature of the Christian gospel with themes of black emancipation and American identity in much the same way as did the 1925 editorial "Our Group Are Fundamentalists in Religion."

Such views did not pass unchallenged by those in the black community who opposed fundamentalism and possessed a manifestly different perspective on its relationship to the history of slavery and abolition. These opponents came not only from liberal pulpits and liberal churches—that is, from those on the "other side" of the religious spectrum in the fundamentalist-modernist controversy. They also included some members of the community who were on the religious periphery or outside the religious spectrum altogether—people whom historian Jeffrey Moran has classified as the "secular black elite."[8] Both modernists and secularists opposed fundamentalism on the grounds that it undermined the intellectual credibility of the race, and thus retarded hope for social progress. Hence, it is not surprising that such critics pushed back against fundamentalists' attempts to associate themselves with the historical legacy of emancipation and racial advancement. Refusing to cede fundamentalists the moral high ground of freedom and emancipation, critics sought instead to turn the tables by aligning this religious perspective with the great national sin of slavery. Not only should the fundamentalists (black *or* white) be denied their identification with the ideals of American freedom, opponents reasoned, but they should rightly be identified with the forces of slavery and oppression instead.

One such member of the "secular black elite," and a fierce opponent of fundamentalism, was Ernest Rice McKinney, himself the grandson of a West Virginia Baptist minister. In addition to being a minister, McKinney's grandfather was involved in union work as a coal miner, and so Ernest Rice McKinney came to imbibe his grandfather's dedication to union activism while eschewing his religious commitments. As his own career progressed, McKinney became an aggressive labor organizer, a founding member of the Conference for Progressive Labor Action, and a devoted voice for black workers' rights and for the full integration of blacks into American life and society.[9] He also became a harsh critic of the religious fundamentalism that he observed within the black community. With biting invective, McKinney took the occasion of an August 1925 editorial column in the Chicago *Broad Ax* to reflect on Protestant fundamentalism in light of the recently concluded Scopes trial in Tennessee. The fundamentalists' "persecution of . . . Dr. [Harry Emerson] Fosdick and Prof. Scopes" placed them squarely in the legacy of the persecution of Galileo, the Spanish Inquisition, the Salem Witch Trials, and even the crucifixion of Jesus, for "it was NOT the Fundamentalists who followed Jesus of Nazareth, but it was THEY WHO CRUCIFIED HIM." In the process of leveling these charges, McKinney excoriated fundamentalists of both races as "imbeciles and morons" who "get a volcanic eruption sensation in the head when they try to think." Having left no doubt as to his personal estimation of this brand of religionists, he proceeded to lay out his caustic argument against any sort of positive fundamentalist presence in the American historical narrative:

> These people don't know or refuse to believe that the progress of the world has been brought about by the Skeptics, Agnostics, Atheists, Radicals and Free Thinkers. Whoever heard of a Conservative or a Fundamentalist precipitating progress at anytime or anywhere? How could they when their look is always backward? The advance of civilization necessitates a push and a pull forward. The Fundamentalist simply sits by the brake and holds it down tight. He doesn't know why he does it. All that he

knows is that Change and Light are poison to him. It was the heterodox who destroyed slavery in America and England. The Orthodox Fundamentalists wanted slavery to continue.

Insofar as fundamentalists deserved to identify with any element of the American past, McKinney made clear, it was with the wickedness and backwardness of racism and slavery, not with the ideals of emancipation and freedom. He even implied that blacks who adopted the fundamentalist worldview were not fully or authentically part of the race's freedom struggle—such people amounted to "white southerners with Negro mothers [and] Negroes with white fathers."[10]

More than just a one-off critique, this idea recurred in McKinney's editorial writing. In another 1925 column McKinney set out to denounce black fundamentalists as intellectually backward impediments to the race, once again invoking the specter of slavery to press his point. It was "the Fundamentalists in the protestant Episcopal Church," he said, "who were the backbone of slavery in the South." Fundamentalism, therefore, represented "a barrier, an obstacle to civilization to climb over and batter down." This was especially true, in McKinney's estimation, within the African American community itself because of the high number of influential black fundamentalist ministers: "The Negro race is filled to overflowing with these 'Fundamentalist' gentlemen. . . . They keep us poor, ignorant, and weak. But some day, we will revolt and then someone will have to get another job or starve."[11] Thus, according to McKinney, to be a fundamentalist was to entwine oneself with the worst of white culture, with the advocates of slavery and racism. Black fundamentalist ministers constituted roadblocks in the race's quest for freedom and equality, and therefore true racial progress required a decisive movement *away* from fundamentalist religion.

Others argued in much the same vein. In a 1927 column in the *Chicago Defender*, George Singleton castigated "the form of Christianity worshiped . . . by the gloriously orthodox and the manifestly fundamentalist" as "crass superstition, literalism and formalism" with no utility whatsoever for the African American race. In fact, blacks who adopted such fundamentalist perspectives were practicing "a hand-me-down religion from the American white man from slavery days."[12] Not only was black fundamentalism to be rhetorically linked to the propagation of slavery, but as far as Singleton was concerned it represented an artifact of slavery itself, and was thus entirely worthless to African Americans. This was the religion that had been imposed from without onto African slaves by their racist oppressors. What meaningful utility, then, could it possibly have for the race? Once again, for blacks to adopt a fundamentalist identity was here portrayed as a foundational betrayal of their own blackness.

Along similar lines, a 1932 column in the *Chicago Defender* honoring the nineteenth-century agnostic and Civil War veteran Robert Ingersoll severely chastised the "amen brethren" of the black community who identified with the Christian fundamentalism of William Jennings Bryan, calling them "long on shouts but short on reasoning." Ingersoll, the columnist chided, "fought for your liberty and rights when the 'Bible-backs' were preaching that slavery was God's work.... Your ministers who paint him as your enemy forgot to tell you that."[13] Once again, the *Defender* linked fundamentalist religion with the great American sin of slavery, and blacks who participated in such religion were considered to be shamefully working contrary to the interests of the race as a whole. Moreover, as in McKinney's evaluation, black fundamentalist ministers were found to be instrumental in perpetuating this dynamic within the black community, and therefore culpable for cozying up to the very forces that had upheld slavery in the first place. Far from a theological tradition in line with the virtuous ideals of freedom and liberty, fundamentalism according to these critics was a relic of the dark side of American history, a remnant of a sinister and sinful past.

But the contestation over fundamentalist identity extended well beyond rhetoric about slavery and emancipation. Black fundamentalists presented their religious tradition as intimately intertwined with the propagation of liberty and democracy itself. Their detractors, on the other hand, painted them as unalterably and diametrically opposed to the American ideals, enshrined in the Constitution, of free speech, free thought, and religious toleration. Consider once again John Albert Johnson's sermon that grounded the emancipatory spirit of the nineteenth century in the steadfast religious character of the United States and the unchanging gospel of salvation "by Grace through faith." After asserting that the spirit of emancipation sprang forth from the nation's essentially Christian character, Johnson went on to expand his discussion beyond slavery and abolition. "Emancipation from what?" he queried. "From everything that hinders the development into the perfect nation, the perfect man."[14]

For Johnson, then, the traditional, unchanging doctrines of the Christian faith not only undergirded the literal emancipation of African Americans from their long nightmare of enslavement, but also provided the cultural bedrock on which rested the future progress of the American people and the fuller realization of the American ideals of freedom and liberty on both national and personal levels. "The future of the Negro," Johnson concluded, "depends more upon character than upon anything else. He must stand fast in his liberty."[15] One can hardly avoid the conclusion, given the surrounding context of the sermon, that the "character" upon which the race's future depended was substantially religious in nature, but it also had a clear political correlation in the willingness to steadfastly contend for "liberty." Just as America's Christian character had motivated the abolition of slavery in the nineteenth century, Johnson implied, so the same Christian character would nurture into full bloom the American commitment to liberty, especially for blacks, as both the nation and the race strove ever closer toward perfection. This sentiment, connecting racial progress with a historic Christian nationalism, would be striking enough in a vacuum, but it is even more so considering that it rang forth with the authority and weight of the pulpit behind it.

## "The Cross, Where Freedom's Sword Was Forged"

If Johnson might be said to have sounded the chime of Christian nationalism, then his younger colleague Isaac Reed Berry rang out the theme of "Christian America" like thunderous church bells. Just as Berry's anti-modernist polemics were aggressively forthright, so too his treatment of America's religious heritage left little room for subtlety or doubt regarding his position. The United States was an intrinsically Christian nation, whose successes and failures were to be viewed through the lens of the nation's relationship to God. Because of this outlook, Berry felt comfortable placing central figures of the American mythos such as George Washington, Benjamin Franklin, and Abraham Lincoln alongside the apostle Paul, Martin Luther, the Wesley brothers, and Francis

Asbury as some among "the multitudes of saints that have gone forward in the work of God, and . . . have been sustained by a clearer faith in God's presence and God's leading," relying for their success on "the same source of divine presence [that] prevails in the whole great array of Christian workers everywhere."[16] The fact that this list of "saints . . . in the work of God" was simply a passing reference in a sermon introduction, and not the focus of the sermon itself—indeed, the fact that Berry felt no need to justify or defend his inclusion of American political figures on the list at all—shows that, for Berry, the Christian nature of the American experiment was simply an assumed truth. The United States was innately and intimately connected to Christianity and "the work of God" in the world.

The country's status as a divinely sanctioned project, of course, did not absolve it from the duty of Christian faithfulness. Much like Israel's covenant with God in the Old Testament, if righteous fidelity to Christian ideals was to be rewarded with God's blessings, so too was infidelity a precursor to God's judgment. Berry made this general principle clear in a sermon about the wickedness of the northern kingdom of Israel prior to its downfall at the hands of Assyria. Having laid out the biblical record of God's wayward and rebellious people, he turned his gaze to the United States: "To banish God from the counsel of government, to shut him out of the education of youth, to build homes without him, is to write concerning the people of our future the record of Israel. God wiped them out of his sight. . . . If ye forsake God and serve strange gods, then he will turn and do you hurt, and consume you after that he has done you good."[17] Elsewhere he invoked the example of the Babylonian conquest of Judah to demonstrate that "the nation that forgets God shall perish. . . . Fools mock sin, but a day is coming when it will register its retribution in flowers of fire and will leave only ashes to tell the story of their guilt and folly."[18] But never did Berry more strikingly apply this principle than when he characterized the 1929 stock market crash (and, by implication, the subsequent Great Depression) as God's judgment against the materialistic greed of a nation drifting away from godliness:

> Listen to the prophet's question: Will a man rob God? Yes, Israel did it in the long ago, and Christian people are doing it today. America—Christian America—the Croesus among the nations of the earth is doing

it today.... Look back to only a short time ago when, in that fearful crash of stocks, in three tragic days, twenty-five billions of dollars were swept away—twenty-five billions of dollars.... This pleasure-mad, gaze-crazy, gold-thirsty generation has forgotten God and robbed God. That is why the stocks plunged into the abyss of wreck and ruin, and fortunes were swept away overnight.[19]

Berry's conspicuous invocation of the phrase "Christian America," paired with his description of the market crash as divine punishment for national infidelity, offers a clear vision of America as a country founded on, and still intrinsically beholden to, a specifically Christian framework.

Such a paradigm was hammered home even more forcefully in Berry's conclusion to the same sermon: "Oh, God grant that not only as individuals may we be faithful, but as a Christian nation as well.... And let us remember that our Christian as well as our civil liberty was first purchased with the priceless blood of the Divine Son of God."[20] Three major elements converged in this crescendo of religious-patriotic fervor: the identification of the United States as an explicitly "Christian nation," the express connection between American civil liberty and the blood of Christ, and the emphatic doctrinal insistence on the divinity of Jesus. All three were to be understood as working together. The deity of Christ, as Berry had made clear in his anti-modernist polemics, was ineluctably linked to Jesus's blood atonement, which purchased "Christian liberty" in deliverance from sin; Christian liberty and Christian doctrine, in turn, undergirded America's unique foundational commitment to civil liberty, since the founders were "saints ... in the work of God"; and finally, due to this godly founding, the United States continued even into the present as a specifically "Christian nation," with the attendant expectation that the people's degree of faithfulness to Christian principles and doctrines would elicit either divine blessing or retribution. Berry's praise for the nation's founding character and the American ideal of civil liberty was, in this case, ineluctably intertwined with his fundamentalist convictions about Christ's deity and substitutionary atonement.

All of these themes that appear across Berry's sermonic corpus— from the saintly stature of the founders, to America's divinely sanctioned founding, to the tethering of American freedom directly to Calvary's cross—were again harnessed together in a sermon that also conspicuously turned the question of "Christian America" toward the plight of the black community itself. Given the subject matter, it seems appropriate that Berry chose to simply title this sermon with a date: "July 4, 1931." Partly an ode to the greatness of Christian America and partly a jeremiad entreating the nation to renew its Christian faithfulness, Berry's reflections on Independence Day weekend of 1931 alternated between celebrating a divinely blessed heritage and warning about the impieties of the present. Beginning by setting the nation's identity within the lineage of the New England Puritans and their invocation of "the name of God," Berry surveyed the great advances and material blessings that had since characterized America's growth: "Today a vast domain is ours," with "more than a hundred million people and 2/3 of the gold in the world"—a nation eighteen times the size of Spain, thirty-one times Italy, and sixty-one times that of England and Wales, which within the lifespan of a single man had progressed from traversing the country in a covered wagon to a Pullman Car to an airplane. "With the fear of God in their hearts," he intoned, "the men of the Mayflower were able to establish on our New England shore an Empire that in 300 years has become the marvel of the world."[21]

And yet despite the enormity of God's special provision in the growth and success of the American experiment, Berry sorrowfully related that many Americans had begun to ignore God, thinking of their homeland as "a great country which we have built up by the might of our power and for the honor of ourselves." This attitude of arrogant self-aggrandizement carried with it serious perils. Berry pointed to the biblical example of Nebuchadnezzar, King of Babylon, who in the fourth chapter of Daniel had likewise preened with the words, "Is not this the great Babylon which I have built up by the might of my power and for the honor of my majesty?" Because he tried to snatch for himself the glory rightfully due to God, Nebuchadnezzar was stricken with insanity and caused to live like a wild beast. This tale served as a warning for modern Americans. With the proper fear of God, the Puritans had laid the foundations of a marvelous, vast nation; without such a proper fear, even "the wisest political institutions and the most astute statecraft" were insufficient to guard the country from its besetting ills—a list of which included "predatory wealth profiteering, sabotage, lynching, camouflaging slavery, bribery, bootlegging," and finally "liberty's death."[22] Notably, this list not only includes generalized social and moral ills, but also two specific examples of moral evil specifically calibrated to the black experience in America—lynching and the legacy of slavery. The lynching tree, encapsulating the fear of extrajudicial violence and indiscriminate murder that daily faced black Americans, was thus a blight on the United States' proud heritage as a "Christian nation." This barbaric practice represented a fundamental betrayal of both God *and* country— the accursed result of a people losing their fear of God, and along with it their own national soul.

Likewise the problem of "camouflaging slavery" stood as an indictment of America's refusal to rightly honor God. A somewhat nebulous turn of phrase, it may have referred to the Jim Crow system as a whole, which arose from the ashes of slavery as a way to continue legally oppressing the black populace. Or perhaps it was meant to evoke the Sisyphean system of sharecropping and tenant farming, which all too often amounted to a method of subjugating black workers under the guise of free labor (a plight for disadvantaged black farmers who, in the words of historian C. Vann Woodward, "not only worked the white man's land but worked it with a white man's plow drawn by a white man's mule").[23] Perhaps "camouflaging slavery" referred to the fallout of slavery more generally, encompassing both of these twin realities. In any case, if the soul of the nation had once been strong enough to abolish a moral evil of the magnitude of chattel slavery, the degree to which Americans now ignored God allowed for the rise and perpetuation of new legal systems of oppression to take its place. The nation's inception in "the fear of God" and its historic overflow of divine blessings bespoke a sense of the country's special standing as a sort of new Israel; yet at the same time, the persistence of racially charged evils such as lynching and the social legacy of slavery (as well as more general moral ills such as drunkenness, corruption, and usury) warned that the dividing line between Israel and Babylon was frighteningly permeable.

How could the United States combat this slide toward Babylon? Hope still abounded that "great America [will be] greater yet," not through greater material wealth but through greater "fruits of the Spirit, which are love, joy, peace and righteousness." The solution to modern problems lay in looking back toward the heritage and tradition that had made

America great in the first place: "What America needs just now is an old-fashioned revival of religion." Berry quickly yoked this revival theme of recapturing the old-time religion to American patriotism, producing a blend of iconic American and Christian imagery that is worth quoting at length:

> Let there be a revival of the patriotism of 1776 and the noble precepts of George Washington, who pleaded for the right of life, liberty, and the pursuit of happiness. Let us never forget Washington at Valley Forge, in the snow on bended knee, praying for the guidance of Almighty God. Let there be a revival of the patriotism of Jesus Christ, who said, "Render unto Caesar the things that are Caesar's, and unto God the things that are God's." Let there be a revival of the Gospel of Jesus Christ, the Christ, who, when they offered him a crown chose the cross, that through faith in him millions might have life in this world and in the world to come. America needs today to bow the knee at the foot of the cross, where freedom's sword was forged.[24]

The intense interconnection and steady progression here from "the patriotism of 1776" to "the patriotism of Jesus Christ" to "the Gospel of Jesus Christ" is difficult to miss. All three elements were central to America's heritage of divine blessing, and the nation's slide away from godliness mandated a "revival" of all three. A scene embedded in the American mythic imagination, the iconic image of George Washington kneeling in prayer at Valley Forge encapsulated what Berry called the "patriotism of 1776." In contrast to the haughty example of Nebuchadnezzar, Washington's prayer offered a visual depiction of a would-be nation humbly subordinate to God's will and submissively seeking his guidance, even as it prepared to fight for its identity and sovereignty. This understanding of founding-era patriotism neatly accorded with Berry's notion of the "patriotism of Jesus Christ." By invoking the well-known synoptic passage on paying taxes to Caesar (Matthew 22:21, Mark 12:17, and Luke 20:25), Berry pressed the idea that expressions of patriotic devotion by no means stood at odds with the Christian faith, for Christ here allowed for multiple categories of devotion ("to Caesar" and "to God"). The "patriotism of Jesus Christ," then, justified the propriety of American patriotic fervor. American patriotism received the divine stamp of approval, so long as, following in the example of George Washington's "patriotism of 1776," the nation "rendered unto God the things that are God's"—honor, glory, and fidelity.

Finally, these considerations culminated in the need for a revival of "the Gospel of Jesus Christ," centered on his sacrificial death and salvific work on the cross. Christ "chose the cross" (and along with it the spiritual liberation of humanity), even when "they offered him a crown"—a prioritization of the eternal over the temporal, which only reinforced the idea that a rightful ordering of priorities would entail an American patriotism wholly yielded to the direction and guidance of God. Moreover, given Berry's strong sentiments on the issue of Christ's atonement, there is little doubt that his references to Christ's salvific work on the cross entail a firm commitment to the fundamentalist understanding of substitutionary atonement; after all, those who denied the necessity and salvific power of Christ's literal bloodshed amounted to "infidels" and "dupes of Satan" who rejected the true gospel of Christ in favor of a "gospel of works."[25] Any true revitalization of American patriotism, then—aligning as it must with the founders' ideals of godly submission ("the patriotism of 1776") and Christ's own teaching ("the patriotism of Jesus Christ")—must also by necessity be tethered to a legitimate spiritual revival of the true gospel of Christ, including his divine nature, his sacrificial atoning death, his resurrection, and eternal life for the faithful. Just as he had elsewhere woven together the themes of civil and spiritual freedom in declaring that Americans' "civil liberty was first purchased with the priceless blood of the Divine Son of God," so here he insisted that "America needs today to bow the knee at the foot of the cross, where freedom's sword was forged."[26]

Thus, to stem the rising tide of moral wickedness facing the nation, and even more specifically to crush the ignominious legacies of slavery that persistently plagued the black community through the daily realities of lynching and Jim Crow segregation, the United Sates had to turn back to the bloodied body of the divine Christ on the cross. The "sword" of American freedom was evidently forged alongside the spiritual freedom from sin and damnation won at the cross—a claim that explicitly linked American civic virtue with the doctrines of Christ's deity and atonement. Likewise, the ideals of freedom and justice that were enshrined in "the Mt. Sinai of our Constitution" were also overtly tied to "the blood of the divine Son of God." Without Christ's divinity and atoning blood, there could be no American experiment, let alone a "glorious destiny," which might, among other things, finally effect African Americans' liberation from the daily experiences of racism and injustice and achieve their full participation in America's founding promises of liberty. These fundamentalist bellwethers were for Berry foundational to the nation's founding ideals, to its continued flourishing, and to the fulfillment of its erstwhile promise of freedom and justice for *all*—including black Americans. If his elder predecessor in ministry John Albert Johnson had sounded notes of a Christian nationalism intrinsically tied to the American ideals of freedom and liberty, Berry's lengthy reflections on the nature of "Christian America" amplified those notes into an overpowering symphonic crescendo. Unabashed, he knit together themes of American civil liberty, freedom, race, and national prosperity with considerations of spiritual salvation, Christ's divinity, the atoning virtue of the crucifixion, and the preeminence of God's moral law. In the process he wove a "Christian nationalist" tapestry that favorably juxtaposed images of American and Christian devotion—Valley Forge and the foot of Calvary's cross; Washington's martial garb and the "sword of freedom"; the Constitution and Sinai's stone tablets; American civil liberty and "the priceless blood of the Divine Son of God." Thus for blacks to lay claim to American identity, along with its promises of freedom and justice, required a similar commitment to a Christian identity that embraced the old, fundamental doctrines.[27]

\* \* \*

While reflections on the history and identity of the United States animated the Christian nationalist perspectives of ministers such as Johnson and Berry, international political concerns over the years likewise prompted some black fundamentalists to reflect on the relationship between their religious convictions and the nation's character. In 1915, for instance, in the shadow of the Great War, Chicago minister Edward Franklin Williams preached a sermon on Psalm 44:20–21 titled "Forgetting God and Stretching Out Our Hands toward a Strange God." A longtime pastor in Chicago, Williams's ministry lasted into the late 1910s and evinced both a steadfast commitment to teaching doctrines that had by this time come to be identified as "fundamentals" (at least in the context of *The Fundamentals*, which was completed in 1915) and a penchant for biting polemical evaluations of the modernist liberal theology that had already begun to coalesce in the late-nineteenth and early twentieth century.[28] In his sermon Williams contemplated the relationship between orthodox Christianity, the terrors of the modern world, and the position of the United States in international affairs. "Has Xty [Christianity] failed?" he asked in his sermon notes, reflecting on the horrors of a world at war. "Xty concerns primarily the soul [and provides] a supply of moral force for it. . . . It is not Xty wh[ich] has caused this war but the lack of it." Williams not only dissociated true Christianity from the violence and horrors of war, but also drew a sharp moral distinction between Christianity and science; while the Christian religion commanded men to seek God's kingdom in lieu of material things, he argued, "Science teaches men how to kill each other. . . . HERE the god worshipped is the god of war, Satan, not Xt [Christ]."[29]

Even as he condemned warfare as Satan-worship, Williams also lifted up the United States as a moral exemplar, arguing that while "the administration and industry of Prussia, all its prosperity has been opposed to morality," this state of affairs was "utterly unlike [the condition] of the U.S." If the Central Powers were "opposed to morality," then the United States was in contrast a purveyor of morality, perhaps even of the "moral force" that Williams considered so central to orthodox Christianity itself. Further commingling religious and patriotic sentiments, Williams concluded that the lessons for his listeners should be "the necessity of a personal faith," "the need of ability to withstand temptation," and "the necessity of national protection by a reasonable defense."[30] By pairing personal faith and national defense as homiletical applications for this particular Sunday morning's pulpit ministry, Williams mixed personal and corporate, sacred and secular, faith and the fight. This staunch preacher, whose teaching ministry was suffused with the traditional doctrinal pillars of fundamentalism, evidently saw an intimate connection between Christian morality and American identity in the midst of an international conflict that would ultimately elicit America's intervention as a self-appointed purveyor of democracy on the global stage.

Two decades later, in the face of another international threat to American national interests and national security, similar perspectives persisted. With communism posing a potential danger to American interests both domestically and internationally in the 1930s, James Madison Nabrit Sr., president of the American Baptist Theological Seminary in Nashville, weighed in about the future of the African American race. The Nabrit family's subsequent storied history of civil rights activism speaks to the values instilled by Nabrit into his sons: James M. Nabrit, Jr. went on to work closely with the NAACP Legal Defense Fund during his legal career, including serving as a strategist for *Brown v. Board of Education*, while Samuel Nabrit provided support to Texas Southern students who initiated the civil rights protests in Houston in the early 1960s during his tenure as president of Texas Southern University.[31] Given his family's later trajectory, it is no surprise that James M. Nabrit, Sr. also displayed a deep concern not only for Christian orthodoxy but also for the social well being of the black community at large during his presidency at ABTS.

So, as Nabrit took up his pen in 1937 to address the urgent need for formal theological education among black leaders, he reflected on the relationship between racial advancement and looming foreign threats facing the nation. There were two foes lurking in the modern world that black ministers absolutely must be prepared to confront with force, Nabrit warned: the twin threats of communism and religious liberalism. "The rise of Communism," he argued, "threatens to destroy utterly all that has been accomplished, and turn the religious faith of the Negro into ashes . . . and the rise of liberalism in religion . . . means substitution of morality, human goodness and mere culture for the old-fashioned regeneration and spiritual power. Against these two new foes the minister must bring not sound but sense."[32] As Nabrit rhetorically paired communism and theological liberalism as threats to blacks, he likewise implicitly paired democracy and theological conservatism. If communism must be combatted by black clergymen because of its potential to "turn the religious faith of the Negro into ashes," then American democracy was by default a means of protecting the race; if religious liberalism threatened to undermine the foundational pillars of "old-fashioned regeneration and spiritual power," then adherence to the "old-fashioned" fundamental doctrines was the solution. Indeed, if communism and religious liberalism were paired as, respectively, the preeminent political and theological threats to the black church, then American democracy and Christian fundamentalism were in like fashion implicitly tied together as the political and theological remedy that could protect the African American community.

But while the likes of Nabrit, John Albert Johnson, Isaac Reed Berry, and Edward Franklin Williams propounded these ideas from their local pulpits or from their administrative offices, perhaps never was the connectivity of fundamentalism, black racial identity, and Americanism given a more public and prominent vocalization than in September 1925, when the president of the largest black Baptist denomination in the country—the National Baptist Convention (NBC)—took to the floor of the national convention meeting to deliver his annual address. Lacey Kirk Williams, who even as a little boy growing up in the rural South had always enjoyed pretending to be a preacher, had by the 1920s become one of the most respected and recognizable ministerial voices in the black religious community.[33] So as he stood to deliver his third annual presidential address to the convention, he did so with the full knowledge that his voice carried a great deal of weight.

Perhaps the most notable element of Williams' convention address was his extended consideration and adjudication of the fundamentalist-modernist controversy. As we have already seen in chapter 3, Williams excoriated modernists as false teachers who would shipwreck the faith of their acolytes, exhorting his convention to stand with the fundamentalists on biblical, historical, and epistemological grounds.[34] Modernism, he declared, was a betrayal of the biblical doctrines represented by the "old time religion," and to embrace it would "tarnish and discredit the vital heritage" bequeathed by the black founders of the NBC itself.[35] But that was not all; Williams also invoked both African American racial progress and American democratic citizenship in connection with National Baptist religious identity. The National Baptist churches, he said, represented "the only group of religionists who may illustrate that Negroes can live under popular government, enjoy its favors and rights, and share and help to carry its burdens and responsibilities."[36] In essence, the success of black Baptists to faithfully govern themselves constituted the means by which African Americans could lay full claim to the "favors," "rights," and "responsibilities" of democratic government. And the success of the NBC itself, as we have previously seen, was intricately tied in Williams's rhetoric to doctrinal fidelity on the "fundamentals" of the faith.

Having already identified fundamentalist doctrine with true biblical Christianity and denominational fidelity—endorsing fundamentalist doctrine as "accept[ing] the teachings of scripture" and condemning modernism as a "shipwreck of the faith" which needed to be "wisely combatted"—Lacey Kirk Williams turned *immediately* to the issue of race relations, and in doing so, he again invoked categories of American citizenship and democratic participation as essential markers of racial progress. The church, he urged, was called to take the *leading* role in American culture on this issue by seeing "inter-racial cooperation substituted for race antagonism . . . and brotherly kindness for prejudice and cruel jealousies." In fact, the role of the church in this task was so central that it could brook no challenge: "We cannot let go unchallenged the efforts made by some secular and semi-secular organizations to transfer from the church the right and authority to say the true and final word in racial matters."[37]

In pushing for social solutions that would allow blacks to participate more fully in the American democratic ideal, Williams saw advocating for black education as one of the church's foremost duties (a consistent theme throughout Williams's life and ministry).[38] While some in the white establishment might be "skeptical [of] and indifferent" to the value of educating the black community, he declared, "let it be known that Negroes are Americans with an undivided devotion. They realize that a correlative of America's best citizenship is Education. They have proven their patriotism under circumstances more exacting than any white man knows. They have proven their ability to acquire education and that money thus spent is a state's safest and most profitable investment." Hence, the church was given the duty to actively press for state-supported black education, and this on the explicit basis of patriotism. Education here was associated with the ideal of American citizenship, and the state's interest in offering more educational opportunities for African Americans was based on both the black race's past "proven patriotism" and their future promise of becoming a "profitable investment" as part of "America's best citizenship." Here, religious, racial, and national categories overlapped substantially.[39]

Another problem that Williams addressed was the need for African Americans to have full, unencumbered access to the ballot. Otherwise "[the Negro] is not a full, free man, or an accepted and fully accredited American citizen. The right and privileges of a democracy, yea, of

America, as between races, cannot be arbitrarily bestowed. We need the Ballot to help save ourselves, and more to help save those who would deprive us of it." Once again racial progress was tightly connected with themes of American democracy, American citizenship, and the rightful leadership of the church in pressing for social change. Indeed, after laying out the educational and political solutions to race antagonism, Williams proceeded to reaffirm orthodox Christianity's leading role in this entire endeavor. It was the duty of true Christianity "to change the first and original thinking of whites on the Race Problem." Indeed, in Williams's view, the American race problem was not "solely an economic and a political question. . . . It is above all a moral and a religious question."⁴⁰ For Lacey Kirk Williams, as for James Madison Nabrit Sr. and others, the well-being of the black community and the advancement of the race involved laying claim to the American ideals of citizenship, liberty for all, and democracy itself; and the foundation from which the race could attain and defend these essential virtues of American identity was a commitment to the teachings of the race's religious leaders of the past, to formal education, and to the biblical and historical orthodoxy represented in the main doctrines of fundamentalism.

In direct contradistinction to such claims, however, stood the critics whose denunciations of fundamentalist religion cast it not only as a hindrance to racial progress but also as altogether opposed to the American ideals of free speech and constitutional democracy. Such arguments appeared repeatedly in the *Chicago Defender*, one of the most widely circulated African American periodicals of the day. In 1929, for instance, the *Defender* cited "the fundamentalism of southern democratic clerics" and the concomitant "sectional bigotry opposed to human freedom" as quintessentially representative of "the worst of Democracy."⁴¹ Or recall once again the *Defender*'s editorial valorizing the agnostic Civil War veteran Robert Ingersoll. Even as the author sought to link fundamentalism with slavery and to display the virtues of Ingersoll as a free thinker, he also offered William Jennings Bryan as a pointed counterexample, as someone "who died fighting for fundamentalism in Christianity, [and] was also fighting against your fundamental rights in the Constitution."⁴² In this context fundamentalists were portrayed not only as undermining American virtues, but as disrespecting the very foundation of the American democratic system itself—the Constitution.

Similar arguments made their way into the black press with some regularity in the immediate aftermath of the Scopes trial. An article from the NAACP Press Service in August 1925 attacked Tennessee fundamentalists as "the same people who permit lynching and make bastardy legal in order to render their race 'pure'" and disparaged the Dayton proceeding as "a menace and warning, . . . a challenge to Religion, Science, and Democracy."[43] Presumably, this evaluation of fundamentalism as innately anti-democratic would likewise apply to members of the black community who supported Williams Jennings Bryan or his partisans in the Scopes trial. Published within a month of Lacey Kirk Williams's convention speech in September 1925, this article diametrically opposed the NBC president's evaluation of fundamentalism relative to the black community. While Williams saw modernism as a danger to be combatted and fundamentalism as the basis for theological and racial fidelity, the NAACP Press Service presented a portrait of fundamentalism as racially oppressive, socially regressive, religiously obtuse, antiscientific, and a danger to the very democratic ideals upon which America was founded. Both sides in the debate over fundamentalism in the black community pressed their cases by appealing to racial and national identity, but they did so in completely opposite ways.

In a similar vein, an article from the *Norfolk Journal and Guide* the following year demonstrated that concerns over southern fundamentalism and the specter of the Scopes trial did not fade quickly from the minds of the opponents of fundamentalism in the black press. In a September 1926 editorial provocatively titled "American Intolerance and the Menace of a State Church," the author contended that the "rising tide of Fundamentalism," as most obviously manifested in the prior year's Scopes trial, represented a clear and present threat to the foundational American values of free thought, religious toleration, and separation of church and state. In fact, this "rising tide" of fundamentalism functionally amounted to "the establishment of a State Church in Tennessee" and a slap in the face of the First Amendment. Freedom of conscience in matters of religion represented "one of the chief glories of the Federal Constitution," and thus the fundamentalist intolerance illustrated in the Scopes trial was portrayed as corrosive to both American founding ideals and the founding documents themselves. Moreover, in a skillful rhetorical twist, the editorialist paralleled fundamentalist intolerance with that of the Roman Catholic Church, "which champions the right of the church to govern the temporal as well as the spiritual life of the people." This argument was surely calculated to agitate a group that typically considered Catholicism to be a false, or at least seriously deficient, religion. Pressing this metaphor forward, the editorial exclaimed that the pressing need was for a "New Luther" to rise up in order to "kill American intolerance." This intolerance so closely associated with dogmatic fundamentalism was perceived not only as religious, but also racial in character, as demonstrated by the author's concluding observation that "intolerance and race prejudice sleep in the same bed and are all but indistinguishable."[44] By implication, not only did African Americans who embraced such an "intolerant" religious tradition aid and abet whites in subverting the basic American ideals of free thought and freedom of religion, but they also became complicit in the racial prejudice and bigotry that was so often associated with the fundamentalist movement. Far from Lacey Kirk Williams's assessment of the church's leading role in subduing racial antagonism or from James M. Nabrit's rhetorical pairing of fundamentalist doctrine and American democracy as stalwart protectors of the black community, here the religious exclusivism of the fundamentalist position was directly tied to the racial exclusivism of Jim Crow white supremacy. As the dispute over fundamentalism raged on, both proponents and detractors argued on the basis of racial identity and American virtues—the former lauding fundamentalist religion as a foundational building block for the black community's access to the full experience of American citizenship and the latter casting it as essentially subversive of the best aspects of both blackness and Americanism.

* * *

The very fact that the fundamentalist movement and the doctrinal sentiments surrounding it prompted such substantial disagreement and debate among African Americans is in itself notable. Indeed, the very existence of such an argument within the black community itself presupposes that fundamentalism had a meaningful presence within the ranks of black Protestant clergy and laymen. This assumption on the part of the historical actors considered herein constitutes a compelling challenge to most prevailing historiographical approaches that either remain essentially silent on the topic of race or expressly deny, by definition, the possibility that African Americans could be fundamentalists at all. Contrary to these historiographical occlusions, it seems clear that African Americans on both sides of the issue asserted that fundamentalism was present in the community; the question was whether embracing it was good or bad for the race. The fact that the "fundamentalism" described among African Americans was less of the institutional variety and much more of the broader historical-theological variety may partly explain their absence from historical accounts; but even so, the reality that black people from across the religious spectrum identified fundamentalists in their midst (either positively or negatively) must prompt us to take seriously the idea that fundamentalism was not a merely white phenomenon that confronted black Americans from an external point of origin, but it also represented a cultural, social, and theological impulse that manifested from within black communities and churches.

Moreover, not only were black fundamentalists present in the community, but their racial identity significantly mattered to the way that they applied their religious convictions. These debates within the African American community offer a window into the intersecting lines of racial and religious identity that were being discussed and contested during the era of Jim Crow. As disputes over fundamentalism unfolded, proponents and detractors demonstrated sharply divergent perspectives as they fought over the contested battleground of American identity. Attempting to integrate their experiences of both religion and race, black fundamentalists tied their religious identity innately to conceptions of racial progress and American virtue in numerous ways.

Some, like John Albert Johnson and Isaac Reed Berry, laid their claim to legitimacy as partakers in the American experiment by way of their understanding of America as an essentially Christian nation. According to this view, the inherently Christian character of the nation and its people manifested in the promotion of personal liberty (a value concretized by, among other things, the abolition of slavery) and in a democratic order that served to propagate morality and Christian freedom. Staking claim to this concept of a Christian America allowed them to see themselves as both proponents of racial advancement and adherents to a historic American identity rooted in historical Christian orthodoxy. In some cases they saw their fundamentalism as a vehicle for racial progress, as in the case of Lacey Kirk Williams, for whom the faithful church, committed to the "old time" fundamentalist doctrines, represented both a means for identifying with black religious leaders of the past and the primary engine for driving the race toward fuller access to the benefits, responsibilities, and rights of American identity and citizenship. For people like these, theirs was a fundamentalism doctrinally aligned with that of their white counterparts, but specifically applied in the context of their own racial consciousness. They tied their conservative faith to progressive reforms on behalf of the race.

On the other hand, black critics of fundamentalism eschewed both the concept of a Christian nationalist identity and the idea of fundamentalist Protestantism as an engine for social progress, emphasizing instead an understanding of fundamentalism as inherently opposed to the values of religious toleration and free thought. In this way, the two sides diverged on their conceptualizations of American identity and the circumstances of racial advancement. Detractors linked the theological intolerance and exclusivity of fundamentalism to racial intolerance, and conversely, they connected the proliferation of more liberal or modernist thinking to racial advancement, thus portraying black adherents to fundamentalist dogma as being not only out of step with essential American values but also stumbling blocks to racial progress. Both sides undoubtedly sought the ultimate good of their race, but in their approaches they demonstrated significant differences in their evaluations of Americanism and the value of theological dogmatism. Whether those fundamentalists within the black community represented a religion of racial progress or a religion of racial regress, therefore, remained an open and contested question.

Perhaps it should come as no surprise that pro- and antifundamentalist factions emerged in the black community with respect to the ever-pressing issue of racial advancement. After all, not only was fundamentalism itself a contentious issue during this period, but African Americans' drive to find ways to combat the oppression of Jim Crow also produced numerous strategies and movements, as well as leaders who clashed with one another—be they Booker T. Washington and W. E. B. Du Bois, Du Bois and Marcus Garvey, or (much later) Martin Luther King Jr. and Malcolm X. With this in mind, the fact that black fundamentalists pursued the cause of racial progress in ways that sometimes differed from their more vociferous critics makes sense. A common recognition of the problem of racial oppression did not necessarily entail a common solution. Yet the testimony presented here demonstrates that black fundamentalists ought not be dismissed out of hand as obstacles and barriers to African American progress. In a variety of ways, black fundamentalists proudly proclaimed the alignment between their religious convictions and the interests of their race as a whole. Whether leading their congregations toward direct political engagement, as we saw with John L. Henry, overtly applying core fundamentalist doctrines to racial issues, as we saw with John Albert Johnson and Isaac Reed Berry, rhetorically connecting fundamentalist theology with racial fidelity and the need for governmental support for civil rights, as we saw with L. K. Williams, or seeking to secure better and more accessible education for theologically conservative clergymen, as we saw with the ABTS project, these historical figures connected their conservative fundamentalist theology with activities designed to challenge some aspect of the racial oppression and inequality that had been institutionalized under the white supremacist system of Jim Crow. In this sense, then, black fundamentalists applied their conservative theology in ways that were sometimes far from socially or politically conservative insofar as they aimed to contravene or transform the social and political status quo. Much as their detractors might have wanted to paint these black fundamentalists as regressive albatrosses hung around the neck of their entire racial group, their own testimony shows a concern for racial justice that belies such a dismissive evaluation. Indeed, taken on their own terms, these historical actors might rightly be understood as being, in a perhaps provocative turn of phrase, *progressive* fundamentalists.

# Conclusion

The presidential election of 2016 proved to be an exceptionally divisive moment in the United States along both religious and racial lines. An overwhelming majority of white evangelicals gave their vocal support to Donald Trump, while many people of color, both within and without conservative evangelical circles, expressed deep concerns and fears about Trump as a conduit for overt racism and white nationalism spilling into America's social mainstream—fears that stemmed both from the rising visibility of the alt-right in 2016 as well as racially charged statements from candidate Trump himself. In the immediate aftermath of President Trump's election, Jemar Tisby took to the airwaves to express his frustration. Tisby is an African American who identifies with the Reformed theological tradition, one of the more generally theologically conservative streams within the American evangelical landscape. And so, as a graduate of the conservative Reformed Theological Seminary, a member of a predominantly white Reformed church, and an active public commentator on racial issues in the church, Tisby found himself in an uncomfortable position. As he reflected on the wave of white evangelical support for Trump, even in the midst of a campaign that appeared to give an increasingly visible platform to the white nationalist alt-right movement, Tisby offered his visceral response: "Here it is, just the raw honest truth. I really, this Sunday, don't feel safe worshiping with white people."

These comments kicked off a storm of controversy, and Tisby soon offered clarification in his blog on the Reformed African American Network website. "I am *not* saying that I feel physically unsafe around white Christians or churches," he explained. "I am, however, highlighting the impact of white evangelical support for this man. Right now I feel misunderstood, alienated, and anxious. . . . That so many white Christians have overlooked or simply don't understand this reality indicates a troubling lack of understanding across racial lines."[1] Less than a year later, on the 500th anniversary of the beginning of the Protestant Reformation, Tisby led his organization to change its name from the "Reformed African American Network" to "The Witness: A Black Christian Collective." With the prior year's post-election hubbub undoubtedly still in mind, Tisby explained that including "Reformed" in the organization's name had brought along with it the tendency "to make faith overly intellectual and theoretical," and so he and his compatriots had realized that "while there is always a place for theological clarity, we did not want our work to end there." Changing the organization's name to "The Witness: A Black Christian Collective" was intended to represent the conjunction of their commitment to historic Christian orthodoxy and their desire to apply their theology in a way that "affirms the embodied experiences of black people as significant and within the scope of Christian dialogue and application."[2]

Jemar Tisby's experience is just one of many that demonstrate the disjunction that often exists at the intersection of race and religion in the United States. Even in a context of intense theological unity on many central doctrinal issues, Tisby is not unique in feeling "misunderstood, alienated, and anxious" when white peers seemingly fail to grapple with the deeply ingrained concerns that emerge out of his experiences as a black American. Because of the historical legacy of slavery, racial discrimination, Jim Crow, segregation, and white supremacy in the United States, racial context can significantly influence the type of social and political concerns toward which many people press their theological applications. This is true now, and it was true a century ago.

This reality raises a problem when considering movements such as early American Protestant fundamentalism that include manifestations on both an expressly historical-theological level and a social, political, and institutional level. If the historical-theological and the social-political are considered to be inexorably and necessarily conjoined, then social orientation becomes sufficiently definitional to membership in a religious group as to exclude many of those who would self-identify with the movement on a historical-theological basis. In the case of fundamentalism this means that a particular conservative brand of social and cultural militancy has often come to be definitionally identified with the movement, thus excluding many African Americans who may have identified themselves as fundamentalists in religion but whose political and social concerns were oriented more toward racial equality and advancement. The vastly different social circumstances facing whites and blacks in the Jim Crow era meant that, even in the face of theological unity on the fundamental doctrines of the Christian faith, the issues garnering social concern and theological application varied widely from one side of the color line to the other. This being the case, it is easy to see why scholars have typically treated fundamentalism as an essentially white movement. The most widely visible leaders pushing fundamentalist issues in the political and social spheres—those with the largest platforms, the most social capital, and the biggest institutions—*were* white, and they were usually operating out of a context that assumed the white conservative racial politics of the day. Hence, if these political and institutional affiliations are indeed considered to be absolutely definitional, then it is no wonder that African Americans have been left out of the picture.

There is, then, an irony in the fact that, much as they were marginalized by early white fundamentalist leaders, conservative black Christians have likewise been excluded from histories of early Protestant fundamentalism—and this despite the fact that numerous black Protestants identified themselves and were identified by others as fundamentalists. This is why the historical-theological approach embraced in this book is helpful. In disentangling the historical-theological roots of fundamentalism from its specific social and institutional manifestations in the white community, as well as from the racial assumptions that often accompanied white fundamentalists' cultural stances, this approach offers a way for heretofore muted fundamentalist voices from the black community to be heard. This strategy is not by any means intended to denigrate or minimize the importance of the social and institutional approach to studying fundamentalism, but it aims to offer another perspective that adds to our multifaceted picture of early fundamentalists.

Adopting this historical-theological approach allows us to grapple with the explicit commentary we find in the black press regarding the widespread influence of fundamentalism among African Americans— ranging from the triumphal declaration of a Virginia editorialist that "the Afro-American people are Fundamentalists" to the lament from the pen of Ernest Rice McKinney that the race was "filled to overflowing" with fundamentalist impediments to modernization and progress. It allows us to identify and to consider on their own terms black churchmen such as African Methodist J. G. Robinson or National Baptist Lacey Kirk Williams, who explicitly aligned themselves in print and speech with the fundamentalism of their day, over against the innovations of modernist theology that they saw as a threat to the both church and the race.

Moreover, the identification of these black fundamentalists in the historical record in turn offers a deeper reading of the social commitments associated with and stemming from this type of theology. While fundamentalist religion has long been associated with a certain brand of conservative social activity, the experience of black fundamentalists suggests that their theologically conservative convictions could be applied in a variety of social and political directions. Locating fundamentalism in a black social context changes some of the social applications that emerge from the theology, because the oppressive circumstances of Jim Crow drove issues of racial equality to the forefront of black fundamentalists' minds in a way that was impossible for their white counterparts to experience. As with the experience of Jemar Tisby, and as in the story of the Southern Baptist resolution on the "alt-right" with which this book opened, so it was with the early fundamentalists: theological unity across racial lines was no guarantee that political and social uniformity would follow.

## ACKNOWLEDGMENTS

Writing a book is often a solitary task, but it is by no stretch of the imagination a solo undertaking. Throughout this lengthy project, the initial conception of which stretches back well over half a decade, I have been blessed with many fellow travelers whose support, encouragement, feedback, and critiques have helped shape this book into its final form. While a truly full and exhaustive accounting of all those to whom I stand indebted may be rendered impossible by limitations not only of space but also of a fallible memory, I am entirely certain that I am in such a fortunate position today thanks in large part to the many friends, teachers, and colleagues whose paths have crossed (and in many gratifying cases, re-crossed) mine throughout this academic and professional journey. To each and every one, I offer my gratitude.

Reflecting on those who were especially instrumental in bringing this project to life, I must start with my editor at New York University Press, Jennifer Hammer. Not only was she invested in this idea from the outset, but her ongoing commitment and involvement throughout the entire process has been invaluable. Jennifer's consistent editorial feedback and eye for detail unquestionably made this book stronger and more cohesive than it otherwise might have been. Without her support, along with the hard work of the entire amazing team at the press, this book would not be a reality.

I was also fortunate to receive encouragement and constructive criticism at many points throughout this project, stretching back years, from colleagues in a variety of professional and academic settings. In some cases this interaction was extensive, in other cases more limited, but in all cases it was deeply appreciated. Whether it was reading specific chapters, commenting on related conference papers and journal articles, discussing the overarching research concept, offering feedback on proposals, pointing me toward new sources, or any number of other boons, many colleagues on the academic side invested time and thought into my work; they include Albert Broussard, Felipe Hinojosa, Robin Veldman, A. G. Miller, Phil Sinitiere, Vaughn Booker, Violet Johnson, Lerone Martin, Mary Beth Mathews, Matthew Hall, John Wilsey, April Hatfield, Walter Kamphoefner, Rob Mackin, Chris Cantwell, and Margaret Mitchell, among others, and my thanks go to all of them. Two more people deserve particular mention here, as well. Mindy Bergman, who has served as the executive director of Interdisciplinary Critical Studies throughout my first two years as a faculty member at Texas A&M, has been an indefatigable supporter of my work ever since the moment we met in 2018; the knowledge that she has always had my back has been a gift and an encouragement. Last but not least, perhaps no person is more directly responsible for my academic career path than Miles Mullin, who has been a constant mentor, teacher, supporter, and friend. Little did I know what was in store when I first walked into his history class.

A research project can only be as good as its sources, and so I also owe thanks to the staff members of the archives where I conducted the majority of my research—the Amistad Research Center at Tulane, the Schomburg Center in New York, and the Southern Baptist Historical Library and Archives in Nashville. Good historians, in my estimation, would be in vanishingly short supply without good archivists, and I feel lucky to have interacted with so many archival staff who were unfailingly helpful. Particular thanks are due also to Taffey Hall, the director and head archivist of the SBHLA, whose professionalism, diligence, and kindness is a true credit to her institution, and whose assistance was indispensable during my research trips to Nashville.

Finally, in myriad ways both large and small, my family shares a part in this work. My wife, Silvana, has been a source of unflagging support and steadfast encouragement from day one. Her love, confidence, companionship, and trust drive me to be a better person each day, and I can unequivocally say that I would never have made it to where I am now without her; I owe her my eternal gratitude for more than I could ever adequately express here. Our two daughters, young as they are, have also played a role in this project—they have kept me grounded, providing constant reminders that the most important and meaningful things in life stand beyond the reach of professional vicissitudes. Likewise, our church family's steady exhortations and prayers have been a source of sustenance during the inevitable days of difficulty that attend any project as lengthy as this one. My brother, Michael, offered welcome hospitality after long days spent in the archives in Nashville, and he even charitably allowed me to talk his ear off about my day's findings from time to time. And last of all, I cannot conclude without offering a word of loving appreciation to my parents, Mac and Barbara Bare. Not only did they introduce me from childhood to a religious faith that has largely steered my career toward the study of American religious history, but they always believed in me and pushed me to be my best, even when I doubted myself. They were my first—and remain my longest tenured—supporters, and therefore it is to them that I dedicate this book.

# NOTES

## INTRODUCTION

1 Green, "Resolution Condemning White Supremacy Causes Chaos at the Southern Baptist Convention."
2 For the full text of the resolution, see "On the Anti-Gospel of Alt-Right White Supremacy."
3 Green, "Resolution Condemning White Supremacy."
4 "Does the Southern Baptist Convention Still Have a Stain on It?"
5 For sociological analysis of this phenomenon in the context of modern American evangelicalism, see Emerson and Smith, *Divided By Faith*; Shelton and Emerson, *Blacks and Whites in Christian America*. Emerson and Smith find a contrast between white evangelicals' emphasis on individualism and blacks' emphasis on collective identity and structural concerns. Shelton and Emerson discuss how America's legacy of racial discrimination shaped five "building blocks" of black Protestantism that distinguish it from white Protestant faith and practice. For multidisciplinary reflections in the wake of Emerson and Smith's landmark study, see Hawkins and Sinitiere, *Christians and the Color Line*.
6 There is perhaps no clearer example of such rhetorical dividing lines being drawn than J. Gresham Machen's *Christianity and Liberalism*, which argued that modernism (or "liberalism") did not represent merely an alternative strain of Christianity, but was an entirely different religion altogether. Thus, modernism was an entirely *anti*-Christian movement, in contrast with true Christianity, which was characterized by adherence to the "fundamental" doctrines of the historic faith.
7 David Harrington Watt, "Fundamentalists of the 1920s and 1930s," 23; Nancy T. Ammerman, "North American Protestant Fundamentalism," 3.
8 The emerging neo-evangelicalism of the 1940s, led by men like Carl F. H. Henry, was in some ways a continuation of fundamentalist doctrinal perspectives (carrying on many of the same conservative theological positions and arguments), while at the same time representing a reaction against certain fundamentalists' proclivities toward strict separatism and cultural disengagement. See Carl F. H. Henry, *The Uneasy Conscience of Modern Fundamentalism*.

For an excellent example of the interplay between the fundamentalist tradition and the rise of midcentury neo-evangelicalism, see George Marsden's history of Fuller Theological Seminary, *Reforming Fundamentalism*. Other titles in this vein include Hart, *Defending the Faith*; Bendroth, *Fundamentalists in the*

*City*; Hankins, *American Evangelicals*; Hankins, *Francis Schaeffer and the Shaping of Evangelical America*; Sutton, *American Apocalypse*; Wacker, *America's Pastor*; Gloege, *Guaranteed Pure*; and Hall and Strachan, *Essential Evangelicalism*.

9  In some respects, this evaluation of the black fundamentalist presence accords with Gayraud S. Wilmore's contention that "there has been and continues to be a significant difference between black religion and white religion in their approaches to social reality and social change." However, many of the voices in this book would certainly dispute his contention that Christian expressions of black protest constitute an "accident of history" rather than an authentically Christian development, as well as his view that the black church of the first half of the twentieth century was largely characterized by "brokenness and insipidity." Wilmore, *Black Religion and Black Radicalism*, xiii, 165, 169.

10  For example, in "Black Protestantism as Expressed in Ecumenical Activity," Mary R. Sawyer associates conservative black religion in the context of Jim Crow with passivity on the issues of segregation and racial advancement (284–85). In fact, as Paul Harvey points out, ever since W. E. B. Du Bois, scholars of black religious institutions have "veered between visions of liberatory potential and sociological explorations of why these poetically powerful institutions so often apparently failed to act as engines of social progress" (*Bounds of Their Habitation*, 142). On this count, my work accords with Ingrid Overacker's analysis that, while historical scholarship often "regretfully dismisses or bitterly excoriates the church for failing to address the pressing social and political issues crucial to the lives and fortunes of African Americans from the turn of the century to the advent of World War II," in fact black Christians "relied upon faith to motivate them to continue to challenge racism during the first four decades of the twentieth century" (*The African American Church Community in Rochester*, 4).

Similarly, Allison Calhoun-Brown and Sandra L. Barnes have pointedly challenged the strict association between religious conservatism and accommodationist social/political stances. Calhoun-Brown demonstrates in "While Marching to Zion" that the "otherworldly" religious orientation of conservative traditions does not necessarily depress expressions of racial empowerment, while Barnes argues in "Priestly and Prophetic Influences" and (with Nwosu) in "Black Church Electoral and Protest Politics" that religious conservatives display both a willingness to engage in political/social activism and a desire to rhetorically align themselves with the resistance/protest tradition of African American religion. Others, such as Eric McDaniel and Christopher Ellison, argue in "God's Party?" that a conservative commitment to biblical literalism within the African American "interpretive community" actually produces support for progressive social and economic policies.

11  A note on terminology: The terms "conservative" and "progressive" are not intended to necessarily connote the array of specific political and social commitments or programs that typically fall under those headings in the rhetoric of today's American political landscape. The words are used here according to their

more general definitions, so that "conservative" entails a desire to preserve or restore traditional conditions (such as the social status quo) and to limit social change, while "progressive" conveys an attitude favoring changes or reforms that break from the status quo.

For instance, historian Wallace Best characterizes the famed National Baptist president Lacey Kirk Williams (who receives significant consideration in this book) as "progressive on issues of race . . . [but] a staunch social and political conservative." (I would add, also a theological conservative.) He further notes Williams's racial progressivism relative to his "articulate stances on fair labor, unobstructed access to the ballot, and denunciations of segregation," while attributing to Williams's social conservatism his rebukes of "'cheaters,' policy players, gamblers, and society matrons," his resolute "fight against the 'curse of liquor,'" his steadfast support of Prohibition, and his support for the Republican Party (*Passionately Human, No Less Divine*, 16).

12 Mary Beth Swetnam Mathews, *Doctrine and Race*. Some other forays into somewhat more circumscribed aspects of fundamentalism and race include Moran, "Reading Race into the Scopes Trial"; Moran, "The Scopes Trial and Southern Fundamentalism"; Miller, "The Construction of a Black Fundamentalist Worldview."
13 Mathews, *Doctrine and Race*, 3.
14 Mathews, *Doctrine and Race*, 4–6.
15 Matthews' work in *Doctrine and Race* follows up on her previous work on fundamentalism, including most notably *Rethinking Zion*, in which she argues that northern print media sought to rhetorically relocate fundamentalism to the South by painting and conjoining exaggerated stereotypes of both fundamentalists and southerners as anti-modern, anti-intellectual, backward, racist, violent, and culturally militant. Yet despite this emphasis on the rhetorical connection drawn between fundamentalism and the American South, black voices appear only sparingly throughout *Rethinking Zion*—an issue that Mathews forthrightly acknowledges as a problem of sources: "The few times black voices appear in this book are, from my investigation, the few times that black voices managed to make themselves heard in the white discussion" (xiv). This absence of black Americans from the discussions of (white) fundamentalism seems to be part of what prompted Mathews to write *Doctrine and Race*. Yet even with her engagement in *Doctrine and Race*, Mathews still appears to view fundamentalism as a racially circumscribed movement about which blacks were *aware* but in which they did not actively *participate*. This view fails to fully account for not only the theological congruencies that spanned the racial gap along doctrinally fundamentalist fault lines (such as detailed explications of fundamentalist doctrines as foundational to the Christian faith, as well as explicit condemnations of modernism as a betrayal of historic Christianity), but also the testimony within the black community itself of a "fundamentalist" presence in religious thought and practice.
16 Mathews, *Doctrine and Race*, 85.
17 Mathews, *Doctrine and Race*, 6, 69, 71.

18 In addition to the previously noted work of Jeffrey P. Moran and Albert G. Miller, Sylvester A. Johnson's *African American Religions* also offers some consideration of the relationship between what he terms "evangelical fundamentalism," American civil religion, and civil rights in the 1950s and 1960s (325–41). However, this is not immediately related to the issue at hand here, since Johnson's discussion of fundamentalism only briefly and tangentially mentions earlier decades, and he appears to utilize a rather broad conception of fundamentalism as being more or less interchangeable with evangelicalism.

19 George Marsden's seminal work *Fundamentalism and American Culture*, for instance, describes fundamentalism as entailing an attitude of militant opposition not only to modernist theology, but also to *cultural* changes that were emerging at the same time and were often tied to modernism. Hence, anti-evolution crusades (illustrated most famously by the Scopes trial) are often treated as definitional to fundamentalism (4).

20 Sandeen, *The Roots of Fundamentalism*, xiii, xv. More recently, Matthew Avery Sutton has argued in this vein in *American Apocalypse*, where he describes fundamentalism as "a distinct movement" made up of "radical evangelical apocalypticists," led by "an interdenominational network of white preachers, evangelists, writers, and Bible institute teachers" (112).

21 Carpenter, *Revive Us Again*, xii. See also Carpenter, "Fundamentalist Institutions and the Rise of Evangelical Protestantism, 1929–1942."

22 Hankins, *God's Rascal*; Trollinger, *God's Empire*.

23 Trollinger, *God's Empire*, 7.

24 Trollinger, *God's Empire*, 71; Hankins, *God's Rascal*, 161–70.

25 Glass, *Strangers in Zion*, x.

26 Glass, *Strangers in Zion*, 71.

27 Lienesch, *In the Beginning*, 90.

28 Lienesch, *In the Beginning*, 39.

29 Lienesch, *In the Beginning*, 39. Lienesch draws upon Moran, "Reading Race into the Scopes Trial" and "The Scopes Trial and Southern Fundamentalism in Black and White."

30 Marsden, *Fundamentalism and American Culture*, 4.

31 See also Marsden, "Fundamentalism as an American Phenomenon," where Marsden identifies fundamentalism as "militantly opposed" to both "modernist theology and the cultural change associated with it" and as a movement that "stressed the supernatural" and whose most distinctive doctrines were biblical inerrancy, divine creation, and dispensational premillennialism.

32 Marsden, *Fundamentalism and American Culture*, 159.

33 Jeffrey Moran, for example, states that while there were black Protestants who affirmed certain fundamentalist doctrinal convictions, the fundamentalist emphasis on cultural militancy was the dividing line that excluded blacks from the movement: "Some conservative white evangelicals shifted to support fundamentalist Protestantism, leaving their black brethren upholding once-shared beliefs

but rejecting the white fundamentalists' emphasis on aggressive cultural battles" ("The Scopes Trial and Southern Fundamentalism," 95–96).
34 Watt, "Fundamentalists of the 1920s and 1930s," 23–24.
35 Marsden, *Fundamentalism and American Culture*, 324.
36 "Our Group Are Fundamentalists in Religion," *Norfolk Journal and Guide*, June 13, 1925.
37 Prothero, *Religious Literacy*, 5–7; Prothero, *Religion Matters*, 6–7; Gaustad, "American History, with and without Religion."
38 Noll, *America's God*, 3–6.
39 Raboteau, *A Fire in the Bones*, 9.
40 Blain, Cameron, and Farmer, Introduction, 3–4.
41 Raboteau, *Canaan Land*, 78.
42 A tendency toward ecclesiastical and organizational separatism has also been sometimes treated as an essential aspect of fundamentalist thought and behavior. However, evangelical historian Nathan Finn's work on Baptist fundamentalism in the South has challenged the ubiquity and necessity of this characteristic. Finn helpfully differentiates between "separatist fundamentalists," who saw strict separation to be imperative, and "denominational fundamentalists," who desired to be voices of conservative influence within their denominations. See Finn, "The Development of Baptist Fundamentalism in the South, 1940–1980."

Such categorization might also be reflected in Robert Ashworth's 1924 account of the development of fundamentalist contingents within the Northern Baptist Convention. Ashworth differentiates between the "more moderate" fundamentalists who were somewhat conciliatory toward the rest of the convention, as represented by J. C. Massee and the Committee on Conferences on Baptist Fundamentals, and the "more radical" fundamentalists who pressed "a more drastic and aggressive program" influenced by the likes of William Bell Riley and John Roach Straton. See Ashworth, "The Fundamentalist Movement among the Baptists," 625, 628.
43 This is one advantage of taking the historical-theological approach, which allows for the examination of fundamentalist theology and fundamentalist theological influences within the black community even apart from official institutional affiliations.
44 Hence, for example, Jehovah's Witnesses and other Unitarian groups would not be considered fundamentalists, despite the fact that they profess both supernaturalism and biblicism, because they deny (among other things) that Jesus Christ is the eternal divine second person of the Trinity.
45 Fosdick, "Shall the Fundamentalists Win?," 418.

## CHAPTER 1. "FILLED TO OVERFLOWING"
1 "Our Group Are Fundamentalists in Religion," *Norfolk Journal and Guide*, June 13, 1925.
2 In recent years, a few scholars have begun to focus on some specific aspects of black fundamentalism, but the movement as a whole still appears to lack much in

the way of notable integration into the wider literature on early-twentieth century Protestant fundamentalism. On race and the Scopes Trial, see Moran, "Reading Race into the Scopes Trial" and "The Scopes Trial and Southern Fundamentalism in Black and White." On the role of Bible schools in black fundamentalism see Miller, "The Construction of a Black Fundamentalist Worldview."

While the topic of black religion generally lacks integration into the larger body of scholarship on fundamentalism, the one major exception comes in Mary Beth Swetnam Mathews's *Doctrine and Race*, which examines the interactions between black Protestants and fundamentalism during the interwar period. Still, Matthews does not appear to consider fundamentalism to be a phenomenon that was expressed or experienced within black churches; rather, she sees it more as an external force that demanded engagement than as an authentic internal expression of black religiosity. For instance, Mathews regularly distinguishes between "fundamentalists" on the one hand and "black Protestants" or "African-American evangelicals" on the other hand (10). In this vein, she posits that black Baptists and Methodists "declined to self-identify as fundamentalists" (69). She argues that "African American Baptists and Methodists did not explicitly embrace or reject fundamentalism," that "African American Protestants defined modernism as a white-only term," and that black Baptists and Methodists "would not side with modernism, but they could not live with fundamentalism either" (6, 8, 71). Even when quoting *National Baptist Union-Review* editor J. H. Frank as explicitly describing himself and others of his denomination as "fundamentalist," Mathews shies away from that terminology, referring to Frank and his ilk as *allies* of the fundamentalists, but not fundamentalists themselves (54–55).

3 Harnack, *What Is Christianity?*, 161–62.
4 Marsden, "Fundamentalism as an American Phenomenon," 215.
5 On J. Frank Norris's views about race, see Hankins, *God's Rascal*, chap. 8.
6 Marsden, *Fundamentalism and American Culture*, 324. Jeffrey Moran likewise identifies a connection between fundamentalists' institutionalized culture wars and African Americans' exclusion from discussions of fundamentalism: "Some conservative white evangelicals shifted to support fundamentalist Protestantism, leaving their black brethren upholding once-shared beliefs but rejecting the white fundamentalists' emphasis on aggressive cultural battles" ("The Scopes Trial and Southern Fundamentalism," 95–96).
7 Mathews's *Doctrine and Race* keeps an exclusive focus on the denominational newspapers of the AME, the AME Zion, and the two major National Baptist bodies. This chapter, on the other hand, incorporates mostly secular black weeklies to see the discussions and debates surrounding fundamentalism outside of a strictly ecclesiastical context.
8 For a discussion of the enormous influence of African American newspapers in the early and mid-twentieth century, see Gregory, *The Southern Diaspora*, 49–54, 124–131, 388. According to Gregory, the pioneering *Chicago Defender* was the first

black newspaper to sell widely not only in its own region but also in the South, claiming by 1920 a circulation of 230,000. Widespread national circulation and influence also characterized a number of other black weeklies, including the *New York Amsterdam News*, the *Pittsburgh Courier*, the *Afro-American*, the *Norfolk Journal and Guide*, and the *Atlanta World*, each of which appear in this chapter.

9 Untitled opinion column, *Negro Star* (Wichita), January 11, 1924, 4.
10 The *Atlanta World* began as a weekly, but transitioned to a daily format in 1932. For simplicity's sake, given its origins as a weekly newspaper and its transition in the middle of the chronological period here under consideration, it is incorporated into this chapter's discussion of weeklies.
11 Murphy, Melton, and Ward, *Encyclopedia of African American Religions*, 841.
12 "Bishop Noah Williams Proposes 'Real' Divinity School," *Atlanta Daily World*, March 23, 1935, 1.
13 Bishop Noah W. Williams, "Touring the Holy Land," *Atlanta Daily World*, March 30, 1935, 1.
14 Gibson, *The African Methodist Shield*; Baxter, *The Doctrine & Discipline of the A.M.E. Church*, 38–49.
15 Twiss, "Ernest Rice McKinney," 96; Moran, *American Genesis*, 88–89.
16 Ernest Rice McKinney, "This Week," *New York Amsterdam News*, April 15, 1925, 9.
17 Ernest Rice McKinney, "This Week: Skeptics, Agnostics, Atheists, Infidels and Free Thinkers," *Broad Ax* (Chicago), August 15, 1925, 2.
18 "Walker's Tabernacle Baptist Church," *Atlanta Daily World*, November 11, 1932, 3a.
19 "Being Boomed," *Plaindealer* (Topeka), April 7, 1939, 4.
20 *The Red Book of Houston*, 76.
21 Wright, *The Encyclopaedia of African Methodism*, 202.
22 Louis R. Lautier, "Howard 'Prexy' Warns against Sophistication," *Pittsburgh Courier*, June 9, 1928, 10.
23 Gary Dorrien reports that in 1931 Adam Clayton Powell responded passionately to H. L. Mencken's "bigoted screed claiming that black Americans had no accomplished thinkers and its ministers were ignorant fundamentalists." Powell agreed that fundamentalism was "a negation of every intellectual decency," but he sought to counter Mencken's attack on black America by providing a list of many black ministers who "were modern, progressive, learned, and emphatically not fundamentalist"—a list that included Dr. Mordecai Johnson (*The New Abolition*, 441).
24 Throughout this book, names given with the use of first and middle initials reflect historical usage in primary source documents. For certain historical figures, primary sources use a variety of different naming conventions. In these cases, references in the text may also vary.
25 P. B. Y. Jr., "The Henry Brothers, Evangelists, Put Over Their Fundamentalism with Modern Embellishments," *Norfolk Journal and Guide*, September 16, 1933, 24.
26 P. B. Y. Jr., "The Henry Brothers"; Elliott Freeman Jr., "The Whirling Hub," *Afro-American*, October 28, 1933, 19; "Manager of the Henry Brothers Dies Suddenly,"

*Norfolk Journal and Guide*, July 27, 1935, 9; "Rev O. D. Henry Buried in $650 Casket; Evangelist Stricken Sun. in Roanoke," *Afro-American*, August 3, 1935, 18; Elliott Freeman Jr., "The Whirling Hub," *Afro-American*, November 4, 1933, 7.

27  "Henry Brothers Say They Were Threatened," *Afro-American*, June 23, 1934, 20.

28  Louis R. Lautier, "Capital Spotlight," *Afro-American*, July 29, 1933, 1–2; Elliott Freeman Jr., "Henry Bros. Get Cold Shoulder in Boston," *Afro-American*, October 28, 1933, 19; "Theme Song, Hand Clapping Feature Revival of Henry Brothers in D.C.," *Afro-American*, July 22, 1933, 2.

29  P. B. Y. Jr., "The Henry Brothers." Regarding the Henrys' "celebrity" stature, an article from the *Afro-American* in 1933, which publicized that three of the brothers began preaching at the age of ten or younger, reads very much like a celebrity-profile entertainment piece: "Dad of Henry Brothers Is a Native of MD," *Afro-American*, September 23, 1933, 8.

30  Freeman, "Henry Bros. Get Cold Shoulder in Boston"; "Evangelists Travel in Limousine," *Norfolk Journal and Guide*, September 23, 1933, A3. On luxury cars and preachers' "commercial celebrity," see Martin, *Preaching on Wax*, 140–44, 148–49.

31  "Poisoning of One of Henry Bros. Mystery," *Afro-American*, July 22, 1933, 1.

32  Elliott Freeman Jr., "Boston Jugs Evangelist Henry," *Afro-American*, July 14, 1934, 1; E. W. Clark, "Evangelist and Officer Stage Fight," *Atlanta Daily World*, July 28, 1934, 6; "Women Faint, Men Weep as Accused Pastor Preaches," *Afro-American*, September 22, 1934, 3; "Henry Evangelists Are under Fire in Richmond," *Afro-American*, July 20, 1935, 6; "Rev. Henry Locked Out of Church as Rumors Circulate," *Afro-American*, April 6, 1935, 10; "Boston Congregation Ejects Wilbert Henry," *Afro-American*, May 18, 1935, 3.

33  P. B. Y. Jr., "The Henry Brothers."

34  "Henry Brothers, Evangelists, Are Baptist Fundamentalists," *Afro-American*, August 5, 1933, 11.

35  Marsden, "Fundamentalism as an American Phenomenon." Interestingly enough, Marsden's third doctrinal distinctive, dispensational premillennialism, appears to have been a topic of somewhat less regular discussion among many self-identified black fundamentalists. Yet eschatology was not wholly absent from the conversation. In 1935 Bishop Noah W. Williams reported to the Associated Negro Press about his journey through the Holy Land. In the process, he joined his express avowal of premillennialism with his conviction that the only reason to read the Bible is "if you believe it is the Inspired Word of God" and his exhortation that anyone who does not believe in biblical inspiration should "quit pretending." Williams's endorsement of premillennialism, however, did not specifically entail the dispensational brand. Noah W. Williams, "Touring the Holy Land," *Atlanta Daily World*, March 30, 1935, 1.

36  Freeman, "Henry Bros. Get Cold Shoulder in Boston"; Freeman, "The Whirling Hub," October 28, 1933.

37  Untitled opinion column, *Negro Star* (Wichita), January 11, 1924, 4.

38  Ashworth, "The Fundamentalist Movement among the Baptists," 627.

39 J. M. Nabrit Sr., "The Need of a Trained Leadership for Negroes," *Home and Foreign Fields*, July 1937, The Southern Baptist Commission on the American Baptist Seminary Records, AR 630, Box 2, Folder 66, Southern Baptist Historical Library and Archives, Nashville, TN.
40 "Clergymen Uphold Religious Revolt," *New York Amsterdam News*, December 31, 1930, 11.
41 Newman, *Freedom's Prophet*.
42 I. P. Reynolds, "What Sam of Auburn Avenue Says," *Atlanta Daily World*, February 21, 1932, 8.
43 "The World Is Lining Up," *Cleveland Gazette*, June 6, 1925, 2.
44 Discussions of the "literal interpretation" of the Bible have the potential to lead to some confusion. The idea of biblical literalism typically pointed to the specific doctrine of biblical inspiration (and the concomitant issues of inerrancy and infallibility). Interpreting the Bible "literally" was generally meant to imply that the words of the Bible were to be considered the literal words of God himself—that is, the Bible's origin was divine, its very words (not just its ideas) were inspired by God, and hence its content was wholly trustworthy and reflective of God's own perfection. "Literal" interpretation did not entail an elimination of genre-specific interpretation, however; the poetic and metaphorical language of the Psalms, for instance, was by necessity recognized even by "literalists." So, Psalm 1's description of the righteous man as "a tree planted by streams of water" did not require biblical literalists to conclude that righteous men were literally trees or that they ought to literally plant themselves next to rivers. However, in other genres (such as historical narrative and prophetic literature), straightforward claims and statements were taken as literally as possible, such that, for example, the claim in Joshua 10:13 that "the sun stood still" for a whole day was understood to mean exactly that—that God had supernaturally and miraculously provided for the sun to remain in the sky longer than ever before in order to allow the Israelites to destroy the Amorites.
45 This is entirely consonant with the convictions of white fundamentalists as seen so clearly, for example, in the essays touching on science, creation, and the Genesis narrative in Torrey and Dixon, *The Fundamentals*.
46 "Ask Me Another," *Chicago Defender*, October 8, 1927, A8.
47 George A. Singleton, "Religion Worth Having," *Chicago Defender*, October 15, 1927, A2.
48 Singleton was not alone in his dismissal of theologically conservative Christianity, with its commitment to supernatural and otherworldly doctrines (in his words, "superstition, literalism and formalism"), as mere accommodation to the oppressive white culture and therefore unfit to advance African American interests. Such ideas are also reflected in the writings of Ernest Rice McKinney quoted in this chapter, and chapter 5 will deal in more detail with this type of argument. This sentiment in some ways anticipates E. Franklin Frazier's argument in *The Negro Church in America* that Christianity represented a foreign tradition that black

slaves eventually adopted due to their "subordination and isolation in American society" and the complete destruction of their social heritage (82). Yet in contrast to Singleton's assertion, Albert J. Raboteau has contended in *Slave Religion* (290, 333) that slaves' Christianity, even as it was in many notable ways an "otherworldly" religion, provided the basis for the slaves to resist the prevailing culture by declaring the fundamental incompatibility between orthodox Christianity and the practice of slavery. Hence, the otherworldly Christianity toward which Singleton was so hostile was not merely an accommodationist adoption of the prevailing "white man's" religion, but actually represented an opportunity for blacks to assert their own agency and resist the oppressive status quo.

Other scholars have likewise affirmed the agency of black slaves in adopting and adapting the Christian religion to fit their circumstances. Eugene Genovese, far from seeing slave Christianity as a purely accommodationist capitulation to the prevailing white culture, identifies elements of resistance and counterculture in slave religion: "The slaves reshaped the Christianity they had embraced; they conquered the religion of those who had conquered them" (*Roll, Jordan, Roll*, 212). William E. Montgomery similarly contends that the egalitarianism inherent in the revivalist doctrines of the Great Awakenings, centering as they did on the conversion experience and the equal standing of all individuals before God, provided an opening for black slaves to connect the Christian gospel with their own emancipation: "The power of the conversion experience pierced all conventional social barriers, rendering privilege irrelevant and elevating all of God's creatures to the same condition. . . . The social and political ramifications of evangelical doctrine reverberated through the South during the late eighteenth and early nineteenth centuries. The inference that blacks drew from the gospel was their liberation from slavery" (*Under Their Own Vine and Fig Tree*, 20).

49 "We Run Everything Says L. K. Williams," *Afro-American*, February 18, 1928, 1.
50 "The Third Annual Address of Dr. L. K. Williams, President," 15. More extensive consideration of this particularly notable oration is offered in chapters 3 and 5.
51 Williams also helped found the American Baptist Theological Seminary—a cooperative effort between white Southern Baptists and black National Baptists to create a school for educating black Baptist clergy. The story of ABTS, including Williams's participation and the school's confessional and institutional relationship to fundamentalist theology, is examined in more detail in chapter 4.
52 For an examination of the fundamentalist origins of the anti-evolution movement, see Lienesch, *In the Beginning*.
53 Floyd J. Calvin, "The Digest," *Pittsburgh Courier*, August 8, 1925, 16.
54 Mathews, *Doctrine and Race*, 87.
55 Alma Booker, "Is Evolution Based Upon a Guess?" *Pittsburgh Courier*, August 8, 1925, 5.
56 Thomas L. Dabney, "Quarrel between Religion and Science," *Afro-American*, August 1, 1925, 13.

57 William Pickens, "Don Quixote Bryan, Fundamentalism," *Norfolk Journal and Guide*, January 12, 1924, 5.
58 "The Bookshelf," *Chicago Defender*, February 27, 1926, A1.
59 Watt, "Fundamentalists of the 1920s and 1930s," 23–24.
60 Moran, "The Scopes Trial and Southern Fundamentalism," 95–96.
61 Lincoln, *Race, Religion, and the Continuing American Dilemma*, 96.
62 "Our Group Are Fundamentalists in Religion."
63 "We Run Everything Says L. K. Williams"; "Ignores School Row in Address," *New York Amsterdam News*, February 22, 1928, 10; "Controversy Sidestepped by Williams," *Chicago Defender*, February 25, 1928, 2.
64 For analysis of Williams's 1925 address to the Convention, see chapters 3 and 5.
65 "Baptist Theological Seminary for Negroes Dedicated Sunday," *Nashville Banner*, September 15, 1924, The Southern Baptist Commission on the American Baptist Seminary Records, AR 630, Box 5, Folder 23, Southern Baptist Historical Library and Archives, Nashville, TN. For more on the American Baptist Theological Seminary, see chapter 4.
66 For a detailed study on the print media's role in creating the association between the South and fundamentalism, see Mathews, *Rethinking Zion*.
67 "The Springfield Sun Throws a Little Light on 'Texas Justice,'" *Pittsburgh Courier*, November 27, 1926, A8; "Empire State of Ignorance," *Pittsburgh Courier*, November 27, 1926, A8.
68 Kelly Miller, "Kelly Miller Says," *Afro-American*, November 21, 1925, 11.
69 "September Crisis Scores Prejudiced Fundamentalist," *Philadelphia Tribune*, August 22, 1925, 15.
70 Wendell P. Dabney, "Reflections of Dabney," *Spokesman* (Chicago), February 4, 1933, 4.
71 Ernest Rice McKinney, "This Week: Skeptics, Agnostics, Atheists, Infidels and Free Thinkers."
72 "American Intolerance and Menace of a State Church," *Norfolk Journal and Guide*, September 11, 1926, 12.
73 "What the Republican Party Can't Be," *Chicago Defender*, November 9, 1929, A2.
74 Ernest Rice McKinney, "This Week," April 15, 1925.
75 "Claim Church Holds Southerners Back," *Plaindealer* (Topeka), March 29, 1935, 2; "Says Negro Church Holds Rase [sic] Back in South," *Wyandotte Echo*, March 29, 1935, 1.
76 While the discussion here is concerned primarily with Christian discourse, this principle that upright social action was essential to true religion extended well beyond the explicitly Christian realm into other faith traditions and even into black secularist intellectual reflections. Consider Alain Locke, whom religious studies scholar David Weinfeld evaluates in "Isolated Believer" as both an adherent to the Baha'i faith and an influential secularist thinker. Locke "valued religion as universal rather than particular," and argued that it was a fallacy to look upon creeds as "the essential elements without which true religion means nothing" (87).

For Locke, religions "served a pragmatic function in this world, not the next" (95), meaning that "without a peaceful payoff in *this* world, monotheistic belief was not worth much" (92). As a result, he considered Christianity to be "an enemy of racial progress" (94).

77  Roscoe Simmons, "The Week," *Chicago Defender*, December 15, 1923, A1; Roscoe Simmons, "The Week," *Chicago Defender*, December 29, 1923, 11; Roscoe Simmons, "The Week," *Chicago Defender*, September 20, 1924, A3.
78  "Ignores School Row in Address."
79  Best, *Langston's Salvation*, 61.
80  A. Clayton Powell Sr., "The Silent Church," *New York Amsterdam News*, February 16, 1935, 8.
81  J. Raymond Henderson, "This Thing Called Religion," *Pittsburgh Courier*, May 30, 1931, 19.
82  Singleton, "Religion Worth Having."
83  "Churchgoers Sign Up," *Afro-American*, March 30, 1935, 1.

## CHAPTER 2. FORMULATING THE FAITH

1  Hankins, *God's Rascal*, 119–20, 165–66; J. Frank Norris to Jane Hartwell, December 28, 1928, quoted in Mathews, *Doctrine and Race*, 28.
2  "Our Group Are Fundamentalists in Religion"; McKinney, "This Week," April 15, 1925.
3  The phrase "faith once delivered to the saints"—often used to describe the idea that the doctrinal core (or fundamentals) of the Christian faith is unchanging through the ages—comes from Jude 1:3, which reads: "Beloved, although I was very eager to write to you about our common salvation, I found it necessary to write appealing to you to contend for the faith that was once for all delivered to the saints" (English Standard Version [ESV]).
4  Subjective personal experience still did play some role in fundamentalist thinking, even in *The Fundamentals*. See, for example, E. Y. Mullins, "The Testimony of Christian Experience," 315.
5  Fosdick, "Shall the Fundamentalists Win?" 422.
6  Blum and Harvey, *The Color of Christ*, 185.
7  Glass, *Strangers in Zion*, 71.
8  Hankins, *God's Rascal*, 162, 167.
9  Curtis Lee Laws, "The Negro and Roman Catholicism," *Watchman Examiner* 19, no. 9 (1931), 265.
10  The characterization of African Americans as "naturally religious" dates back to antebellum romantic racialists and is intimately connected to the idea of intellectual inferiority. Evans, *The Burden of Black Religion*, 36–37.
11  Blain, Cameron, and Farmer, Introduction, 3.
12  From the beginning there have been numerous lists of the "five fundamentals," albeit with some variations. In a 1924 article chronicling the early fundamentalist conflicts in the Northern Baptist Convention, Robert Ashworth stated that

the "particular doctrines of which the Fundamentalists consider themselves to be the advocates and defenders are those of a miraculously inspired Bible, . . . the miraculous Virgin Birth, a substitutionary atonement, the bodily resurrection of Jesus, and his second coming" ("The Fundamentalist Movement among the Baptists," 611). Later in the article he quotes at length from a 1921 letter penned by the convention's fundamentalist contingent, which offered a slightly different list. This enumeration failed to mention the virgin birth, adding in its place "the deity of the Lord Jesus Christ" (620).

In *Are Southern Baptists "Evangelicals"?* James Leo Garrett, Jr., E. Glenn Hinson, and James E. Tull trace several iterations of the "five fundamentals" that have been utilized by historians over the years. They are chosen from six or seven fundamental doctrines: biblical inerrancy, the deity of Christ, the virgin birth, substitutionary atonement, Christ's bodily resurrection and second coming (sometimes presented as a single point of faith, and sometimes split into two), and the miracle-working power of Christ (48–49).

In at least one instance, self-professed heirs to the fundamentalist movement combined Christ's deity and his virgin birth into a single doctrinal point in their list of "fundamentals," while distinguishing Christ's resurrection and literal second coming as two separate doctrines; Dobson and Hindson, *The Fundamentalist Phenomenon*, 7.

Numerous scholars have pointed to the five-point resolution of the 1910 General Assembly of the Presbyterian Church, U.S.A. (subsequently reaffirmed in 1916 and 1923) as the model for a five-point fundamentalist formula. Nodding to the 1910 declaration as the likely source of such a formulation, Ernest Sandeen lists inerrancy, the virgin birth, the atonement, the resurrection, and Christ's miracle-working power (*The Roots of Fundamentalism*, xiv–xv). George Marsden likewise identifies the General Assembly's 1910 statement as the source of the "famous five points," which he summarizes similarly to Sandeen (*Fundamentalism and American Culture*, 117). See also Simpson, *Modern Christian Theology*, 298, and Mathers, *Battle for Orthodoxy*, 27–29. Interestingly, Simpson's summary of the Presbyterian statement differs in one major way from that of Sandeen and Marsden. In lieu of "miracle-working power" (Sandeen) or "authenticity of the miracles" (Marsden), Simpson lists "the deity of Jesus." This difference stems from the General Assembly's fifth article, which states that Jesus "showed his power and love by working mighty miracles," but also later affirmed that these miracles "were signs of the divine power of our Lord."

Between Ashworth's testimony from the 1920s, Garrett, Hinson, and Tull's analysis of various formulations, and numerous invocations and interpretations of the 1910 Presbyterian statement, there appears to be a relatively circumscribed spectrum of six or seven doctrines that appear variously as part of the "five fundamentals." Moreover, some of these often overlap or hew together, as seen in the pairing of Christ's bodily resurrection and second coming or in the overlap between "deity of Christ" and "miracle working power." Therefore, my discussion of the "five fundamentals" includes biblical inspiration/inerrancy, Christ's deity, the virgin birth, substitutionary atonement, and the bodily resurrection and bodily return of Christ (considered together due to their shared emphasis on the literal, physical, bodily work of the resurrected Christ).

13  Among those figures examined in this chapter, even those who did not explicitly use the term "fundamentals" or "fundamentalist" in defining their own position would fall into the "doctrinal fundamentalist" category as laid out in this book's introduction. This category also takes into account, of course, the overt antimodernist polemics that constitute the focus of chapter 3.

14  George Biddle, "The Fundamentals," *Star of Zion*, September 8, 1921.

15  While a few sermonic references appear in the current chapter out of necessity, sermonic discourse is not the main point of focus. Sermons, representing in their form and authority a substantially different and unique type of communication, are a central focus of chapter 3.

16  Martin, *Preaching on Wax*, 70–72, 90.

17  The concept of using a "dialectical spectrum" in lieu of a strict dichotomy reflects the approach of C. Eric Lincoln and Lawrence H. Mamiya in *The Black Church in the African American Experience*. Lincoln and Mamiya offer a "dialectical model of the black church," which includes various sets of dialectical polarities with the understanding that any given church body could fall within a range of possible locations on the resulting spectrum. If we apply this model to issues pertinent to the fundamentalist/modernist controversy, we can understand how, even within the "fundamentalist" range of the spectrum, there could be substantial internecine arguments and disagreements, such as between plenary verbal and mechanical dictation views of inspiration, or between penal and moral-government views of substitutionary atonement.

Scholars such as Allison Calhoun-Brown (political science) and Sandra L. Barnes (sociology) have used Lincoln and Mamiya's suggested dialectical pairings to argue for more nuanced views of the relationship between conservative theology and political/social action among African American Christians. In "While Marching to Zion" Calhoun-Brown challenges the assumption that the "otherworldly/this-worldly" and "resistance/accommodation" dialectics are intrinsically linked. In "Priestly and Prophetic Influences" Barnes argues that black churches all across the "priestly/prophetic" spectrum are involved in social and political activism, and in "Black Church Electoral and Protest Politics" she and Nwosu also point out that when religious conservatives and progressives find themselves in opposition to one another on social issues, both sides position themselves as being in line with the resistance/protest tradition of the black church and consider their opponents to be accommodationists.

18  Finn, "John R. Rice, Bob Jones Jr. and the 'Mechanical Dictation' Controversy."

19  L. W. Munhall, in discussing 2 Peter 1:21, asserts, "This passage does not justify the so-called 'mechanical theory of inspiration.' Such theory is nowhere taught in the

Scriptures" ("Inspiration," 56). George Bishop argues that the testimony of Exodus 4:11–12 and 2 Corinthians 13:3 "looks very much like what has been stigmatized as the 'mechanical theory.' It surely makes the writer a mere organ" ("The Testimony of the Scriptures to Themselves," 94).

20 Gray, "The Inspiration of the Bible," 12. Emphasis in the original.
21 Ehrman, "Why Textual Criticism Is 'Safe' for Conservative Christians."
22 Mary Beth Swetnam Mathews discusses Eli George Biddle at some length in *Doctrine and Race*, 75, 82–86, 96. Despite the fact that Biddle expressly identified as a proponent of the fundamentals and he consigned to hell anyone who rejected the fundamental doctrines, Mathews is unwilling to categorize him as a fundamentalist. This unwillingness apparently stems from the fact that, as Mathews demonstrates, Biddle drifted away from dispensational eschatology, he argued for an essential compatibility between religion and science, and he used the word "motherhood" in conjunction with "Fatherhood" to describe God's relationship to his creation. As will become clear later in this chapter, Biddle's eschatological ambivalence regarding particular millennial theories and his view of science and religion are consonant with early fundamentalism as expressed in Torrey and Dixon's volumes on *The Fundamentals*. Biddle's use of "motherhood" would very likely have earned the ire of some white fundamentalist leaders, such as J. Frank Norris, but it is a relatively minor oddity that does not appear to infringe on any central fundamentalist doctrine in Biddle's exposition of the faith. Moreover, Biddle's own use of capitalization qualitatively distinguishes between "Fatherhood" (capitalized) on the one hand, which reflects the Bible's testimony to "Father" as a personal name and an essential relational element of Trinitarian theology, and "motherhood" (uncapitalized) on the other hand, which seemingly reflects an analogical description of certain elements of God's actions and disposition toward creation (see Isaiah 66:13, Psalm 131:2, Matthew 23:37). This appears to be a relatively thin basis upon which to disqualify Biddle from being a fundamentalist, especially in the face of his own testimony on the issue of "the fundamentals."
23 Biddle, "The Fundamentals."
24 Biddle, "The Fundamentals."
25 E. George Biddle, "The Bible a God-Inspired Book," *Star of Zion*, June 1, 1922.
26 Munhall, "Inspiration," 45; Hague, "The History of the Higher Criticism," 20; Pitzer, "The Wisdom of This World," 47–48. All four volumes of *The Fundamentals* are replete with similar references.
27 Biddle, "The Bible a God-Inspired Book."
28 Orr, "Science and the Christian Faith," 336.
29 Kyle, "The Recent Testimony of Archaeology to the Scriptures," 330.
30 Biddle, "The Bible a God-Inspired Book"; Gray, "The Inspiration of the Bible," 14; Freeman, *Handbook of Bible Manners and Customs*, 6.
31 Mathews argues that "the lack of mention of *The Fundamentals* [by black ministers] again begs the question of whether the booklets really were sent to every minister in the United States and Canada, or whether they were sent to every

white minister in the United States and Canada.... It would seem that [black ministers] did not possess Lyman Stewart's books" (*Doctrine and Race*, 86).
32 Biddle, "The Bible a God-Inspired Book."
33 A note on biblical quotations: When quoting biblical material as it appears directly in a primary source, such as an article or a sermon manuscript, the verses will appear in the translation used by the source (typically the King James Version [KJV]). Otherwise, all references to biblical texts—for instance, to more fully contextualize an argument or to explain an allusion that appears in a primary source—will come from the English Standard Version (ESV) for the purposes of modern readability.
34 Caven, "The Testimony of Christ to the Old Testament," 203, 218; Hague, "The Doctrinal Value of the First Chapters of Genesis," 287; Hague, "The History of the Higher Criticism," 22, 34.
35 Biddle, "The Bible a God-Inspired Book"; Torrey, "Tributes to Christ and the Bible by Brainy Men," 369.

    Other examples of similar exegesis and usage of 2 Timothy 3:16 and 2 Peter 1:21 include Bettex, "The Bible and Modern Criticism," 91; Caven, "The Testimony of Christ to the Old Testament," 212; Gray, "The Inspiration of the Bible," 20; Munhall, "Inspiration," 56.
36 Biddle's use of the "Road to Emmaus" pericope from Luke 24 also appears with some frequency in *The Fundamentals*.
37 W. H. Davenport, "Bishop L. W. Kyles Applauded While Delivering Sentiment of Bishops to Delegates," *Star of Zion*, May 15, 1924.
38 For other examples of this sort of sentiment among black writers and speakers of the era, see chapters 1 and 5.
39 "Women of Two Races Discuss Negro Equality," *Star of Zion*, November 6, 1930. This unequivocally theologically liberal message at a women's conference located at Fosdick's Riverside Church could support the link between gender progressivism and theological progressivism posited by Betty A. DeBerg in *Ungodly Women*. While I disagree with the causal sequence proposed by DeBerg (she argues that the desire to preserve Victorian gender norms was the underlying factor driving fundamentalists' theological/doctrinal considerations), there does appear to be a correlative link between the gender and theological spectrums. Evelyn Brooks Higginbotham also discusses the development of "feminist theology" among black Baptist women in connection with the "age of liberal theology" in *Righteous Discontent*, 136–42.
40 Pelikan, *The Christian Tradition*, vol. 1, chap. 2. Pelikan also draws a connection between second-century Marcionism and nineteenth-century biblical criticism, an observation that Mrs. Wallace's words at the 1930 women's conference seem to further validate (see *The Christian Tradition*, 1:23).
41 Biddle, "The Bible a God-Inspired Book."
42 While fundamentalists are most often characterized in the historiography as essentially separatist in nature, Nathan Finn draws a helpful and needful distinction

between different types of fundamentalists on the basis of differing modes of "conservative dissent." "Separatist fundamentalists" saw strict organizational and denominational separation as an imperative, while "denominational fundamentalists" saw their personal opposition to theological progressivism as a reason to remain in their denominations as agents of conservative influence. Finn writes:

> For denominational fundamentalists, contending for the faith did not have to result in abandoning mainline denominations that were infected with progressive theology. Rather, faithful conservatives should fight to purge their churches and denominations of any theology or practice that threatened Christian orthodoxy. Many denominational fundamentalists rejected the label 'fundamentalist' for the very reason that they chose to fight the progressives in their denominations rather than separating from those denominations. The very idea of denominational fundamentalism as a particular approach to conservative dissent has been almost totally ignored by historians. ("The Development of Baptist Fundamentalism in the South," 15)

Many of the nonseparatist black fundamentalists considered in this book, such as Eli George Biddle, may fit into this "denominational fundamentalist" category, with some caveats. Firstly, some did indeed show a willingness to expressly identify as fundamentalists even within their denominations. Moreover, their willingness to associate with theological liberals was motivated not only by the desire for denominational reform but also by the common imperative of racial advancement.

43 Angell and Pinn, *Social Protest Thought in the African Methodist Episcopal Church*, xxiv.
44 J. G. Robinson, "Preachers—Modernists and Fundamentalists," *Star of Zion*, January 30, 1936.
45 Rauschenbusch, *A Theology for the Social Gospel*, 131, 144, 148, 150–51.
46 Grossman, *Land of Hope*, 171–72.
47 Blum, *W. E. B. Du Bois*, 8, 22, 45–46, 49–50, 91–92, 99–101, 103, 114–15, 160; Best, *Passionately Human, No Less Divine*, 4, 72, 74; Best, *Langston's Salvation*, 18–22, 61–63, 157, 172, 186; Savage, "Biblical and Historical Imperatives," 379; Sernett, "Re-Readings," 454–55; Pinn and Pinn, *Fortress Introduction to Black Church History*, 127–28.
48 Du Bois, *The Negro Church*, 189.
49 Blum, *W. E. B. Du Bois*, 50, 114.
50 Zuckerman, "The Sociology of Religion of W.E.B. Du Bois."
51 See Raboteau, *Slave Religion*, esp. chap. 5.
52 Dickerson, *The African Methodist Episcopal Church*, 286.
53 On the subject of Du Bois's view of the liberating potential of the social gospel, Edward Blum frames Du Bois as an early precursor and an "unheralded father" of the black liberation theology that was formally developed later in the work of thinkers such as James H. Cone and James Deotis Roberts. Blum argues that Du Bois's reflections on Christ presaged black liberation theology's emphasis on the

blackness of Christ and of God, as well as the emphasis on God's essential affiliation with the oppressed. Blum, *W. E. B. Du Bois*, 8, 13, 17, 139–40.

Cone's early works developing black liberation theology include *Black Theology and Black Power*, *A Black Theology of Liberation*, and *God of the Oppressed*. For an early articulation of Roberts's reflections on black liberation theology see his *A Black Political Theology*. For a sampling of Roberts's developing thoughts on black theology over the course of his career, see his *Black Religion, Black Theology*.

For historical reflections on interpretations of Jesus relative to race, see Blum and Harvey, *The Color of Christ*; Prothero, *American Jesus*, esp. chap. 6.

54 Robinson, "Preachers—Modernists and Fundamentalists."
55 Robinson, "Preachers—Modernists and Fundamentalists."
56 Bettex, "The Bible and Modern Criticism," 88.
57 Gaebelein, "Fulfilled Prophecy a Potent Argument for the Bible," 143; Munhall, "Inspiration," 60.
58 Gray, "The Inspiration of the Bible," 16.
59 In addition to the consideration here relating to the unincorporated National Baptist Convention, see also the analysis in chapters 3 and 5 of L. K. Williams' 1925 convention address to the incorporated National Baptist Convention, as well as the consideration in chapter 4 of the doctrinal controversies that attended the incorporated body's educational joint venture with Southern Baptists, the American Baptist Theological Seminary.
60 Mathews, *Doctrine and Race*, 55.
61 J. H. Frank, "White Baptists," *National Baptist Union-Review*, April 17, 1926; "How to Study the Bible," *National Baptist Union-Review*, March 27, 1926. Quoted in Mathews, *Doctrine and Race*, 54, 65.
62 Mathews, *Doctrine and Race*, 65.
63 Pierson, "The Testimony of the Organic Unity of the Bible," 103.
64 John Albert Johnson, "Critique of Adolf Harnack's *Christianity and History*," John Albert Johnson Papers, Box 1, Folder 4, Schomburg Center for Research in Black Culture, New York Public Library, New York (hereafter cited as Johnson Papers).
65 John Albert Johnson, "The Faithful Minister," 5, 7–8, Johnson Papers, Box 1, Folder 4. Emphasis in the original.
66 Examples of this sort of argumentation recur throughout Christian history, bolstering Johnson's claim (and similar claims of fundamentalist scholars in general) to be representing a longstanding orthodox tradition of the church. For example, the second-century church father Irenaeus of Lyons argued in *Against Heresies* for the inspiration and unity of the Old and New Testaments on the basis of both the Old Testament's prophetic testimony about Christ and the testimony of Jesus in John 5 about the nature and authority of the Old Testament:

> The Old Testament Scriptures, and those written by Moses in particular, do everywhere make mention of the Son of God, and foretell his advent and passion. From this fact if follows that they were inspired by one and the

same God. Wherefore also John does appropriately relate that the Lord said to the Jews: "Ye search the Scriptures, in which ye think ye have eternal life; these are they which testify of me. And ye are not willing to come unto Me, that ye may have life." How therefore did the Scriptures testify of Him, unless they were from one and the same Father, instructing men beforehand as to the advent of His Son, and foretelling the salvation brought in by Him? (464)

Irenaeus later uses John 5:46–47 to argue that the words of Moses in the Old Testament are in fact the words of Christ himself, at once affirming and connecting the doctrines of biblical inspiration and the deity of Christ: "But since the writings of Moses are the words of Christ, He does Himself declare to the Jews, as John has recorded in the Gospel: 'If ye had believed Moses, ye would have believed Me: for he wrote of Me. But if ye believe not his writings, neither will ye believe My words.' He thus indicates in the clearest manner that the writings of Moses are His words" (*Against Heresies*, 473).

Origen of Alexandria argued similarly in the third century, using Jesus's testimony in John 5 to connect belief in Christ with belief in the authority and veracity of the Scriptures: "For as 'if they believed Moses they would have believed Jesus,' so if they had believed the prophets they would have received Him who had been the subject of prophecy. But disbelieving Him they also disbelieve them, and cut off and confine in prison the prophetic word, and hold it dead and divided, and in no way wholesome, since they do not understand it" (*Commentary on the Gospel of Matthew*, 429).

Such argumentation emerged likewise from the Protestant Reformation—the common broad tradition from which the fundamentalists hailed. French reformer John Calvin, for instance, drew on Jesus's testimony in John 5:46 to affirm the Bible's authority and the duty of true Christians to defend it against outside attacks. For Calvin, Jesus's words of rebuke to the Jews that "if you believed Moses, you would also believe me" constituted a call to the defense of the full scope of the inspired Scriptures (*Commentary on the Gospel According to John*, 224).

67 John Albert Johnson, "Inspiration," 2–3, 6–7, Johnson Papers, Box 1, Folder 4.
68 John Albert Johnson, "The Preacher's Chief Study," Johnson Papers, Box 1, Folder 5.
69 Gray's argument in *The Fundamentals* drawing an explicit connection between the sinlessness of the incarnate Word and the inerrancy of the written Word proceeds as follows: "Is it not with the written Word as with the incarnate Word? Is Jesus Christ to be regarded as imperfect because His character has never been perfectly reproduced before us? Can He be the incarnate Word unless He were absolutely without sin? And by the same token, can the scriptures be the written word unless they were inerrant?" ("The Inspiration of the Bible," 13).
70 Johnson, "Inspiration," 6, 8–9.
71 Johnson, "Critique of Adolf Harnack's *Christianity and History*."

72 John Albert Johnson, "The Doctrine of the Incarnation," Johnson Papers, Box 1, Folder 4.
73 Such claims were sometimes leveled by antifundamentalist voices in the black press, such as George A. Singleton (see chapter 1 for a discussion of some of Singleton's criticisms). In "Religion Worth Having," an October 1927 article for the *Chicago Defender*, Singleton lamented that so many African Americans clung to a fundamentalist version of Christianity that he characterized as a "hand-me-down . . . from the American white man" and thus a religion utterly unsuited for the black race.
74 Horace Hovey to E. F. Williams, October 16, 1876, Edward Franklin Williams Papers, Box 7, Folder 2, Amistad Research Center at Tulane University, New Orleans, LA (hereafter cited as Williams Papers); Ellen B. Taft to E. F. Williams, December 14, 1876, Williams Papers, Box 7, Folder 2; Toronto correspondent to E. F. Williams, December 8, 1876, Williams Papers, Box 7, Folder 2; Horace Hovey to E. F. Williams, January 27, 1877, Williams Papers, Box 7, Folder 3; Frank Dyer to E. F. Williams, April 5, 1906, Williams Papers, Box 10, Folder 12.
75 Frank Dyer to E. F. Williams, April 5, 1906.
76 Edward Franklin Williams, "Preparatory Lecture: The Practical Nature of the Christian Religion," February 27, 1889, Williams Papers, Box 19, Folder 12.
77 In *Something Within* Fredrick C. Harris provides a worthwhile consideration of the assumed connection between otherworldliness and social/political passivity (what he calls the "opiate theory"), along with the inverse position (what he calls the "inspiration theory"). He offers the "multidimensionality of religion" as a more nuanced approach to the topic, treating religious faith and practice in the black community as diverse and variegated rather than as "discrete and unitary" (4–9, 135–36). See also Calhoun-Brown, "While Marching to Zion"; Barnes, "Priestly and Prophetic Influences"; Barnes and Nwosu, "Black Church Electoral and Protest Politics"; McDaniel and Ellison, "God's Party?."
78 For example, Paul Harvey associates black churches' community engagement with an embrace of the social gospel movement, in opposition to a focus on spiritual doctrinal matters such as the afterlife. Harvey argues that in the first half of the twentieth century, "Both Southern and Northern black churches engaged in much community work. In doing so, they applied the ideas of the social gospel movement, which emphasized emulating Jesus' life in practical works of caring for people rather than focusing on the spiritual afterlife" (*Through the Storm, Through the Night*, 88).
79 Edward Franklin Williams, Easter sermon, March 27, 1910, Williams Papers, Box 19, Folder 13. Even as Williams regularly exhorted his congregants toward this sort of interpersonal compassion, social service, and righteous living in this world, he also leveled attacks on social gospel theology (see chapter 3).
80 Biddle, "The Fundamentals"; Biddle, "The Bible a God-Inspired Book."

81  For an example of an early scholarly voice among the fundamentalists repeatedly using "vicarious" and "substitutionary" synonymously with respect to Christ's atonement, see Hague, "At-One-Ment by Propitiation."
82  Johnson, "The Atonement," 64, 72.
83  Johnson, "Critique of Adolf Harnack's *Christianity and History.*"
84  Edward Franklin Williams spoke of Christ's atonement in relation to "the position in the moral government of God which is given one on condition of faith in Jesus Christ" ("Righteousness," September 18, 1904, Williams Papers, Box 19, Folder 12). John Stock's contribution to *The Fundamentals* included similar language, suggesting that editors R. A. Torrey and A. C. Dixon likely saw such conceptions as within the bounds of fundamentalist orthodoxy: "A so called Saviour, whose only power to save lies in the excellent moral precepts that He gave, and the pure life that He lived; who is no longer the God-man, but the mere man; whose blood had no sacrificial atoning or propitiatory power in the moral government of Jehovah, but was simply a martyr's witness to a superior system of ethics—is not the Saviour of the four Gospels, or of Paul, or Peter, or John" (Stock, "The God-Man," 281).
85  Isaac Reed Berry, "God's One Essential for Salvation," n.d., Isaac Reed Berry Papers, Box 1, Folder 69, Schomburg Center for Research in Black Culture, New York Public Library, New York.
86  Penn-Lewis, "Satan and His Kingdom," 188–89. Emphases in the original.
87  Further points of congruity between Isaac Reed Berry's preaching and *The Fundamentals* are considered in chapter 3.
88  Robinson, "Preachers—Modernists and Fundamentalists."
89  Mathews, *Doctrine and Race*, 82. For an extended consideration of the historical connection between premillennial theology and twentieth-century American evangelicalism, see Sutton, *American Apocalypse*.
90  Bishop Noah W. Williams, "Touring the Holy Land," *Atlanta Daily World*, March 30, 1935, 1.
91  Ashworth, "The Fundamentalist Movement among the Baptists," 611–12.
92  E. P. Alldredge to L. R. Scarborough, March 1, 1921, Eugene Perry Alldredge Papers, AR 795-134, Box 15, Folder 3, Southern Baptist Historical Library and Archives, Nashville, TN. Alldredge, who figures prominently in chapter 4's examination of the American Baptist Theological Seminary, falls explicitly into Nathan Finn's category of "denominational fundamentalists" ("The Development of Baptist Fundamentalism," 143–44).
93  Erdman, "The Coming of Christ," 301, 312.

## CHAPTER 3. POLEMICS FROM THE PULPIT

1  Marsh, *God's Long Summer*, 22–23; Isaac Reed Berry, "Paul In Athens," n.d., Isaac Reed Berry Papers, Box 3, Folder 140, Schomburg Center for Research in Black Culture, New York Public Library, New York (hereafter cited as Berry Papers). Most of Berry's sermon manuscripts are undated.

2 Luther, *Sermons on the Gospel of St. John Chapters 14–16*, 170.
3 W. E. B. Du Bois famously noted that "the preacher is the most unique personality developed by the Negro on American soil. A leader, a politician, an orator, a 'boss,' an intriguer, an idealist,—all these he is, and ever, too, the centre of a group of men, now twenty, now a thousand in number" (*The Souls of Black Folk*, 116).

Contemporaneous with Du Bois, William A. Daniel's 1925 sociological survey of black theological education concluded that "[black theological] students were in substantial agreement that the consensus of opinion among the churchgoers of their home communities is that ministers are 'called of God' in a supernatural way." Daniel proceeded to quote one such student, saying, "I believe men are called to the ministry not by any actual sound they hear, but I believe they see a vision from God" (*The Education of Negro Ministers*, 71–72).

In his study of mid-twentieth century African American preaching in Macon County, Georgia, William H. Pipes likewise noted that "the old-time Negro preacher is not merely a speaker with a speech: he is the 'Man of God' with God's message to me—the instrument through which the Father talks to His children" (*Say Amen, Brother!*, 90).

Henry Mitchell also affirmed this element of Pipes's perspective on black preaching, amidst his argument that black religion reflects a confluence of West African and Euro-American cultural streams:

> Black preaching has always assumed that preaching must be an *experience*, not merely a clever idea. It involves the totality of a person and is, consciously or not, concerned to organize feeling tones around the text. It is understood that no such demanding enterprise can be undertaken inside human limitations, and so the understandings of spirit possession, deeply imbedded in African religion, have informed our entire history. Educated black preachers have never agreed with the tradition that eschews preparation, but all are agreed that no mere man can prepare enough to calculate, choreograph, and control the trialogue between the preacher, the congregation, and the very Spirit of God. Black preaching, in the best of all its traditional strands, still assumes that God Himself speaks through men who give themselves to Him in prayer and sincere preparation for the preaching event. ("Two Streams of Tradition," 73–74)

Edward Wheeler has addressed the idea of the black minister as paradoxically both intimately connected to and profoundly separate or set-apart from his community on the dual basis of his divine endowment and his role as an exemplar and an agent of social uplift for the community: "The key to understanding the paradox of the separateness of the preachers from their communities is found in the position a man assumed when he became a minister in the black community: as a minister, he was set apart. . . . The call to the ministry and the confirmation of that call by the community placed the minister in a high place of influence that had consequences for his activity in uplifting the race.... As a public figure held in high esteem, he had a sacred trust." In demonstrating the high expectations placed upon black ministers, Wheeler quotes from AME Bishop W. J. Gaines, "The ministry is not a profession, but a calling... the high and holy functions which belong to it can be discharged only by the man who has been set apart to it, anointed by the Holy Ghost and divinely endowed for its peculiar and special responsibilities." Likewise, he also quotes one of Gaines's contemporaries, John B. L. Williams, to the same effect: "The Christian pulpit has ever been acknowledged to be a great power for good among all people. Coming as it does divinely commissioned and bearing to man a divine message, it has a claim upon the attention and the acceptance of mankind.... To the Christian pulpit the people look for the loftiest ideals of life. In this respect the Negro more than any other people has been largely dependent upon the pulpit" (*Uplifting the Race*, 22–24).

Charles Hamilton has commented on the closeness of the relationship between the African American minister and his congregants, including his authoritative voice in their lives: "A discussion of religion among church-affiliated blacks will frequently include the phrase 'my pastor.' And when the phrase is used, there is a strong sense of mutual, personal attachment. The speaker will quote his pastor, cite him authoritatively, tell what his pastor has done for him, what the pastor said in his sermon last Sunday. There is a feeling of trust and mutual loyalty not found in other relationships" (*The Black Preacher in America*, 19).

4 The willingness to make racial applications, especially applications related to structural issues in society, reflects in part the "survival" and "justice" building blocks in Shelton and Emerson's sociological analysis of black Protestantism in *Blacks and Whites in Christian America*.
5 Edward Franklin Williams, Easter sermon, March 27, 1910, Edward Franklin Williams Papers, Box 19, Folder 13, Amistad Research Center at Tulane University, New Orleans, LA (hereafter cited as Williams Papers).
6 Williams, Easter sermon.
7 Edward Franklin Williams, "The Simplicity Which Is in Christ," February 26, 1905, Williams Papers, Box 19, Folder 12.
8 Williams, "The Simplicity Which Is in Christ."
9 Rauschenbusch, *A Theology for the Social Gospel*, 7–8.
10 Williams, "The Simplicity Which Is in Christ."
11 Wright, *The Encyclopaedia of African Methodism*, 321–23, 336, 341, 477, 586–87.
12 Johnson, "Critique of Adolf Harnack's *Christianity and History*"; John Albert Johnson, "The Faithful Minister," Johnson Papers, Box 1, Folder 4.
13 John Albert Johnson, "The Christian Ministry," Johnson Papers, Box 1, Folder 4.
14 Johnson, "The Christian Ministry."
15 The idea that fundamentalism was inherently regressive in nature—that is, unable and unwilling to address real problems facing the world—comes across plainly in the writings and speeches of modernists of the era. For example, Harry Emer-

son Fosdick said the following in his famous oration "Shall the Fundamentalists Win?":

> Multitudes of young men and women at this season of the year are graduating from our schools of learning, thousands of them Christians who may make us older ones ashamed by the sincerity of their devotion to God's will on earth. They are not thinking in ancient terms that leave ideas of progress out. They cannot think in those terms. There could be no greater tragedy than that the Fundamentalists should shut the door of the Christian fellowship against such.... [What is] needed, if we are to reach a happy solution of this problem, is a clear insight into the main issues of modern Christianity and a sense of penitent shame that the Christian church should be quarreling over little matters when the world is dying of great needs. If, during the war, when the nations were wrestling upon the very brink of hell and at times all seemed lost, you chanced to hear two men in an altercation about some minor matter of sectarian denominationalism, could you restrain your indignation? You said, "What can you do with folks like this who, in the face of colossal issues, play with the tiddlywinks and peccadillos of religion?" So now, when from the terrific questions of this generation one is called away by the noise of this Fundamentalist controversy, he thinks it almost unforgivable that men should tithe mint and anise and cumin, and quarrel over them, when the world is perishing for the lack of the weightier matters of the law, justice, and mercy, and faith. (422–23)

16 Johnson, "The Christian Ministry."
17 Johnson, "The Christian Ministry."
18 Johnson, "The Christian Ministry."
19 Johnson's view is obviously set in complete opposition to the modernist view, represented by the likes of Walter Rauschenbusch and Harry Emerson Fosdick, that fundamentalist theological emphases were regressive and that Christianity must adapt its theological content to fit the needs and sensibilities of the modern age. Rauschenbusch wrote in this vein that "the social gospel joins with all modern thought in the feeling that the old theology does not give us a Christ who is truly personal," and so the social gospel sought "the adjustment of the Christian message" because "if we seek to keep Christian doctrine unchanged, we shall ensure its abandonment" (*A Theology for the Social Gospel*, 7, 148). Fosdick similarly claimed that fundamentalists think "in ancient terms that leave ideas of progress out" and dismissed their "tiddlywinks and peccadillos of religion" as insufficient to address the modern world's social needs ("Shall the Fundamentalists Win?," 422–23).
20 For examination of the "prophetic" tradition in the African American church, and its relationship to racial activism during the era of Jim Crow, see David Chappell, *A Stone of Hope*. For a sociological perspective on this prophetic tradition, see the analysis of the "priestly vs. prophetic church function" dialectic in Lincoln and Mamiya, *The Black Church in the African American Experience*.

21 John Albert Johnson, "The Outlook," Johnson Papers, Box 1, Folder 4. Although the sermon manuscript is undated, several clues offer hints about when the message was delivered. While his ministry stretched from 1875 to 1928, the sermon's repeated references to the United States as "this nation" indicate that he was ministering in America at the time the sermon was preached, ruling out most of the first two decades of his ministry that were spent in Canada and Bermuda; he also served as the AME's resident bishop in South Africa from 1908 to 1916. The sermon's rhetorical treatment of the nineteenth century as a completed whole and its bookmarked opening/closing remarks indicating a concern for the African American people's future in the twentieth century ("to every century comes its own message . . ."; "the future of the negro depends . . .") seem to point toward either an early twentieth century date prior to his departure for South Africa (sometime between 1900 and 1908) or a date after his return from South Africa. What weighs slightly in favor the latter date range is that Johnson intentionally included a worldwide perspective in his concern for black advancement, noting that "the future of the negro" should entail "his ability to hold his own as a permanent factor in the world's civilization, and against the aggressions of his enemies in this country, or indeed in any country."
22 Isaac Reed Berry, "A Conversation with Christ," n.d., Berry Papers, Box 1, Folder 28.
23 Isaac Reed Berry, "Hell," n.d., Berry Papers, Box 2, Folder 80.
24 A. C. Dixon, "Evangelism: Old and New," *The Watchman* 86, no. 6 (February 11, 1904): 10–12.
25 Berry, "Hell."
26 Procter, "What Christ Teaches Concerning Future Retribution," 59, 63.
27 Berry, "Hell."
28 As noted in chapter 2, nearly one-third (twenty-eight out of ninety) of the essays in *The Fundamentals* were specifically devoted to some aspect of the doctrine of scripture, many of them engaging directly with the issue of higher biblical criticism.
29 Isaac Reed Berry, "Asleep in Gethsemane," n.d., Berry Papers, Box 1, Folder 3.
30 While Berry's sermon "An Attempt to Destroy God's World, Rejecting the Saving Word," n.d., Berry Papers, Box 1, Folder 4, is undated (as are almost all of his sermon manuscripts), several pages of this particular handwritten manuscript appear to have been written on the backsides of letters that Berry had begun to compose but left unfinished. The dates on these aborted letters range from November to December 1923, leading to the conclusion that the sermon was preached either in December 1923 or in early 1924.
31 Berry, "An Attempt to Destroy God's World."
32 Berry, "An Attempt to Destroy God's World."
33 Isaac Reed Berry, "A Lost Bible Is Found," n.d., Berry Papers, Box 2, Folder 112.
34 Berry, "Paul in Athens"; Isaac Reed Berry, "Church Unity," n.d., Berry Papers, Box 1, Folder 24.

35  Berry, "A Lost Bible Is Found."
36  Isaac Reed Berry, "Heaven's Great Magnet," n.d., Berry Papers, Box 2, Folder 79.
37  Isaac Reed Berry, "God's One Essential for Salvation," n.d., Berry Papers, Box 1, Folder 69.
38  Matthew 7:21–23 reads: "Not everyone who says to me, 'Lord, Lord,' will enter the kingdom of heaven, but the one who does the will of my Father who is in heaven. On that day many will say to me, 'Lord, Lord, did we not prophesy in your name, and cast out demons in your name, and do many mighty works in your name?' And then will I declare to them, 'I never knew you; depart from me, you workers of lawlessness'" (ESV).
39  Berry, "God's One Essential for Salvation."
40  Berry, "God's One Essential for Salvation."
41  The very fact that Berry used the somewhat technical theological term "propitiation" throughout his sermon without stopping to explain its meaning indicates that substitutionary atonement (and various corollaries) was a sufficiently common theme in his pulpit ministry as to be assumed as part of the general congregational knowledge.
42  Isaac Reed Berry, "The Brotherhood of Man," n.d., Berry Papers, Box 1, Folder 8.
43  Berry, "The Brotherhood of Man"; Isaac Reed Berry, "1 Corinthians 2:2," n.d., Berry Papers, Box 1, Folder 30.
44  Berry, "The Brotherhood of Man"; Berry, "Heaven's Great Magnet." In numerous other sermonic contexts as well Berry affirmed that the church's preeminent mission was to preach that "Christ died to save men from their sins," to "evangelize the world," to "save men and to furnish an earthly spiritual home for the people of God," and the like. See Isaac Reed Berry, "The Inevitability of God's Law, or a Terrible Penalty," n.d., Berry Papers, Box 2, Folder 86; Isaac Reed Berry, "Holy War," n.d., Berry Papers, Box 2, Folder 82.
45  Berry, "The Brotherhood of Man."
46  Interracial sex had been a longstanding point of agitation for the white ruling elite dating back to the colonial era. Kathleen Brown argues that sexual regulation was closely tied to the social construction of racial categories in colonial Virginia, as black sexuality was imbued with "the power to taint" (*Good Wives, Nasty Wenches, and Anxious Patriarchs*, chap. 6). Winthrop Jordan likewise discusses the construction of racial-sexual categories in colonial America based on power dynamics and psychological impulses (*The White Man's Burden*, chap. 4).
47  Berry, "The Brotherhood of Man."
48  The testimony of Isaac Berry and others in this chapter challenges the common assumption that a theological emphasis on "otherworldly" elements of Christianity necessarily indicates a propensity toward social accommodation rather than resistance. In this respect, this chapter aligns with the sociological research of Allison Calhoun-Brown, who has shown in "While Marching to Zion" that in modern black churches an otherworldly orientation does not depress racial empowerment, but rather manifests in different *types* of racial activism. Similarly,

Sandra L. Barnes and Oluchi Nwosu have argued in "Black Church Electoral and Protest Politics" that even as religious conservatives and religious progressives within today's black community disagree on social issues such as gay marriage, both sides rhetorically align themselves with the resistance/protest tradition while categorizing their opponents as accommodationists. These scholars' conclusions about modern black churches also accord with the testimony of the early-twentieth century voices catalogued here.

49 Isaac Reed Berry, "The Fool in Christ," n.d., Berry Papers, Box 1, Folder 56.
50 Isaac Reed Berry, "Church Unity," n.d., Berry Papers, Box 1, Folder 24.
51 Berry, "Heaven's Great Magnet."
52 Isaac Reed Berry, "Taking God at His Word," n.d., Berry Papers, Box 3, Folder 194.
53 C. S. Lewis's formulation of the trilemma argument can be found in his book *Mere Christianity*.
54 For consideration of "gospel hip-hop" in the context of interracial engagement and cross-cultural interactions, see Sinitiere, "Interracialism and American Christianity," 149–52.

Relative to the phenomenon of "gospel hip-hop," Berry's content here actually compares very favorably to the expressions offered by some Reformed artists in the genre. In particular, Berry's litany of Christ in the Old Testament is very similar to the formulation of the same theme by the artist Result in his track titled "Show Me," from his 2016 album *The Elementology* (Columbus, GA: Wrath and Grace Productions).

55 Isaac Reed Berry, "The Question of the Centuries," n.d., Berry Papers, Box 3, Folder 159; Isaac Reed Berry, "The Cost of Being Loyal to Christ," n.d., Berry Papers, Box 1, Folder 31.
56 Isaac Reed Berry, "Blessedness in Sight," n.d., Berry Papers, Box 1, Folder 6.
57 Berry, "Blessedness in Sight."
58 Berry, "Blessedness in Sight."
59 Berry, "Blessedness in Sight"; Williams, *Torchbearers of Democracy*, esp. chap. 7.
60 Horace, "*Crowned with Glory and Honor*," 38, 53–54, 57, 66.
61 Noted historian Milton Sernett characterizes L. K. Williams as a "progressive" minister in his primary source reader's introduction to one of Williams's essays. The fact that as notable a scholarly voice as Sernett's would do so illustrates the importance of distinguishing between theological conservatism and social or political conservatism. Sernett identifies Williams as a wholesale "progressive" minister on the basis of his commitment to social activism in the community, thus implicitly reinforcing the idea that progressive social or political attitudes stood indelibly apart from (or even contrary to) conservative attitudes on theology (*African American Religious History*, 372). In this paradigm, then, L. K. Williams is flatly considered to be a member of the "progressive clergy" due to his social outlook. Yet Williams subverts this assumption in that he was a conservative in his theology (even, according to his 1925 NBC presidential address, a fundamentalist), but a progressive challenger to the social status quo in some of his political

and social convictions, particularly with respect to race. This important nuance is lost when social or political tendencies are considered sufficient grounds for applying the wholesale label of "progressive clergy." Thus, conjoining or conflating the spectrum of theological conservatism/progressivism with that of political conservatism/progressivism serves to obscure as much as it illumines; to classify Williams flatly as a progressive minister—a categorization that would easily include any number of theological liberals and modernists against whom he was militating in his 1925 convention address—seems to unnecessarily and unwisely discount the significance of theological conviction on its own terms.

62 "The Third Annual Address of Dr. L. K. Williams, President," 14–15.
63 "The Third Annual Address," 14.
64 The biblical text reads as follows: "This charge I entrust to you, Timothy, my child, in accordance with the prophecies previously made about you, that by them you may wage the good warfare, holding faith and a good conscience. By rejecting this, some have made shipwreck of their faith, among whom are Hymenaeus and Alexander, whom I have handed over to Satan that they may learn not to blaspheme" (1 Timothy 1:18–20, ESV). The intimate connections in this passage between the rejection of apostolic doctrine, blasphemy, the "shipwreck" of one's faith, and being given over to Satan are unmistakable, as L. K. Williams himself undoubtedly knew when he selected his allusion to this particular text.
65 "The Third Annual Address," 14.
66 "The Third Annual Address," 15.
67 It seems fitting that Williams included E. C. Morris alongside Charles Spurgeon in his list. As Williams's predecessor in the convention presidency, Morris also appeared to hold Spurgeon in high regard, even invoking him as a shining example of traditional Baptist doctrine and heritage during his own presidential convention address in 1899 (*Sermons, Addresses and Reminiscences*, 102).

  Black Baptist evangelist I. Benjamin Toliver organized Mt. Aria Baptist Church (later First Baptist Church) in Taylor, Texas, in 1886. L. K. Williams, whose youth and young adulthood were spent mainly in Texas, served as the second pastor of Mt. Aria Baptist (Williamson County Historical Commission, "Historical Marker: First Baptist Church," accessed May 1, 2019, www.wilcohistory.org).
68 "The Third Annual Address," 15.
69 "The Third Annual Address," 15.
70 This element of Williams's speech receives more consideration in chapter 5. His positioning of the NBC as an avenue for political pressure reflects Evelyn Brooks Higginbotham's description of the denomination as a "social space in which to critique openly the United States government, its laws, and its institutions" (*Righteous Discontent*, 12).
71 "The Third Annual Address," 15–16. Williams has at times been labeled as a proponent of the social gospel, but his rather explicit criticism of the social gospel paradigm here, in addition to his affirmation of the fundamentalist posi-

tion, seems to belie such a categorization. For example, Gayraud Wilmore lists Williams as a social gospel exponent alongside Reverdy C. Ransom and Adam Clayton Powell (*Black Religion and Black Radicalism*, 160–61), as do Anne Pinn and Anthony Pinn in their *Fortress Introduction to Black Church History* (127).

72 Williams, "Effects of Urbanization on Religious Life," 374.

73 Williams's formulation of "passionately human, but no less divine" inspired the title of Wallace Best's book about Chicago's "new sacred order" brought on by the Great Migration. Best rightly identifies Williams's phrase as indicating the sacredness of religious work in the world. Best links the phrase to the historic Trinitarian doctrine of *homoousios*, that God the Son is "of the same nature" as God the Father (*Passionately Human, No Less Divine*, 18).

Yet theologically, Williams's formulation seems to allude more directly to the doctrine of the hypostatic union—that two distinct natures, one fully human and one fully divine, are united in the single person of Jesus Christ. Just as the full divinity of Christ in no way detracted from his full humanity but rather was united with it, so the spiritual mission of the Christian ministry does not detract from the church's social significance but rather upholds it. Just as Christ is "fully human and fully divine," so Williams saw the church's mission as being "passionately human, but no less divine."

74 Recall, for example, the argument offered by the *Norfolk Journal and Guide* editorialist, which opens chapter 1, that the fundamentalist faith "has brought [the race] thus far, and the belief is general that it is sufficient to carry us further in the enlargement of higher and better things in human life and living.... Yes, the Afro-American people are Fundamentalists, and they can give a reason for the faith that is in them by pointing to what they have become in this free Nation from what they began in the days of the Colonies" ("Our Group Are Fundamentalists in Religion"). This line of argument is substantially congruent with Williams's approach here in September 1925, positing a direct connection between fundamentalist fidelity and racial advancement (both past and future).

75 "The Third Annual Address," 14–15.

76 "The Third Annual Address," 3.

77 For an analysis of the widespread drive among African Americans for full participation in the American democratic identity during and immediately after World War I, see Williams, *Torchbearers of Democracy*. Other works covering later periods likewise consider similar themes regarding Americanism and military conflicts; they include Dudziak, *Cold War Civil Rights*, which considers civil rights advances in the context of America's foreign image during the Cold War, and Phillips's *War! What Is It Good For?*, which contrasts the perspectives of elite and working-class blacks regarding the utility of military service as a means of staking claim to the full rights of American citizenship. With less of a military focus, William Tuttle's *Race Riot* similarly includes the drive for democratic participation and respect as one of several factors in the July 1919 Chicago race riot.

78 "The Third Annual Address," 15.

## CHAPTER 4. RELIGIOUS EDUCATION AND INTERRACIAL COOPERATION

1. Ford Porter to R. W. Hailey, October 21, 1936, The Southern Baptist Commission on the American Baptist Seminary Records, AR 630, Box 5, Folder 39, Southern Baptist Historical Library and Archives, Nashville, TN (hereafter cited as Commission on ABTS Records).
2. While institutional separatism was not absolutely essential to the fundamentalist perspective (Finn, "The Development of Baptist Fundamentalism in the South"), there was undeniably a separatist bent among many white fundamentalist leaders and institutions, which was not so clearly mirrored among African Americans. Figures such as George Biddle, John Albert Johnson, or Isaac Berry evinced little desire to separate from their denominational bodies even when significant modernist perspectives were being advanced by their fellow religionists.
3. Miller, "The Construction of a Black Fundamentalist Worldview," 718–19.
4. The idea of "interracial cooperation" here describes conscious efforts to engage in joint endeavors across racial lines that entail not only cultural exchange, but also deliberate cooperation, purposeful fellowship, and a substantial distribution of authority and control between black and white participants. This falls somewhere between Paul Harvey's categories of "racial interchange" and "Christian interracialism" in his analysis of southern religious-racial development (*Freedom's Coming*, 2–3). Harvey's concept of "racial interchange" describes "the exchange of southern religious cultures between white and black believers," particularly in expressions of "folk culture" such as music or oratorical style. The interracial cooperation surrounding ABTS involved some of this, but also pointedly built formal, cooperative institutional connections between the nation's largest white and black Baptist denominations. Harvey's "Christian interracialism" entails "self-consciously political efforts to undermine the system of southern racial hierarchy"; the aims of the ABTS project, on the other hand, were more theological than political, and though not designed to eliminate the South's racial system wholesale, it did offer implicit (and occasionally explicit) theological challenges to certain limited elements of the Jim Crow order—even to the point, as we will see later, of prompting one prominent Southern Baptist to suggest admitting black graduates of ABTS to a white Southern Baptist seminary. In this respect, the "interracial cooperation" of the ABTS project aligns more with Phillip Sinitiere's slightly broader definition of Christian interracialism as "constructive social interactions and collaboration across racial and ethnic boundaries—existential engagement inspired by religious ideals and religious teachings—in the interest of undercutting sanctioned divisions" ("Interracialism and American Christianity," 136).
5. Miller, "The Construction of a Black Fundamentalist Worldview," 719.
6. Miller, "The Construction of a Black Fundamentalist Worldview," 719–24. For Miller's analysis of the Southern Bible Institute, see 719–21; for his analysis of Carver Bible Institute, see 721–24.

7   Another locus for interracial cooperation in the late-nineteenth and early-twentieth century was between certain southern black and northern white Baptist women who "worked in a cooperative fashion rare for the times," thereby showing that "divergent motives did not preclude mutual goals" so long as "allegiances and interests overlapped sufficiently to create common ground on which to counter the effects of racial oppression" (Higginbotham, *Righteous Discontent*, 13, 90). This description might also apply in some measure to the ATBS project in general, as well as to the seminary's Women's Auxiliary.
8   Harvey, *Redeeming the South*, 169, 185.
9   Horace, *"Crowned with Glory and Honor,"* 107.
10  Mary Beth Swetnam Mathews's *Doctrine and Race* also mentions ABTS once (169), in an endnote concerning the National Baptist split.
11  "Baptist Theological Seminary for Negroes Dedicated Sunday," *Nashville Banner*, September 15, 1924, Commission on ABTS Records, AR 630, Box 5, Folder 23.
12  A. M. Townsend, "Some Observations on the History of the American Baptist Theological Seminary," April 11, 1951, 1, Commission on ABTS Records, AR 630, Box 3, Folder 24; L. S. Sedberry, "Report on the American Baptist Theological Seminary," n.d., 1, Commission on ABTS Records, AR 630, Box 6, Folder 37.
13  "Minutes of a Joint Meeting of the Two Committees of the Southern Baptist Convention and the National Baptist Convention," September 18, 1913, Commission on ABTS Records, AR 630, Box 1, Folder 1.
14  "Negro Theological Education: Southern Baptist Attitude and Actions, 1913–1938," 4–9, Commission on ABTS Records, AR 630, Box 6, Folder 25.
15  Lillian Horace offers a brief insider's explanation of the National Baptist split and the circumstances surrounding the publishing house dispute (*"Crowned With Glory and Honor,"* 174–75). Evelyn Brooks Higginbotham likewise attributes the National Baptist split to the controversy surrounding the publishing board (*Righteous Discontent*, 164). Mary Beth Swetnam Mathews offers a possible doctrinal component to the denominational split in addition to the commonly cited conflict over the publishing house. Mathews posits that the future trajectory of both bodies' denominational newspapers indicates a theological divide between the more conservative Unincorporated group and the more progressive Incorporated group, though she acknowledges that this is essentially suppositional in nature, since "a clear dichotomy between the two conventions . . . is impossible to identify or defend " (*Doctrine and Race*, 43–44). As we have seen and will continue to see, while the incorporated body certainly included a variety of theological perspectives, it did contain its own contingent of doctrinal fundamentalists.
16  A. M. Townsend to E. Y. Mullins, January 4, 1915, Commission on ABTS Records, AR 630, Box 1, Folder 1.
17  "Negro Theological Education," 10, Commission on ABTS Records, AR 630, Box 6, Folder 25.
18  "Negro Theological Education," 13–14; minutes of board of directors meeting, June 25, 1924, Commission on ABTS Records, AR 630, Box 1, Folder 1.

19 "Minutes of a Joint Meeting of the Two Committees of the Southern Baptist Convention and the National Baptist Convention," September 18, 1913, Commission on ABTS Records, AR 630, Box 1, Folder 1.
20 Largely congruent with A. M. Townsend's 1915 evaluation that ABTS represented "the first effort made by our White brethren of the South toward the education of our Negro Ministry," W. E. B. Du Bois had noted in 1903 that friction often arose between white and black churches on the issue of interracial cooperation because "the white Baptist mission societies have failed to understand the Negro desire for home rule and autonomy, and the Negro recipients have not fully appreciated the help they have received from without" (*The Negro Church*, 153). The structure of the ABTS governing boards, with the numerical advantage for National Baptists, appears to be a step in the direction of white Baptists acknowledging black Baptists' desire for "home rule and autonomy" amidst interracial cooperative efforts.
21 Cooks, "The Historical Development and Future of the Southern Bible Institute," 28–29; Cooks, "The History and Future of the Southern Bible Institute," 152–53.
22 Miller, "The Construction of a Black Fundamentalist Worldview," 721–24.
23 Busto, *King Tiger*, 80.
24 E. P. Alldredge, "The American Baptist Theological Seminary, 1934," 10, Commission on ABTS Records, AR 630, Box 5, Folder 25.
25 J. H. Garnett, Report on the 12th year of operation of the American Baptist Theological Seminary, 1936, Commission on ABTS Records, AR 630, Box 5, Folder 27.
26 J. H. Garnett to E. P. Alldredge, June 18, 1934, Commission on ABTS Records, AR 630, Box 5, Folder 25.
27 "Report of the Joint Commission Meeting," July 6, 1921, Commission on ABTS Records, AR 630, Box 3, Folder 24.
28 "O. L. Hailey: By a Lifelong Acquaintance," Una Roberts Lawrence Collection, AR 631, Box 3, Folder 4, Southern Baptist Historical Library and Archives, Nashville, TN (hereafter cited as Lawrence Collection); Willie May Hall to a cousin (unnamed), Lawrence Collection, AR 631, Box 3, Folder 4.
29 Willie May Hall to a cousin (unnamed).
30 Harvey, *Redeeming the South*, 247.
31 Willie May Hall to a cousin (unnamed).
32 Minutes of board of directors meeting, April 11, 1928, Commission on ABTS Records, AR 630, Box 1, Folder 3.
33 "A Tribute to Dr. O. L. Hailey," *National Baptist Voice*, n.d., Commission on ABTS Records, AR 630, Box 5, Folder 25.
34 Willie May Hall to a cousin (unnamed).
35 Curtis Evans has convincingly demonstrated that the idea that African Americans possess a "natural genius for religion," traceable to the "romantic racialism" of the antebellum era, was rooted in an assumption of black intellectual inferiority. Even as abolitionists featured the portrait of "naturally religious" Africans in their antislavery polemics, this "naturally" superior capacity for "religious feeling" and

"emotion" was expressly contrasted with Anglo-Saxons' "naturally" superior intellectual capacity (*The Burden of Black Religion*, 36–37).
36   O. L. Hailey, "A Plan of Cooperation between the Southern Baptist Convention and the National Baptist Convention," minutes of board of directors meeting, April 11, 1928, Commission on ABTS Records, AR 630, Box 1, Folder 3.
37   As we will see, nearly two decades later the chairman of the Southern Baptist Commission on the seminary would tentatively suggest that Southern Baptist Theological Seminary begin to admit black graduates of ABTS as a hedge against modernist incursions into the black community.
38   Hailey, "A Plan of Cooperation." The intimate connection between the presentation of African Americans as "naturally religious" and the assumption of black intellectual inferiority is described in Evans's *The Burden of Black Religion*.
39   Townsend to Mullins, January 4, 1915. The Negro Baptist Ministers' Conference's conception of ABTS as a unique venture accords well with James Melvin Washington's evaluation of the circumstances that led, in part, to the founding of the National Baptist Convention as a racially and ecclesiastically separate body in 1895: "There were few white Baptist leaders who were open enough to listen to black views, and moderate enough to share social power wherever possible" (*Frustrated Fellowship*, 159).
40   "Report of the Joint Commission Meeting," July 6, 1921, Commission on ABTS Records, AR 630, Box 3, Folder 24.
41   For a historical consideration of racial uplift as a strategy for race advancement in the twentieth century, see Gaines, *Uplifting the Race*. On uplift relative to commercial culture and leisure activities such as music, see Martin, *Preaching on Wax*, 42–48.
42   Explicating the concept of "scientific racism," Matthew Frye Jacobson provides a compelling analysis of the ways in which theories of racial hierarchy, evolutionism, and eugenics served as popular scientific justifications for racist and xenophobic attitudes in the early twentieth century (*Barbarian Virtues*, esp. chap. 4). For analysis of how the scientific racism of the late-nineteenth and early twentieth century related to the common characterization of black religion as "emotional" and "sensual," see Evans, *The Burden of Black Religion*, 121–35.
43   Sutton E. Griggs to the Southern Baptist Convention, 122. Emphases in the original. For background and analysis of the Chicago race riots of 1919, see Tuttle, *Race Riot*; for a broader evaluation of the violence and rioting during the Red Summer of 1919, see Williams, *Torchbearers of Democracy*, esp. chap. 6.
44   Martin, *Preaching on Wax*, 129.
45   Much of the text of Griggs's letter, in both outlook and language, is reminiscent of Booker T. Washington's "Atlanta Compromise" address in which he famously declared, "In all things that are purely social we can be as separate as the fingers, yet one as the hand in all things essential to mutual progress." Griggs's hope that an educated black clergy would "induce a spirit of love" in all men and that it would ensure "no unjust laws, nor unjust administration of laws" recalls Washington's

hope that African Americans being "prepared for the exercise of these privileges [of the law]" might ultimately bring about a "higher good ... in a blotting out of sectional differences and racial animosities and suspicions, in a determination to administer absolute justice, in a willing obedience among all classes to the mandates of law" (Harlan, *The Booker T. Washington Papers*, 3:583–87).

46 Sutton E. Griggs to the Southern Baptist Convention, 122–23.
47 W. H. Davenport, "Bishop L. W. Kyles Applauded While Delivering Sentiment of Bishops to Delegates," *Star of Zion*, May 15, 1924, 1.
48 E. W. D. Isaac to I. J. Van Ness, April 2, 1928, I. J. Van Ness Papers, AR 795-112, Box 16, Folder 6, Southern Baptist Historical Library and Archives, Nashville, TN.
49 "Report of the Commission on the Negro Theological Seminary," *Annual of the Southern Baptist Convention 1920*, 119.
50 E. P. Alldredge to R. W. Riley, April 9, 1949, Commission on ABTS Records, AR 630, Box 3, Folder 27.
51 Finn, "The Development of Baptist Fundamentalism," 143–44.
52 In 1921, just three years prior to the formulation of the ABTS Confession of Faith, Carter G. Woodson devoted a chapter of his *History of the Negro Church* to reflections on the differences between "conservatives" and "progressives" among black Christians. Theologically, Woodson's dichotomy contrasted the conservative's commitment to "the crude notions of Biblical interpretation [and] the grotesque vision of the hereafter" with the progressive's "developed mind [which] found itself unwillingly at war with such extravagant claims and seeking a hearing for a new idea." Socially, this contrast included the conservative's intellectual weakness and hostility toward education over against the progressive's commitment to education on the basis that "there can be little revelation of God where there is arrested mental development" (178–79). ABTS seems to complicate this paradigm. While the school's confession affirmed traditional doctrines about hell and Satan, which presumably fit into Woodson's categorization of conservatives' "grotesque vision of the hereafter," in contrast to progressives' search for "a new idea" in theology, this conservative theology did not manifest in hostility toward education; on the contrary, the very existence of ABTS was based on the idea that ministerial education should be more affordable and accessible to black Baptist clergymen.
53 E. P. Alldredge to A. D. Muse, January 8, 1947, Commission on ABTS Records, AR 630, Box 6, Folder 11.
54 Garrett, *Baptist Theology*, 436.
55 "Confession of Faith Adopted by the American Baptist Theological Seminary, September 13, 1924," Commission on ABTS Records, AR 630, Box 3, Folder 27; "NOBTS Articles of Religious Belief."
56 E. P. Alldredge to A. D. Muse, January 8, 1947.
57 "1925 Baptist Faith and Message Statement of the Southern Baptist Convention."
58 Ashworth, "The Fundamentalist Movement among the Baptists," 627–30. For further examination of the rise of theological liberalism in the Northern Baptist Convention, including the fundamentalists' years-long (yet ill-fated) push for the

Northern Baptists to adopt a confessional standard, see Straub, *The Making of a Battle Royal*.

59 "Confession of Faith"; "1925 Baptist Faith and Message Statement."
60 "The Third Annual Address of Dr. L. K. Williams, President," 14.
61 Minutes of board of directors meeting, March 12, 1924, Commission on ABTS Records, AR 630, Box 1, Folder 1; Minutes of board of directors meeting, June 25, 1924, Commission on ABTS Records, AR 630, Box 1, Folder 1.
62 L. G. Jordan to E. P. Alldredge, August 9, 1938, Commission on ABTS Records, AR 630, Box 5, Folder 58.
63 E. P. Alldredge, "The Seminary Singers," 1936, Commission on ABTS Records, AR 630, Box 5, Folder 27; J. H. Garnett, "High Points in the Operation of the American Bapt. Theological Seminary, 1936-37," Commission on ABTS Records, AR 630, Box 5, Folder 28.
64 Gust E. Carlson to R. W. Hailey, October 20, 1936, Commission on ABTS Records, AR 630, Box 5, Folder 39.
65 "History of First Baptist Church of Princeton, Indiana." Various of Ford Porter's own fundamentalist theological convictions—including his views on sin, salvation, substitutionary atonement, and the literal resurrection—are evident in "God's Simple Plan for Salvation," the gospel tract that he authored in 1933 (accessed January 21, 2020, www.godssimpleplan.org).
66 Ford Porter to R. W. Hailey, October 21, 1936.
67 Mathews, *Doctrine and Race*.
68 L. K. Williams to E. P. Alldredge, March 3, 1930, Commission on ABTS Records, AR 630, Box 7, Folder 43.
69 Mathews, *Doctrine and Race*, 66, 144–45.
70 Yenser, *Who's Who in Colored America*, 198.
71 Minutes of board of directors meeting, April 8, 1925, Commission on ABTS Records, AR 630, Box 1, Folder 1; minutes of executive committee meeting, October 28, 1927, Commission on ABTS Records, AR 630, Box 1, Folder 66.
72 J. H. Garnett to the board of directors, November 7, 1934, Commission on ABTS Records, AR 630, Box 1, Folder 70.
73 Alldredge, "The American Baptist Theological Seminary, 1934"; E. P. Alldredge, Report on the American Baptist Theological Seminary, 1935, Commission on ABTS Records, AR 630, Box 5, Folder 26.
74 J. H. Garnett, Address to the Southeastern Regional Meeting of the National Baptist Convention, February 20, 1936, Commission on ABTS Records, AR 630, Box 5, Folder 27.
75 Wills, *Southern Baptist Theological Seminary*, 275.
76 Alldredge, "The American Baptist Theological Seminary, 1934," 7.
77 Garnett, Address.
78 "Dr. Townsend Finally Defeats Editor Barbour," *National Baptist Voice* 18, no. 32 (1934).
79 J. H. Garnett to E. P. Alldredge, June 18, 1934.

80 J. Pius Barbour, "Is There Religious Freedom at Our Seminary?" *National Baptist Voice*, December 1, 1945, Commission on ABTS Records, AR 630, Box 7, Folder 34.
81 E. P. Alldredge, "Editor Barbour Makes a Bad Suggestion," Commission on ABTS Records, AR 630, Box 7, Folder 34.
82 J. Pius Barbour to E. P. Alldredge, December 27, 1945, Commission on ABTS Records, AR 630, Box 7, Folder 34.
83 D. V. Jemison to E. P. Alldredge, December 18, 1945, Commission on ABTS Records, AR 630, Box 7, Folder 34.
84 D. V. Jemison to E. P. Alldredge, January 5, 1946, Commission on ABTS Records, AR 630, Box 7, Folder 34.
85 E. P. Alldredge to A. D. Muse, January 8, 1947 (emphasis in the original); Porter Routh to L. S. Sedberry, February 28, 1949, Commission on ABTS Records, AR 630, Box 3, Folder 27.
86 E. P. Alldredge to Professor J. J. McNeil, April 9, 1941, Commission on ABTS Records, AR 630, Box 6, Folder 11.
87 E. P. Alldredge to Mrs. C. H. Ray, July 16, 1942, Commission on ABTS Records, AR 630, Box 6, Folder 43.
88 E. P. Alldredge to Ryland Knight, June 2, 1942, Commission on ABTS Records, AR 630, Box 6, Folder 7.
89 J. M. Nabrit, "A Response to a Vote of Thanks for the Southern Baptist Convention," n.d., Commission on ABTS Records, AR 630, Box 6, Folder 19.
90 E. P. Alldredge to A. M. Townsend, October 13, 1943, Commission on ABTS Records, AR 630, Box 7, Folder 32. For a brief summary of Southern Seminary's navigation of questions relating to segregation and integration in the middle decades of the twentieth century, see Wills, *Southern Baptist Theological Seminary*, 413–17. For a broader consideration of the evolving ideas about race and social equality among postwar white evangelicals, see Mullin, "Neoevangelicalism and the Problem of Race in Postwar America."
91 Erdman, "The Church and Socialism," 97–108; Watt, "Fundamentalists of the 1920s and 1930s," 31.
92 J. M. Nabrit, "The Need of a Trained Leadership for Negroes," *Home and Foreign Fields*, July 1937, Commission on ABTS Records, AR 630, Box 2, Folder 66.
93 Ryland Knight, "Southern Baptists and the Negro," n.d., Commission on ABTS Records, AR 630, Box 2, Folder 66.
94 On fundamentalist concerns about race in connection with Catholicism, see Mathews, *Doctrine and Race*; Hankins, *God's Rascal*, esp. chap. 9. On the Catholic Church's relationship with African Americans in the urban North, including the competing Catholic traditions of theological interracialism and residential segregation, see McGreevy, *Parish Boundaries*. On Catholic racialization and interracialism, including considerations of the doctrine of the mystical body of Christ in race relations, see Johnson, *One in Christ*; Johnson, "Healing the Mystical Body." On the development of a "black Catholic" identity during the mid-twentieth

century—that is, a distinctively "black" way of being Catholic—see Cressler, *Authentically Black and Truly Catholic*.
95 Laws, "The Negro and Roman Catholicism," 265.
96 Henry Alford Porter, "Christianity and Race," n.d., Lawrence Collection, AR 631, Box 1, Folder 9.
97 E. P. Alldredge to E. A. Pickup, March 4, 1935, Commission on ABTS Records, AR 630, Box 5, Folder 26; E. P. Alldredge, "To Legalize Interracial Marriage," n.d., Commission on ABTS Records, AR 630, Box 5, Folder 53. Alldredge offers a complementary perspective to that advanced by scholars such as William Glass, who argues that southern fundamentalists used racial topics such as intermarriage as examples of "modernist" threats in order to rally southern white support (*Strangers in Zion*). Alldredge's words and actions indicate that the modernist and Catholic adoption of relatively progressive racial stances also prompted some southern fundamentalists to reach out to blacks in order to promote a better conservative theological consensus and eliminate potential modernist or Catholic footholds in the South.
98 Malry and his fellow Seminary Singers, as noted earlier, were welcomed to perform and give messages in such avowedly fundamentalist churches as Ford Porter's First Baptist Church of Princeton, Indiana. Given the church's identity as a separatist fundamentalist congregation (having rejected American Baptist missionaries in favor of independent Baptist missionaries due to disputes over the fundamentals), Porter's expression of theological congruence with the Singers and the seminary seems to be a point in favor of the school's early fundamentalist bona fides.
99 Illie E. Malry to E. P. Alldredge, April 21, 1937, Commission on ABTS Records, AR 630, Box 6, Folder 11. Malry's confrontation with life in the urban north—specifically Chicago—was also troubling to him due to the presence of new non-Christian movements that were taking root in portions of the black community. In the same letter to Alldredge, he expressed concern that "Some of my people call themselfs [sic] MOSLEMS, being taught ISLAM, by a HINDU somewhere in INDIA. It is a shame for some of our people to be led that way." Malry's reference to India indicates that he was likely alluding to the Ahmadiyya Movement, which according to historian Richard Brent Turner was "until the mid-1950s . . . arguably the most influential community in African-American Islam" (*Islam in the African-American Experience*, 138). Other alternative religious movements were also making inroads in the black community during this era, including Islamic-based groups such as the Moorish Science Temple of America and the Nation of Islam. Historian Judith Weisenfeld helpfully explores these two groups, as well as the Ethiopian Hebrew movement and Father Divine's Peace Mission Movement, as conveyors of new "religio-racial identities" that allowed African Americans to reconceptualize their origins, history, and corporate future amid the social and religious changes brought on by the Great Migration (*New World A-Coming*).

## CHAPTER 5. CONTESTED IDENTITIES

1. Isaac Reed Berry, "July 4, 1931," Berry Papers, Box 2, Folder 99.
2. The phrase "long civil rights movement," intended to offer a new perspective on the foundations of the civil rights movement extending back into the 1930s, was coined by Jacquelyn Dowd Hall in her landmark article "The Long Civil Rights Movement and the Political Uses of the Past." While Hall's articulation of the "long civil rights" thesis constituted a historiographical flashpoint, earlier historians also explored elements of civil rights in these earlier decades. See, for example, Sitkoff, *A New Deal For Blacks*; Egerton, *Speak Now against the Day*. For a brief overview of historiography following on Dowd's "long civil rights" thesis, see Salmond, "'The Long and the Short of It.'"

    For works touching on the propensity of African Americans to use themes of American democracy, American political participation, and American military service in advancing the cause of black civil rights, see Williams, *Torchbearers of Democracy*; Tuttle, *Race Riot*; Phillips, *War! What Is It Good For?*; Leiker, *Racial Borders*; Christian, *Black Soldiers in Jim Crow Texas*.
3. Examples of biblical literalism, creationism, evolution, and intellectual credibility as important elements in the African American community's discussions of fundamentalism can be found in chapter 1.
4. "American Intolerance and Menace of a State Church," *Norfolk Journal and Guide*, September 11, 1926, 12.
5. "Our Group Are Fundamentalists in Religion."
6. For consideration of the terminology of "old-time religion" in relation to Protestant fundamentalism in the black community, see chapter 1.
7. John Albert Johnson, "Faith and Intellect as Factors in Progress," n.d., Johnson Papers, Box 1, Folder 4; Johnson, "The Outlook."
8. Moran, *American Genesis*, 88. See also Lerone Martin's examination of the "new black intelligentsia" (*Preaching on Wax*, 128–31).
9. Twiss, "Ernest Rice McKinney."
10. Ernest Rice McKinney, "This Week: Skeptics, Agnostics, Atheists, Infidels and Free Thinkers," *Broad Ax* (Chicago), August 15, 1925, 2.
11. Ernest Rice McKinney, "This Week," *New York Amsterdam News*, April 15, 1925, 9.
12. George A. Singleton, "Religion Worth Having," *Chicago Defender*, October 15, 1927, A2.
13. "The Week," *Chicago Defender*, April 30, 1932, 1, col. 2.
14. Johnson, "The Outlook."
15. Johnson, "The Outlook."
16. Berry, "1 Corinthians 2:2."
17. Berry, "The Inevitability of God's Law."
18. Isaac Reed Berry, "The Downfall of Judah—Sin Brings Ruin," n.d., Berry Papers, Box 1, Folder 40. Though undated (as the vast majority of Berry's sermon manuscripts were), one page of this sermon manuscript was written on the backside of

a scrapped draft of a letter dated October 26, 1923, placing the likely date of this sermon shortly thereafter.

19   Isaac Reed Berry, "A Priceless Privilege," n.d., Berry Papers, Box 3, Folder 155. While this sermon is not precisely dated, it was likely delivered in the early 1930s since Berry repeatedly referenced the stock market crash of 1929 as an event of recent history and also discussed Roger Babson's September 1929 prediction of the impending crash as a warning that the nation should have heeded.

20   Berry, "A Priceless Privilege." In this context, Berry also draws an interesting parallel between the bloodshed of American soldiers who fought for freedom and the holy, redemptive blood shed by Christ:

> About 16 years ago I saw that bell [the Liberty Bell], and that day I saw a young sailor in the glory of his manhood drop to one knee before that bell, then he arose and bent over and kissed it. And why? Because that was the Liberty Bell which, on that memorable day when the forefathers signed the Declaration of Independence, rang out the glad tidings to the waiting people. For and in the name of that liberty which cost the blood, the blood of noble heroes, every true American is glad to pay his tribute. And let us remember that our Christian as well as our civil liberty was first purchased with the priceless blood of the Divine Son of God.

Liberty *first* purchased by the blood of Christ also later cost the blood of those faithful soldiers who were, in a sense, emulating Christ's sacrifice.

This perspective echoes a sentiment from certain military circles in the World War I era, which cast the American soldier's role as that of a Christ-figure—a theme that historian Jonathan Ebel has discussed as being stoked in the pages of the American military newspaper *Stars and Stripes*: "*The Stars and Stripes* also described the American soldier as an imitator of Christ. Images, articles, and poems emphasized the Christ-likeness of soldiers' sufferings and the atoning regenerative effects of their spilled blood. *The Stars and Stripes'* motives in connecting the American soldier to Christ are far clearer than those of the soldiers themselves. The staff of the paper sought to valorize soldiers and to elevate them above all temporal and, it seems, all eternal critiques" (Ebel, *Faith in the Fight*, 92).

21   Berry, "July 4, 1931."
22   Berry, "July 4, 1931."
23   Berry, "July 4, 1931." Woodward, *Origins of the New South*, 206. On the sharecropping and tenant-farming system and its role in controlling black labor, see Painter, *Exodusters*, chap. 5; Grossman, *Land of Hope*, 26–28; Cohen, *At Freedom's Edge*, 18–22. C. Vann Woodward also addresses the emergence and development of the Jim Crow system, both in *Origins of the New South* and *The Strange Career of Jim Crow*. See also Hahn, *A Nation Under Our Feet*, 366–67, 440–51.
24   Berry, "July 4, 1931."
25   Berry, "God's One Essential For Salvation."
26   Berry, "A Priceless Privilege"; Berry, "July 4, 1931."

27 Berry, "July 4, 1931."
28 For discussion of Edward Franklin Williams's positive instruction on fundamentalist doctrines and his polemics against modernist liberalism, see chapters 2 and 3, respectively. While Williams did not use the term "fundamentalist" to describe himself (the term was not coined until 1920), his ministry did extend into the period after the publication of *The Fundamentals*, and he was undoubtedly aware of the controversy between theological conservatives and liberals that would ultimately come to be labeled the "fundamentalist-modernist controversy." For instance, a colleague wrote to Williams in 1906, seeking to assure him that a revivalist preacher coming to Chicago was untainted by "the modern viewpoint," which might "threaten the very ground-work" of the faith (Frank Dyer to E. F. Williams, April 5, 1906, Williams Papers, Box 10, Folder 12.) With all this in mind, we can see that Williams meets the description of a "doctrinal fundamentalist" as it has been used in this work.
29 Edward Franklin Williams, "Forgetting God and Stretching Out Our Hands toward a Strange God," July 27, 1915, Williams Papers, Box 19, Folder 13.
30 Williams, "Forgetting God."
31 On James M. Nabrit Jr.'s involvement as a strategist in the *Brown v. Board* case, see Katie McCabe and Dovey Johnson Roundtree, *Justice Older Than the Law*, 96–97, 104–7, 119, 128, 132–33. Reflecting on the impact that the religious life of the elder J. M. Nabrit had on the legal career of the younger, Roundtree writes: "And though the fair-skinned Professor Nabrit . . . cut quite a different figure from his fiery father, he had a whole lot of minister in him. The home from which he came was a place infused with Christianity, and though he never uttered an overtly religious word in the classroom, I felt in him a sense of the law as a ministry and of the flow of history as divinely ordained" (96–97).

On Samuel Nabrit's support for the Texas Southern student protesters, see Cole, *No Color Is My Kind*:
> When it became clear that the sit-in movement in Houston was not going to fold, Mayor Cutrer and others increased the pressure on Nabrit. While presidents at other state universities capitulated to white politicians, Sam Nabrit stood firm. . . . He was not afraid to lose his job. He and his wife could afford to live on their savings if necessary. Nabrit viewed the issue as one of citizenship rather than of academic policy. The students had violated no laws or TSU regulations, and he had no desire to control their activities. . . . "Our view then is that it is the democratic right of students to seek remedial measures for social injustices within the framework of law. *We stand with our students.*" (33–34; emphasis in original)

32 J. M. Nabrit, "The Need of a Trained Leadership for Negroes," *Home and Foreign Fields*, July 1937, Commission on ABTS Records, AR 630, Box 2, Folder 66.
33 Horace, *"Crowned with Glory and Honor,"* 38, 202.
34 For an extended analysis of this portion of Williams's address, including his express affirmations of fundamentalism and rebukes of modernism, see chapter 3.

35 "The Third Annual Address of Dr. L. K. Williams," 15.
36 "The Third Annual Address," 3.
37 "The Third Annual Address," 14–15.
38 Horace, in her biography of Williams, repeatedly discusses his passion for education, in terms of both his commitment to his personal education and his conviction about the need for increased educational opportunities for African Americans as a whole.
39 "The Third Annual Address," 15.
40 "The Third Annual Address," 16.
41 "What the Republican Party Can't Be," *Chicago Defender*, November 9, 1929, A2.
42 "The Week," *Chicago Defender*, April 30, 1932, 1, col. 2.
43 "September Crisis Scores Prejudiced Fundamentalist," *Philadelphia Tribune*, August 22, 1925, 15.
44 "American Intolerance and Menace of a State Church," *Norfolk Journal and Guide*, September 11, 1926, 12.

CONCLUSION
1 Tisby, "Trump's Election and Feeling 'Safe' in White Evangelical Churches."
2 Tisby, "The Journey from RAAN to 'The Witness.'"

# SELECTED BIBLIOGRAPHY

"1925 Baptist Faith and Message Statement of the Southern Baptist Convention." The Reformed Reader. Accessed July 10, 2017. www.reformedreader.org.

Ammerman, Nancy T. "North American Protestant Fundamentalism." In *Fundamentalisms Observed*, edited by Martin Marty and R. Scott Appleby, 1–65. Chicago: University of Chicago Press, 1991.

Angell, Stephen W., and Anthony B. Pinn, eds. *Social Protest Thought in the African Methodist Episcopal Church, 1862–1939*. Knoxville: University of Tennessee Press, 2000.

*Annual of the Southern Baptist Convention 1920*. Nashville: Marshall and Bruce Co., 1920.

Ashworth, Robert A. "The Fundamentalist Movement among the Baptists." *Journal of Religion* 4, no. 6 (November 1924): 611–31.

Barnes, Sandra L. "Priestly and Prophetic Influences on Black Church Social Services." *Social Problems* 51, no. 2 (May 2004): 202–21.

Barnes, Sandra L., and Oluchi Nwosu. "Black Church Electoral and Protest Politics from 2002 to 2012: A Social Media Analysis of the Resistance versus Accommodation Dialectic." *Journal of African American Studies* 18, no. 2 (June 2014): 209–35.

Baxter, D. M. *The Doctrine & Discipline of the A.M.E. Church*, 28th rev. ed. Philadelphia: A.M.E. Book Concern, 1924.

Bendroth, Margaret Lamberts. *Fundamentalists in the City: Conflict and Division in Boston's Churches, 1885–1950*. New York: Oxford University Press, 2005.

Best, Wallace D. *Langston's Salvation: American Religion and the Bard of Harlem*. New York: New York University Press, 2017.

———. *Passionately Human, No Less Divine: Religion and Culture in Black Chicago, 1915–1952*. Princeton, NJ: Princeton University Press, 2005.

Bettex, F. "The Bible and Modern Criticism." In *The Fundamentals: A Testimony to the Truth*, edited by R. A. Torrey and A. C. Dixon, 1:76–93. 1917; repr., Grand Rapids, MI: Baker Book House, 1988.

Bishop, George S. "The Testimony of the Scriptures to Themselves." In *The Fundamentals: A Testimony to the Truth*, edited by R. A. Torrey and A. C. Dixon, 2:80–96. 1917; repr., Grand Rapids, MI: Baker Book House, 1988.

Blain, Keisha N., Christopher Cameron, and Ashley D. Farmer, eds. *New Perspectives on the Black Intellectual Tradition*. Evanston, IL: Northwestern University Press, 2018.

———. "Introduction: The Contours of Black Intellectual History." In *New Perspectives on the Black Intellectual Tradition*, edited by Keisha N. Blain, Christopher Cameron, and Ashley D. Farmer, 3–16. Evanston, IL: Northwestern University Press, 2018.

Blum, Edward J. *W. E. B. Du Bois: American Prophet*. Philadelphia: University of Pennsylvania Press, 2007.

Blum, Edward J., and Paul Harvey. *The Color of Christ: The Son of God and the Saga of Race in America*. Chapel Hill: University of North Carolina Press, 2012.

Brown, Kathleen M. *Good Wives, Nasty Wenches, and Anxious Patriarchs: Gender, Race, and Power in Colonial Virginia*. Chapel Hill: University of North Carolina Press, 1996.

Busto, Rudy V. *King Tiger: The Religious Vision of Reies López Tijerina*. Albuquerque: University of New Mexico Press, 2005.

Calhoun-Brown, Allison. "While Marching to Zion: Otherworldliness and Racial Empowerment in the Black Community." *Journal for the Scientific Study of Religion* 37, no. 3 (September 1998): 427–39.

Calvin, John. *Commentary on the Gospel According to John*, vol. 1. Translated by William Pringle. Bellingham, WA: Logos Bible Software, 2010.

Carpenter, Joel A. "Fundamentalist Institutions and the Rise of Evangelical Protestantism, 1929–1942." *Church History* 49, no. 1 (March 1980): 62–75.

———. *Revive Us Again: The Reawakening of American Fundamentalism*. New York: Oxford University Press, 1997.

Caven, William. "The Testimony of Christ to the Old Testament." In *The Fundamentals: A Testimony to the Truth*, edited by R. A. Torrey and A. C. Dixon, 1:201–27. 1917; repr., Grand Rapids, MI: Baker Book House, 1988.

Chappell, David. *A Stone of Hope: Prophetic Religion and the Death of Jim Crow*. Chapel Hill: University of North Carolina Press, 2004.

Christian, Garna L. *Black Soldiers in Jim Crow Texas, 1899–1917*. College Station: Texas A&M University Press, 1995.

Cohen, William. *At Freedom's Edge: Black Mobility and the Southern White Quest for Racial Control, 1861–1915*. Baton Rouge: Louisiana State University Press, 1991.

Cole, Thomas R. *No Color Is My Kind: The Life of Eldrewey Stearns and the Integration of Houston*. Austin: University of Texas Press, 1997.

Cone, James H. *God of the Oppressed*. New York: Seabury Press, 1975.

———. *A Black Theology of Liberation*. Philadelphia: J. B. Lippincott, 1970.

———. *Black Theology and Black Power*. New York: Seabury Press, 1969.

Cooks, Michael J. F. "The History and Future of the Southern Bible Institute: A Post-Secondary School of Biblical Studies for African Americans." *Christian Higher Education* 9, no. 2 (2010): 151–65.

———. "The Historical Development and Future of the Southern Bible Institute." Ed.D. diss., University of North Texas, 2008.

Corrigan, John, ed. *The Oxford Encyclopedia of Religion in America*. New York: Oxford University Press, 2018.

Cressler, Matthew J. *Authentically Black and Truly Catholic: The Rise of Black Catholicism in the Great Migration*. New York: New York University Press, 2017.

Daniel, William A. *The Education of Negro Ministers*. New York: George H. Doran Company, 1925.

DeBerg, Betty A. *Ungodly Women: Gender and the First Wave of American Fundamentalism*. Minneapolis, MN: Fortress Press, 1990.
Dickerson, Dennis C. *The African Methodist Episcopal Church: A History*. New York: Cambridge University Press, 2020.
Dixon, A. C. "Evangelism: Old and New." *The Watchman* 86, no. 6 (February 11, 1904): 10–12.
Dobson, Ed, and Ed Hindson. *The Fundamentalist Phenomenon: The Resurgence of Conservative Christianity*. Edited by Jerry Falwell. Garden City, NY: Doubleday, 1981.
"Does the Southern Baptist Convention Still Have a Stain on It?" *Pulpit and Pen* (blog). June 23, 2017. www.pulpitandpen.org.
Dorrien, Gary. *The New Abolition: W. E. B. Du Bois and the Black Social Gospel*. New Haven, CT: Yale University Press, 2015.
Du Bois, W. E. B. *The Negro Church: Report of a Social Study Made under the Direction of Atlanta University; Together with the Proceedings of the Eighth Conference for the Study of the Negro Problems, Held at Atlanta University, May 26th, 1903*. 1903; repr. with new introduction by Phil Zuckerman, Sandra L. Barnes, and Daniel Cady. Walnut Creek, CA: AltaMira Press, 2003.
———. *The Souls of Black Folk*. 1903; repr. New York: Dover Publications, 1994.
Dudziak, Mary. *Cold War Civil Rights: Race and the Image of American Democracy*. Princeton, NJ: Princeton University Press, 2000.
Ebel, Jonathan. *Faith in the Fight: Religion and the American Solider in the Great War*. Princeton, NJ: Princeton University Press, 2010.
Edward Franklin Williams Papers. Amistad Research Center at Tulane University, New Orleans, LA.
Egerton, John. *Speak Now against the Day: The Generation before the Civil Rights Movement in the South*. New York: Alfred A. Knopf, 1994.
Ehrman, Bart. "Why Textual Criticism Is 'Safe' for Conservative Christians." *The Bart Ehrman Blog: The History & Literature of Early Christianity*, September 11, 2016. www.ehrmanblog.org.
Emerson, Michael O., and Christian Smith. *Divided by Faith: Evangelical Religion and the Problem of Race in America*. New York: Oxford University Press, 2000.
Erdman, Charles R. "The Church and Socialism." In *The Fundamentals: A Testimony to the Truth*, edited by R. A. Torrey and A. C. Dixon, 4:97–108. 1917; repr. Grand Rapids, MI: Baker Book House, 1988.
———. "The Coming of Christ." In *The Fundamentals: A Testimony to the Truth*, edited by R. A. Torrey and A. C. Dixon, 4:301–13. 1917; repr. Grand Rapids, MI: Baker Book House, 1988.
Eugene Perry Alldredge Papers. Southern Baptist Historical Library and Archives, Nashville, TN.
Evans, Curtis J. *The Burden of Black Religion*. New York: Oxford University Press, 2008.
Finn, Nathan A. "John R. Rice, Bob Jones Jr. and the 'Mechanical Dictation' Controversy: Finalizing the Fracturing of Independent Fundamentalism." *Journal of Baptist Studies* 6 (2014): 60–75.

———. "The Development of Baptist Fundamentalism in the South, 1940–1980." Ph.D. diss., Southeastern Baptist Theological Seminary, 2007.

Fosdick, Harry Emerson. "Shall the Fundamentalists Win?" In *American Religions: A Documentary History*, edited by R. Marie Griffith, 418–23. New York: Oxford University Press, 2008.

Frazier, E. Franklin. *The Negro Church in America*. New York: Schocken Books, 1963.

Freeman, James M. *Handbook of Bible Manners and Customs*. New York: Nelson & Phillips, 1875.

Gaebelein, Arno C. "Fulfilled Prophecy a Potent Argument for the Bible." In *The Fundamentals: A Testimony to the Truth*, edited by R. A. Torrey and A. C. Dixon, 2:112–43. 1917; repr. Grand Rapids, MI: Baker Book House, 1988.

Gaines, Kevin K. *Uplifting the Race: Black Leadership, Politics, and Culture in the Twentieth Century*. Chapel Hill: University of North Carolina Press, 1996.

Garrett, James Leo, Jr. *Baptist Theology: A Four-Century Study*. Macon, GA: Mercer University Press, 2009.

Garrett, James Leo, Jr., E. Glenn Hinson, and James E. Tull. *Are Southern Baptists "Evangelicals"?* Macon, GA: Mercer University Press, 1983.

Gaustad, Edwin S. "American History, with and without Religion." *OAH Magazine of History* 6, no. 3 (Winter 1992): 15–18.

Genovese, Eugene D. *Roll, Jordan, Roll: The World the Slaves Made*. New York: Pantheon, 1974.

Gibson, A. B. B. *The African Methodist Shield (Improved): For the Benefit of the Members, Sunday Schools, Allen Christian Endeavor League and Missionary Societies of the African Methodist Episcopal Church*. Macon, GA: published by the author, 1919.

Glass, William R. *Strangers in Zion: Fundamentalists in the South, 1900–1950*. Macon, GA: Mercer University Press, 2001.

Gloege, Timothy. *Guaranteed Pure: The Moody Bible Institute, Business, and the Making of Modern Evangelicalism*. Chapel Hill: University of North Carolina Press, 2015.

Gray, James M. "The Inspiration of the Bible—Definition, Extent, and Proof." In *The Fundamentals: A Testimony to the Truth*, edited by R. A. Torrey and A. C. Dixon, 2:9–43. 1917; repr. Grand Rapids, MI: Baker Book House, 1988.

Green, Emma. "Resolution Condemning White Supremacy Causes Chaos at the Southern Baptist Convention." *The Atlantic*, June 14, 2017. www.theatlantic.com.

Gregory, James N. *The Southern Diaspora: How the Great Migrations of Black and White Southerners Transformed America*. Chapel Hill: University of North Carolina Press, 2005.

Griffith, R. Marie, ed. *American Religions: A Documentary History*. New York: Oxford University Press, 2008.

Griggs, Sutton E. Letter to the Southern Baptist Convention. *Annual of the Southern Baptist Convention 1920*, 121–23. Nashville, TN: Marshall and Bruce Co., 1920.

Grossman, James R. *Land of Hope: Chicago, Black Southerners, and the Great Migration*. Chicago: University of Chicago Press, 1989.

Hague, Dyson. "At-One-Ment by Propitiation." In *The Fundamentals: A Testimony to the Truth*, edited by R. A. Torrey and A. C. Dixon, 3:78–97. 1917; repr. Grand Rapids, MI: Baker Book House, 1988.

———. "The Doctrinal Value of the First Chapters of Genesis." In *The Fundamentals: A Testimony to the Truth*, edited by R. A. Torrey and A. C. Dixon, 1:272–87. 1917; repr. Grand Rapids, MI: Baker Book House, 1988.

———. "The History of the Higher Criticism." In *The Fundamentals: A Testimony to the Truth*, edited by R. A. Torrey and A. C. Dixon, 1:9–42. 1917; repr. Grand Rapids, MI: Baker Book House, 1988.

Hahn, Steven. *A Nation under Our Feet: Black Political Struggles in the Rural South from Slavery to the Great Migration*. Cambridge, MA: The Belknap Press of Harvard University Press, 2005.

Hall, Jacquelyn Dowd. "The Long Civil Rights Movement and the Political Uses of the Past." *Journal of American History* 91, no. 4 (March 2005): 1233–63.

Hall, Matthew J., and Owen Strachan, eds. *Essential Evangelicalism: The Enduring Influence of Carl F. H. Henry*. Wheaton, IL: Crossway, 2015.

Hamilton, Charles V. *The Black Preacher in America*. New York: William Morrow, 1972.

Hankins, Barry. *American Evangelicals: A Contemporary History of a Mainstream Religious Movement*. Lanham, MD: Rowman & Littlefield, 2008.

———. *Francis Schaeffer and the Shaping of Evangelical America*. Grand Rapids, MI: William B. Eerdmans, 2008.

———. *God's Rascal: J. Frank Norris and the Beginnings of Southern Fundamentalism*. Lexington: University Press of Kentucky, 1996.

Harlan, Louis R., ed. *The Booker T. Washington Papers*, vol. 3. Urbana: University of Illinois Press, 1974.

Harnack, Adolf. *What Is Christianity?* Translated by Thomas Bailey Saunders. New York: Harper & Row, 1957.

Harris, Fredrick C. *Something Within: Religion in African-American Political Activism*. New York: Oxford University Press, 1999.

Hart, D. G. *Defending the Faith: J. Gresham Machen and the Crisis of Conservative Protestantism in Modern America*. Phillipsburg, NJ: P&R Publishing, 2003.

Harvey, Paul. *Bounds of Their Habitation: Race and Religion in American History*. Lanham, MD: Rowman & Littlefield, 2017.

———. *Through the Storm, Through the Night: A History of African American Christianity*. Lanham, MD: Rowman & Littlefield, 2011.

———. *Freedom's Coming: Religious Culture and the Shaping of the South from the Civil War through the Civil Rights Era*. Chapel Hill: University of North Carolina Press, 2005.

———. *Redeeming the South: Religious Cultures and Racial Identities among Southern Baptists, 1865–1925*. Chapel Hill: University of North Carolina Press, 1997.

Hawkins, J. Russell, and Phillip Luke Sinitiere, eds. *Christians and the Color Line: Race and Religion after "Divided by Faith."* New York: Oxford University Press, 2014.

Henry, Carl F. H. *The Uneasy Conscience of Modern Fundamentalism*. Grand Rapids, MI: William B. Eerdmans, 1947.

Higginbotham, Evelyn Brooks. *Righteous Discontent: The Women's Movement in the Black Baptist Church, 1880–1920*. Cambridge, MA: Harvard University Press, 1993.

"History of First Baptist Church of Princeton, Indiana." Accessed March 11, 2018. www.fbcprinceton.net.

Horace, Lillian B. *"Crowned with Glory and Honor": The Life of Rev. Lacey Kirk Williams*. Hicksville, NY: Exposition Press, 1978.

I. J. Van Ness Papers. Southern Baptist Historical Library and Archives, Nashville, TN.

Irenaeus of Lyons. *Against Heresies*. In *The Ante-Nicene Fathers: Translations of the Writings of the Fathers down to A.D. 325*, edited by Alexander Roberts, James Donaldson, and A. Cleveland Coxe, vol. 1. Buffalo, NY: Christian Literature Company, 1885–1887.

Isaac Reed Berry Papers. Schomburg Center for Research in Black Culture, New York Public Library, New York.

Jacobsen, Douglas, and William Vance Trollinger Jr., eds. *Re-Forming the Center: American Protestantism, 1900 to the Present*. Grand Rapids, MI: William B. Eerdmans, 1998.

Jacobson, Matthew Frye. *Barbarian Virtues: The United States Encounters Foreign Peoples at Home and Abroad, 1876–1917*. New York: Hill and Wang, 2000.

John Albert Johnson Papers. Schomburg Center for Research in Black Culture, New York Public Library, New York.

Johnson, Franklin. "The Atonement." In *The Fundamentals: A Testimony to the Truth*, edited by R. A. Torrey and A. C. Dixon, 3:64–77. 1917; repr. Grand Rapids, MI: Baker Book House, 1988.

Johnson, Karen J. *One in Christ: Chicago Catholics and the Quest for Interracial Justice*. New York: Oxford University Press, 2018.

———. "Healing the Mystical Body: Catholic Attempts to Overcome the Racial Divide in Chicago, 1930–1948." In *Christians and the Color Line: Race and Religion after "Divided by Faith,"* edited by J. Russell Hawkins and Phillip Luke Sinitiere, 45–71. New York: Oxford University Press, 2014.

Johnson, Sylvester A. *African American Religions, 1500–2000: Colonialism, Democracy, and Freedom*. New York: Cambridge University Press, 2015.

Jordan, Winthrop D. *The White Man's Burden: Historical Origins of Racism in the United States*. New York: Oxford University Press, 1974.

Kyle, M. G. "The Recent Testimony of Archaeology to the Scriptures." In *The Fundamentals: A Testimony to the Truth*, edited by R. A. Torrey and A. C. Dixon, 1:315–33. 1917; repr. Grand Rapids, MI: Baker Book House, 1988.

Leiker, James. *Racial Borders: Black Soldiers along the Rio Grande*. College Station: Texas A&M University Press, 2002.

Lewis, C. S. *Mere Christianity*. London: Geoffrey Bles, 1952.

Lienesch, Michael. *In the Beginning: Fundamentalism, the Scopes Trial, and the Making of the Antievolution Movement*. Chapel Hill: University of North Carolina Press, 2007.

Lincoln, C. Eric. *Race, Religion, and the Continuing American Dilemma*. New York: Hill and Wang, 1984.
Lincoln, C. Eric, ed. *The Black Experience in Religion*. Garden City, NY: Anchor Press, 1974.
Lincoln, C. Eric, and Lawrence H. Mamiya. *The Black Church in the African American Experience*. Durham, NC: Duke University Press, 1990.
Luther, Martin. *Sermons on the Gospel of St. John Chapters 14–16*. In *Luther's Works*, edited by Jaroslav Pelikan, translated by Martin H. Bertram, vol. 24. St. Louis: Concordia Publishing House, 1961.
Machen, J. Gresham. *Christianity and Liberalism*. New York: Macmillan, 1923.
Marsden, George M. *Fundamentalism and American Culture*, 2nd ed. New York: Oxford University Press, 2006.
———. "Fundamentalism as an American Phenomenon: A Comparison with English Evangelicalism." *Church History* 46, no. 2 (June 1977): 215–32.
Marsh, Charles. *God's Long Summer: Stories of Faith and Civil Rights*. Princeton, NJ: Princeton University Press, 1997.
Martin, Lerone A. *Preaching on Wax: The Phonograph and the Shaping of Modern African American Religion*. New York: New York University Press, 2014.
Marty, Martin, and R. Scott Appleby, eds. *Fundamentalisms Observed*. Chicago: University of Chicago Press, 1991.
Mathers, Norman W. *Battle for Orthodoxy: American Religious Thought (1870–1910)*. Eugene, OR: Wipf & Stock, 2018.
Mathews, Mary Beth Swetnam. *Doctrine and Race: African American Evangelicals and Fundamentalism between the Wars*. Tuscaloosa: University of Alabama Press, 2017.
———. *Rethinking Zion: How the Print Media Placed Fundamentalism in the South*. Knoxville: University of Tennessee Press, 2006.
McCabe, Katie, and Dovey Johnson Roundtree. *Justice Older than the Law: The Life of Dovey Johnson Roundtree*. Jackson: University Press of Mississippi, 2009.
McDaniel, Eric L. and Christopher G. Ellison. "God's Party? Race, Religion, and Partisanship over Time." *Political Research Quarterly* 61, no. 2 (June 2008): 180–91.
McGreevy, John T. *Parish Boundaries: The Catholic Encounter with Race in the Twentieth-Century Urban North*. Chicago: University of Chicago Press, 1996.
Miller, Albert G. "The Construction of a Black Fundamentalist Worldview: The Role of Bible Schools." In *African Americans and the Bible*, edited by Vincent L. Wimbush, 712–27. New York: Continuum International, 2000.
Mitchell, Henry. "Two Streams of Tradition." In *The Black Experience in Religion*, edited by C. Eric Lincoln, 70–75. Garden City, NY: Anchor Press, 1974.
Montgomery, William E. *Under Their Own Vine and Fig Tree: The African-American Church in the South, 1865–1900*. Baton Rouge: Louisiana State University Press, 1993.
Moran, Jeffrey P. *American Genesis: The Antievolution Controversies from Scopes to Creation Science*. New York: Oxford University Press, 2012.
———. "The Scopes Trial and Southern Fundamentalism in Black and White: Race, Region, and Religion," *Journal of Southern History* 70, no. 1 (2004): 95–120.

———. "Reading Race into the Scopes Trial: African American Elites, Science, and Fundamentalism." *Journal of American History* 90, no. 3 (December 2003): 891–911.

Morris, E. C. *Sermons, Addresses and Reminiscences and Important Correspondence.* Nashville, TN: National Baptist Publishing Board, 1901.

Mullin, Miles S., II. "Neoevangelicalism and the Problem of Race in Postwar America." In *Christians and the Color Line: Race and Religion after "Divided by Faith,"* edited by J. Russell Hawkins and Phillip Luke Sinitiere, 15–44. New York: Oxford University Press, 2014.

Mullins, E. Y. "The Testimony of Christian Experience." In *The Fundamentals: A Testimony to the Truth,* edited by R. A. Torrey and A. C. Dixon, 4:314–23. 1917; repr. Grand Rapids, MI: Baker Book House, 1988.

Munhall, L. W. "Inspiration." In *The Fundamentals: A Testimony to the Truth,* edited by R. A. Torrey and A. C. Dixon, 2:44–60. 1917; repr. Grand Rapids, MI: Baker Book House, 1988.

Murphy, Larry G., J. Gordon Melton, and Gary L. Ward, eds. *Encyclopedia of African American Religions.* New York: Routledge, 2011.

Newman, Richard S. *Freedom's Prophet: Bishop Richard Allen, the AME Church, and the Black Founding Fathers.* New York: New York University Press, 2008.

"NOBTS Articles of Religious Belief." Accessed January 7, 2020. www.baptistcenter.net.

Noll, Mark A. *America's God: From Jonathan Edwards to Abraham Lincoln.* New York: Oxford University Press, 2002.

"On the Anti-Gospel of Alt-Right White Supremacy." The Southern Baptist Convention. Accessed January 19, 2018. www.sbc.net.

Origen of Alexandria. *Commentary on the Gospel of Matthew.* In *The Ante-Nicene Fathers: Translations of the Writings of the Fathers down to A.D. 325,* edited by Alexander Roberts, James Donaldson, and A. Cleveland Coxe, vol. 9. Buffalo, NY: Christian Literature Company, 1885–1887.

Orr, James. "Science and the Christian Faith." In *The Fundamentals: A Testimony to the Truth,* edited by R. A. Torrey and A. C. Dixon, 1:334–47. 1917; repr. Grand Rapids, MI: Baker Book House, 1988.

Overacker, Ingrid. *The African American Church Community in Rochester, New York, 1900–1940.* Rochester, NY: University of Rochester Press, 1998.

Painter, Nell Irvin. *Exodusters: Black Migration to Kansas after Reconstruction.* New York: Alfred A. Knopf, 1977.

Pelikan, Jaroslav. *The Christian Tradition: A History of the Development of Doctrine,* vol. 1, *The Emergence of the Catholic Tradition (100–600).* Chicago: University of Chicago Press, 1971.

Phillips, Kimberley L. *War! What Is It Good For?: Black Freedom Struggles and the U.S. Military from World War II to Iraq.* Chapel Hill: University of North Carolina Press, 2012.

Pierson, Arthur T. "The Testimony of the Organic Unity of the Bible to Its Inspiration." In *The Fundamentals: A Testimony to the Truth,* edited by R. A. Torrey and A. C. Dixon, 2:97–111. 1917; repr. Grand Rapids, MI: Baker Book House, 1988.

Pinn, Anne H., and Anthony B. Pinn. *Fortress Introduction to Black Church History.* Minneapolis, MN: Fortress Press, 2002.
Pipes, William H. *Say Amen, Brother! Old-Time Negro Preaching: A Study in American Frustration.* 1951; repr. Westport, CT: Negro Universities Press, 1970.
Pitzer, A. W. "The Wisdom of This World." In *The Fundamentals: A Testimony to the Truth,* edited by R. A. Torrey and A. C. Dixon, 4:40–48. 1917; repr. Grand Rapids, MI: Baker Book House, 1988.
Procter, W. C. "What Christ Teaches Concerning Future Retribution." In *The Fundamentals: A Testimony to the Truth,* edited by R. A. Torrey and A. C. Dixon, 3:53–63. 1917; repr. Grand Rapids, MI: Baker Book House, 1988.
Prothero, Stephen. *Religion Matters: An Introduction to the World's Religions.* New York: W. W. Norton, 2020.
———. *Religious Literacy: What Every American Needs to Know—and Doesn't.* New York: HarperCollins, 2007.
———. *American Jesus: How the Son of God Became a National Icon.* New York: Farrar, Straus and Giroux, 2003.
Raboteau, Albert J. *Slave Religion: The "Invisible Institution" in the Antebellum South,* updated ed. New York: Oxford University Press, 2004.
———. *Canaan Land: A Religious History of African Americans.* New York: Oxford University Press, 2001.
———. *A Fire in the Bones: Reflections on African-American Religious History.* Boston: Beacon Press, 1995.
Rauschenbusch, Walter. *A Theology for the Social Gospel.* New York: MacMillan, 1918.
*The Red Book of Houston: A Compendium of Social, Professional, Religious, Educational, and Industrial Interests of Houston's Colored Population.* Houston, TX: Sotex Publishing Company, 1915.
"Report of the Commission on the Negro Theological Seminary." *Annual of the Southern Baptist Convention 1920,* 118–20. Nashville: Marshall and Bruce Co., 1920.
Roberts, Alexander, James Donaldson, and A. Cleveland Coxe, eds. *The Ante-Nicene Fathers: Translations of the Writings of the Fathers down to A.D. 325,* 10 vols. Buffalo, NY: Christian Literature Company, 1885–1887.
Roberts, J. Deotis. *Black Religion, Black Theology: The Collected Essays of J. Deotis Roberts.* Edited by David Emmanuel Goatley. Harrisburg, PA: Trinity Press International, 2003.
———. *A Black Political Theology.* Philadelphia: Westminster Press, 1974.
Salmond, John A. "'The Long and the Short of It': Some Reflections on the Recent Historiography of the Civil Rights Movement." *Australasian Journal of American Studies* 32, no. 1 (July 2013): 53–61.
Sandeen, Ernest R. *The Roots of Fundamentalism: British and American Millenarianism, 1800–1930.* Chicago: University of Chicago Press, 1970.

Savage, Barbara Dianne. "Biblical and Historical Imperatives: Toward a History of Ideas about the Political Role of Black Churches." In *African Americans and the Bible*, edited by Vincent L. Wimbush, 367–88. New York: Continuum International, 2000.

Sawyer, Mary R. "Black Protestantism as Expressed in Ecumenical Activity." In *Re-Forming the Center: American Protestantism, 1900 to the Present*, edited by Douglas Jacobsen and William Vance Trollinger Jr., 284–99. Grand Rapids, MI: William B. Eerdmans, 1998.

Sernett, Milton C. "Re-Readings: The Great Migration and the Bible." In *African Americans and the Bible*, edited by Vincent L. Wimbush, 448–63. New York: Continuum International, 2000.

Sernett, Milton C., ed. *African American Religious History: A Documentary Witness*, 2nd ed. Durham, NC: Duke University Press, 1999.

Shelton, Jason E., and Michael O. Emerson. *Blacks and Whites in Christian America: How Racial Discrimination Shapes Religious Convictions*. New York: New York University Press, 2012.

Simpson, Christopher Ben. *Modern Christian Theology*, 2nd ed. London: T&T Clark, 2020.

Sinitiere, Phillip Luke. "Interracialism and American Christianity." In *The Oxford Encyclopedia of Religion in America*, edited by John Corrigan, 136–59. New York: Oxford University Press, 2018.

Sitkoff, Harvard. *A New Deal for Blacks: The Emergence of Civil Rights as a National Issue; The Depression Decade*. New York: Oxford University Press, 1978.

The Southern Baptist Commission on the American Baptist Seminary Records. Southern Baptist Historical Library and Archives, Nashville, TN.

Stock, John. "The God-Man." In *The Fundamentals: A Testimony to the Truth*, edited by R. A. Torrey and A. C. Dixon, 2:261–81. 1917; repr. Grand Rapids, MI: Baker Book House, 1988.

Straub, Jeffrey Paul. *The Making of a Battle Royal: The Rise of Liberalism in Northern Baptist Life, 1870–1920*. Eugene, OR: Pickwick Publications, 2018.

Sutton, Matthew Avery. *American Apocalypse: A History of Modern Evangelicalism*. Cambridge, MA: The Belknap Press of Harvard University Press, 2014.

"The Third Annual Address of Dr. L. K. Williams, President." *National Baptist Voice* 10, no. 40 (1925): 1, 3–6, 12–16.

Tisby, Jemar. "The Journey from RAAN to 'The Witness: A Black Christian Collective.'" *The Witness* (blog), October 31, 2017. www.thewitnessbcc.com.

———. "Trump's Election and Feeling 'Safe' in White Evangelical Churches." *The Witness* (blog), November 18, 2016. www.thewitnessbcc.com.

Torrey, R. A. "Tributes to Christ and the Bible by Brainy Men Not Known as Active Christians." In *The Fundamentals: A Testimony to the Truth*, edited by R. A. Torrey and A. C. Dixon, 3:363–69. 1917; repr. Grand Rapids, MI: Baker Book House, 1988.

Torrey, R. A., and A. C. Dixon, eds. *The Fundamentals: A Testimony to the Truth*, 4 vols. 1917; repr. Grand Rapids, MI: Baker Book House, 1988.

Trollinger, William V., Jr. *God's Empire: William Bell Riley and Midwestern Fundamentalism*. Madison: University of Wisconsin Press, 1990.

Turner, Henry Brent. *Islam in the African-American Experience*, 2nd ed. Bloomington: Indiana University Press, 2003.

Tuttle, William M., Jr. *Race Riot: Chicago in the Red Summer of 1919*. Urbana: University of Illinois Press, 1970.

Twiss, Pamela. "Ernest Rice McKinney: African American Appalachian, Social Worker, Radical Labor Organizer and Educator." *Journal of Appalachian Studies* 10, no. 1/2 (Spring/Fall 2004): 95–110.

Una Roberts Lawrence Collection. Southern Baptist Historical Library and Archives, Nashville, TN.

Wacker, Grant. *America's Pastor: Billy Graham and the Shaping of a Nation*. Cambridge, MA: The Belknap Press of Harvard University Press, 2014.

Washington, James Melvin. *Frustrated Fellowship: The Black Baptist Quest for Social Power*. Macon, GA: Mercer University Press, 2004.

Watt, David Harrington. "Fundamentalists of the 1920s and 1930s." In *Fundamentalism: Perspectives on a Contested History*, edited by Simon A. Wood and David Harrington Watt, 18–35. Columbia: University of South Carolina Press, 2014.

Weinfeld, David. "Isolated Believer: Alain Locke, Baha'i Secularist." In *New Perspectives on the Black Intellectual Tradition*, edited by Keisha N. Blain, Christopher Cameron, and Ashley D. Farmer, 83–98. Evanston, IL: Northwestern University Press, 2018.

Weisenfeld, Judith. *New World A-Coming: Black Religion and Racial Identity during the Great Migration*. New York: New York University Press, 2016.

Wheeler, Edward L. *Uplifting the Race: The Black Minister in the New South, 1865–1902*. Lanham, MD: University Press of America, 1986.

Williams, Chad L. *Torchbearers of Democracy: African American Soldiers in the World War I Era*. Chapel Hill: University of North Carolina Press, 2010.

Williams, Lacey Kirk. "Effects of Urbanization on Religious Life." In *African American Religious History: A Documentary Witness*, 2nd ed., edited by Milton C. Sernett, 372–75. Durham, NC: Duke University Press, 1999.

Wills, Gregory A. *Southern Baptist Theological Seminary, 1859–2009*. New York: Oxford University Press, 2009.

Wilmore, Gayraud S. *Black Religion and Black Radicalism: An Interpretation of the Religious History of the Afro-American People*, 2nd ed. Maryknoll, NY: Orbis Books, 1983.

Wimbush, Vincent L., ed. *African Americans and the Bible*. New York: Continuum International, 2000.

Wood, Simon A., and David Harrington Watt, eds. *Fundamentalism: Perspectives on a Contested History*. Columbia: University of South Carolina Press, 2014.

Woodson, Carter G. *The History of the Negro Church*, 2nd ed. Washington, DC: Associated Publishers, 1921.

Woodward, C. Vann. *Origins of the New South, 1877–1913*, 2nd ed. Baton Rouge: Louisiana State University Press, 1971.

———. *The Strange Career of Jim Crow*. New York: Oxford University Press, 1955.
Wright, Richard R. Jr. *The Encyclopaedia of African Methodism*. Philadelphia: A.M.E. Book Concern, 1947.
Yenser, Thomas, ed. *Who's Who in Colored America: A Biographical Dictionary of Notable Living Persons of African Descent in America*, 6th ed. Brooklyn, NY: T. Yenser, 1942.
Zuckerman, Phil. "The Sociology of Religion of W.E.B. Du Bois." *Sociology of Religion* 63, no. 2 (Summer 2002): 239–53.

# INDEX

Note: Page numbers in *italics* refer to illustrations.

Abyssinian Baptist Church, Harlem, 51
Adam and Eve narrative, 44, 93
African Methodist Episcopal (AME) Church, 8, 29–30, 40, 71, 94. *See also* Johnson, John Albert
African Methodist Episcopal Zion (AMEZ) Church, 64, 65, 68, 135
*Afro-American*; on anti-lynching campaigns, 53–54, *53*; circulation of, 27; discussions about fundamentalism in, 27; on Henry Brothers, 34, 36; on Ku Klux Klan, 49; "old-time religion" references in, 37; and Scopes trial, 44–45; on Williams (L. K.), 47, 48
Alldredge, Eugene Perry, *154*; and American Baptist Theological Seminary, 129–30, 138–39, 141, 144, 146; and Barbour's progressivism, 149–52; and black students at white seminaries, 153; and "doctrinal fundamentalism," 213n92; and Garnett, 144; and NBC's *National Baptist Voice*, 144; and premillennialism, 84; and Seminary Singers, 142; and textbook concerns, 152; and threat of encroaching religious bodies, 156, 229n97
Allen, Richard, 40
Allen University, Columbia, South Carolina, 29
alt-right movement, 1–2, 185, 188
*American Apocalypse* (Sutton), 196n20

American Baptist Theological Seminary (ABTS), 127; and Barbour's (J. P.) progressivism, 148–51; and Barbour's (R. C.) progressivism, 144–48, 159; combating theological modernism, 123; "Confession of Faith" adopted by, 137–41, 143, 149, 151–52; dedication of first building, 125–26; financial support of, 155, 156; founding of, 122, 123, 202n51; fundamentalist doctrines of, 124–25, 131, 133, 143–44, 157, 229n98; fundraising of, 142; and Garnett's antimodernist message, 145–48; governing structure of, 128–29, 133; Griggs Hall, 125–26, *127*, 147; grill and book shop of, 137; and interracial cooperation/fellowship, 22–23, 122, 123–24, 125, 128, 129–34, 136, 222n4, 223n7, 224n20; leadership/governance of, 23, 123–24; location of, 127–28; origins of, 126–27; presidency of, 128, 132; and racial advancement, 134; racial considerations at, 140; and racial differences, 134–36, 157; and Riley's inauguration, *154*; Seminary Singers, 121, 141–43, 229n98; and underlying racist mores, 125, 132, 140, 157; and Williams (L. K.), 48, 124, 126, 132, 202n51; and Women's Training School, 152, 223n7; and Woodson's criticisms of conservatism, 226n52

247

American identity, 159–63; and Berry's "Christian America," 167–74, 182; democratic participation linked to, 178–79, 221n77; freedom associated with, 162; Johnson on, 163; and National Baptist religious identity, 177; and racial advancement, 179, 182–83; Williams (E. F.) on, 175; and Williams's (L. K.) calls for racial progress, 177–79. *See also* United States of America

A.M.E. Shield (AME), 30

Ammerman, Nancy, 3

antiracism resolution offered at annual meeting of SBC, 1–2, 5, 188

apocalypse and end-times, 83–84

apostasy, 73, 118

Arbor, Edward, 50

*Are Southern Baptists "Evangelicals"?* (Garrett, Hinson, and Tull), 205n12

*Articles of Religious Belief* of the Baptist Bible Institute of New Orleans, 138–39

Asbury, Francis, 167–68

Ashworth, Robert, 84, 197n42, 204n12, 205n12

atheism and threat of modernism, 155

*Atlanta Daily World*, 29–30, 40–41, 199n10

atonement: and AME Church's fundamentalist doctrines, 30; Berry on, 81–82, 104, 169, 173–74, 218n41; Biddle on, 80–81; black theologians' perspectives on, 80–82; and interracial fellowship at ABTS, 131; Johnson on, 81, 96; as one of five fundamentals of the faith, 21, 60, 205n12, 206n12; substitutionary, 30, 60, 80–81, 104–5, 205n12; Williams (E. F.) on, 213n84

"An Attempt to Destroy God's World, Rejecting the Saving Word" (Berry), 102–3, 217n30

Avery Chapel AME Church, Oklahoma City, 32

Baptist Bible Institute of New Orleans, 138–39

Baptist churches: doctrinal disputes in, 73–74; and founding of ABTS, 122; and Henry Brothers, 36; identified as fundamentalists, 74; Williams's (L. K.) advocacy for, 47–48, 51; and Williams's (L. K.) emphasis on fundamentals, 117

*Baptist Faith and Message* (SBC), 139, 140–41

Baptist Ministers' Conference (1928), 43

Barbour, J. Pius, 148–51

Barbour, Russell C., 144–48, 159

Barnes, Sandra L., 194n10, 206n17, 219n48

Berry, Isaac Reed: antimodernist message of, 87–88, 98–112; on atonement, 81–82, 104, 169, 173–74, 218n41; "Christian America" message of, 167–74, 182; and Christian nationalism, 158–59, 231n20; and fidelity to fundamentalist doctrines, 120; and *The Fundamentals*, 100–101, 102; leadership of, 184; on mission of the church, 218n44; and otherworldly message, 218n48

Best, Wallace, 51–52, 195n11, 221n73

Bettex, Frédéric, 73

biblical authority, 74, 75–78, 119, 210n66

biblical inerrancy: adopted across the color line, 54; and biblical literalism, 201n44; Biddle on, 65, 67, 68; at center of modernist controversy, 68; and *Chicago Defender*'s trivia column, 41–42; Davenport on, 68; Gray on, 62, 211n69; and Marsden on tenets of fundamentalism, 196n31; and McKinney's criticisms of fundamentalism, 30; and modernist theology, 69–70, 72–73; as one of five fundamentals of the faith, 60, 205n12, 206n12; as related to biblical inspiration, 62; Robinson on, 69–70, 72–73; Williams (L. K.) on, 43

biblical infallibility: and biblical literalism, 201n44; Biddle on, 65; Johnson on, 75–76; as one of five fundamentals of the faith, 60; as related to biblical inspiration, 62; Robinson on, 72; science's subordination to, 119
biblical inspiration (doctrine): about, 201n44; adopted across the color line, 54, 60–61, 76–77; and AME Church's fundamentalist doctrines, 30; and antievolution attitudes, 45; and Berry's opposition to modernism, 109; Biddle's defense of, 64–68; central importance of, 61, 62; and criticisms of fundamentalism, 44; evident in commercial culture, 61; Frank's defense of, 74–75; and higher-critical threat, 63–67; Johnson on, 75–76; as litmus test for Christianity, 65–66; nuanced theological distinctions regarding, 57; as "old time religion" teaching, 29; as one of five fundamentals of the faith, 60; variety of perspectives on, 61–62
biblicism of fundamentalists, 18, 28, 36, 54, 60–61. *See also* literalism
Biddle, Eli George, 64–69, 80, 83, 207n22, 209n42
Bishop, George, 207n19
Bishop College, 155
black church: and African American identity, 46; communist threat to, 155–56, 157, 176; complexity and diversity within, 17; liberal threat to, 176–77; and racial advancement, 48; social action of, 116–17
*The Black Church in the African American Experience* (Lincoln and Mamiya), 206n17
black intellectual tradition, 17
black press. *See* press/weeklies, black
Blain, Keisha N., 16–17, 59
Blum, Edward, 209n53
*Broad Ax* (Chicago), 164

"The Brotherhood of Man" (Berry), 105–7
Brown, Kathleen, 218n46
Bryan, William Jennings, 12, 44–45, 166, 179, 180

Caesar, biblical passage on, 172
Calhoun-Brown, Allison, 194n10, 206n17, 218n48
Calvin, Floyd J., 43–44
Calvin, John, 75, 211n66
Cameron, Christopher, 16–17, 59
Carpenter, Joel, 9
Carver Bible Institute, 123, 129
Catholic Church and Catholicism, 59, 139, 156–57, 181, 229n97
Cedine Bible Camp and Institute, 123
celebrity preachers, 33, 35–36
Chalcedonian formulation, 70, 78
Chappelle, Brother, 121
*Chicago Defender*: circulation of, 27, 198n8; criticisms of fundamentalism, 50, 165–66; discussions of fundamentalism, 27; on literalism, 42; on racial militancy, 52; on social action resulting from true religion, 50–51
"Christian America" message of Berry, 167–74, 182
*Christian Index*, 155
*Christianity and History* (Harnack), 77
*Christianity and Liberalism* (Machen), 193n6
"The Christian Ministry" (Johnson), 95
Christian nationalism, 158–59, 160, 167, 168–69, 174, 182–83, 231n20
Chrysostom, John, 104
*Church Review*, 69
civil rights movement, 87, 159, 230n2
Civil War, American, 111
Cleveland Gazette, 41
commercial culture, 61
communist threat, 155–56, 157, 175–76
community engagement, 79–80. *See also* social gospel movement

Conference for Progressive Labor Action, 164
confessions of faith, 137–41
conservatives and conservatism: association of fundamentalists with, 90; and conservative-fundamentalist distinction, 21; cultural militancy of, 8, 12–14, 30, 37, 45, 54, 186, 196n33
Constitution of the United States, 173–74, 179
Cornerstone Baptist Church, Arlington, Texas, 1
Costigan-Wagner antilynching bill, 54
*Crisis*, 49, 50
cultural militancy, 12–14, 30, 37, 45, 54, 186–87, 196n33

Dabney, Wendell, 49
Daniel, William A., 214n3
Davenport, W. H., 68
DeBerg, Betty A., 208n39
*Defender Junior*, 42
DeMent, Byron Hoover, 138
democracy: and fundamentalist identity, 166; racial advancement linked to participation in, 178–79, 221n77; and theological conservatism, 176–77; threat of modernism to, 155
denominational fundamentalists, 69, 197n42, 209n42, 213n92
devil, 37–38, 101–2, 104–5, 138, 175
dispensationalism, 83–84
divine creation (doctrine), 28, 30, 36, 41, 54
divinity of Jesus Christ (doctrine): and AME Church's fundamentalist doctrines, 30; Berry on, 109–11, 169, 173–74; Biddle on, 64; Johnson on, 77; as one of five fundamentals of the faith, 21, 60, 205n12, 206n12; and social gospel movement, 94; Williams (L. K.) on, 43, 47, 221n73
Dixon, A. C., 99–100, 101, 213n84

"doctrinal fundamentalism," 19, 206n13, 232n28
*Doctrine and Race* (Mathews), 5–7, 195n15, 198n2, 198n7, 207n22
*The Doctrines and Disciplines* (AME), 30
doctrines of fundamentalist movement: adopted across the color line, 76–77, 85–86; and AME Church, 30; and American Baptist Theological Seminary, 124–25, 131, 133, 138, 143–44; Biddle on, 64–69; centrality of literalism in, 42; combating theological modernism with, 29; complexity and diversity within, 17–18; compromises considered attacks on, 95; and confessions of faith, 137–41; and dispensationalism, 83–84; five fundamentals of, 60, 204–6n12; and identity, 159; and "intellectual inferiority" of blacks, 56, 59; Johnson's perspectives on, 75–78; nuanced distinctions emphasized in, 57, 59–60; "otherworldly," 79–80, 96–97, 194n10, 201n48, 206n17, 212n77, 218n48; racial applications of, 120; and racial division/segregation, 86; and social gospel ideas, 69–72; staple tenets, 36; variety in expressions of, 61–62; Williams (L. K.) on, 115; and Williams's (E. F.) proto-fundamentalism, 78–80. See also *The Fundamentals*; *specific doctrines, including* atonement; *specific tenets, including* biblical inspiration
Dorrien, Gary, 199n23
Du Bois, W. E. B., 71, 183, 209n53, 214n3, 224n20

Easter and physical resurrection, 26, 92
Ebel, Jonathan, 231n20
education and schools: and black seminaries, 48, 122–23, 129, 135 (*see also* American Baptist Theological Seminary); and black students at white seminaries, 153, 222n4, 225n37;

combating theological modernism with, 122; and evolutionary biology, 26, 45; and fears of modernist incursions, 153, 225n37; Nabrit's call for theological, 176; and racial considerations at ABTS, 140; and school curricula, 26, 47, 54; and social action of the church, 116–17; and textbook concerns, 152; Williams's (L. K.) advocacy for, 48, 178, 233n38; Williams's (N. W.) advocacy for, 29–30; and Woodson's criticisms of conservatism, 226n52;

Ellison, Christopher, 194n10

Evangelical Theological College, 129

Evans, Curtis, 224n35

evolutionary biology: and biblical literalism, 41, 44; and "Confession of Faith" adopted by ABTS, 138; fundamentalists' opposition to, 8, 11–12, 13, 26, 41, 43–45; and public school curricula, 26, 45; and racial prejudice, 11; Williams (L. K.) on, 113–14; and Williams's (L. K.) defense of fundamentalism, 118–19. *See also* Scopes trial

Farmer, Ashley D., 16–17, 59

Federal Council of Churches, 137–38, 143, 156

Fellowship Bible Institute, 123

films, religious, 58

Finn, Nathan, 69, 138, 197n42, 208n42

First Baptist Church, Princeton, Indiana, 121, 142, 229n98

Fosdick, Harry Emerson: and Barbour's (R. C.) progressivism, 144; and Berry on "false believers," 105; on conservative-fundamentalist distinction, 21; on intolerance of fundamentalists, 58; McKinney on persecution of, 164; on regressive nature of fundamentalism, 215n15, 216n19

Frank, J. H., 73–75, 198n2

Franklin, Benjamin, 167

Frazier, E. Franklin, 201n48

Freeman, James, 66

*Fundamentalism and American Culture* (Marsden), 12, 196n19

"fundamentalism" term, 3, 13, 18–19

fundamentalist-modernist controversy: and Berry's ministry, 87, 98; black fundamentalists' engagement in, 7; in the black press, 27, 29, 30, 41, 68; and blacks' self-identification as fundamentalists, 3, 7, 19, 27; and diversity in the black church, 17; and fundamentalist movement vs. fundamentalist controversy, 8–9; lack of middle ground in, 41; and literalism, 41, 42, 43; and Methodism, 68; and religious vs. racial identity, 159; and Williams's (L. K.) ministry, 113, 177. *See also* modernism, theological

*The Fundamentals*: about, 4; on atonement, 82–83, 213n84; and Berry, 100–101, 102; and biblical inerrancy, 76, 211n69; on biblical inspiration, 62; and Biddle's theological arguments, 66–67; black ministers' access to, 67, 207n31; on communist threat to the church, 155; and defining fundamentalism, 18; doctrinal emphasis of, 217n28; end-time theories in, 84; and exegetical analysis of fundamentalist theology, 16; on hell, 100; theology reflected across the color line, 60, 76–77; variety in perspectives represented in, 62

Gaebelein, Arno C., 73, 155

Gaines, W. J., 215n3

Garden of Eden, 93

Garnett, James H.: and American Baptist Theological Seminary, 126, 130, *146*, 152; and Barbour's (J. P.) progressivism, 150; and Barbour's (R. C.) progressivism, 144–48, 159; on Hailey's service to ABTS, 132; and Seminary Singers, 142

Garvey, Marcus, 183
Genesis 1–3 (creation narrative), 43–44, 45
Gladden, Washington, 93
Glass, William R., 10–11, 13, 229n97
*God's Empire* (Trollinger), 9–10
"God's One Essential for Salvation" (Berry), 81–82, 104
*God's Rascal* (Hankins), 9–10
Gray, James M., 62, 65, 66, 67, 73, 76, 211n69
Great Depression, 168–69
Great Migration, 27, 229n99
Griggs, Sutton E., 126, 134–35, 225n45
guns, power afforded by, 111–12

Hailey, Orren Luico, 126, 131–33, 137–38, 144
Haitian Revolution, 112
Hall, Jacquelyn Dowd, 230n2
Hamer, Fannie Lou, 87
Hamilton, Charles, 215n3
*Handbook of Bible Manners and Customs* (Freeman), 66
Hankins, Barry, 9–10
Harlem, New York, 51
Harlem Renaissance, 112
Harnack, Adolf, 26, 77, 81
Harris, Fredrick C., 212n77
Harvey, Paul, 124, 194n10, 212n78, 222n4
Heard (Bishop), 40–41
heaven, reality of, 138
hell, doctrine of, 99–101, 138
Henderson, J. Raymond, 52
Henry, Carl F. H., 193n8
Henry, J. I., 33, 34
Henry, J. L., 33, 34, 53, 54, 184
Henry, N. G., 33, 35
Henry, O. D., 33, 34
Henry, W. W., 33, 34, 35
Henry Brothers, 33, 34, 35–36, 37–38, 200n29
Higginbotham, Evelyn Brooks, 208n39, 220n70, 223n15

higher biblical criticism, 63–67, 73, 90–91, 101–4, 148–50, 217n28
historical accounts of fundamentalism: absence of black fundamentalists from, 3, 5–7, 24, 54, 181–82, 187; and fundamentalism as conservative cultural militancy, 8, 12–14; and fundamentalism as institutional movement, 7–12, 14
historical figures, fundamentalists' alignment with, 115–16
historical-theological perspective, 6, 14–20, 60–61, 182, 186–87, 197n43
Holy Spirit, 38–39, 89, 96, 139
Horace, Lillian B., 124, 223n15, 233n38
Howard University, 32
Hubert Harrison Memorial Church, 40
Hughes, Langston, 71
human rights, 52
hypostatic union (doctrine), 77, 117, 221n73

identity: American citizenship and, 162, 166; and Berry's "Christian America," 167–74, 182; black church's custodianship of African American, 46; and doctrines of fundamentalism, 159; and opponents of fundamentalism, 159–60, 183; "Our Group . . . ," editorialist on, 162; and racial progress, 182
Ingersoll, Robert, 166, 179
institutional movement, fundamentalism as, 7–12, 14
"intellectual inferiority" of blacks, 56, 59, 156, 224n35
Interchurch World Movement, 137, 143
International Council of Religious Education, 152
interracial marriage, 107, 120, 229n97
interwar period, 5, 19
Irenaeus of Lyons, 75, 210n66
Ironside, Edmund H., 129

Isaac, E. W. D., 136
Islam, 229n99

Jehioakim, King, 102
Jemison, D. V., 149–50
Jesus Christ: and Berry's "Christian America," 169, 172, 173–74; and biblical inspiration doctrine, 75–76; deity of (see divinity of Jesus Christ); focus on imminent return of, 9; and McKinney's criticisms of fundamentalism, 164; and modernist theology, 92–93; physical resurrection of, 26, 60, 80, 92–93, 138, 205n12, 206n12; sacrifice of (see atonement); second coming of, 21, 60, 83–84, 205n12, 206n12; virgin birth of, 21, 43, 47, 60, 205n12, 206n12; and Wallace's criticisms of fundamentalism, 68–69
Johnson, John Albert: antimodernist perspectives of, 75–78, 94–98, 216n19; on atonement, 81, 96; and Christian nationalism, 167, 174, 182; on doctrinal fundamentals, 75–78, 120; leadership of, 184; and racial advancement, 120, 217n21; on spirit of emancipation, 98, 162–63, 166–67
Johnson, Mordecai, 32–33, 199n23
Johnson, Sylvester A., 196n18
Jordan, Lewis Garnett, 141, 143
Jordan, Winthrop, 218n46
Journal of Religion, 84

King, Martin Luther, Jr., 183
Knight, Ryland, 153, 155–56
Ku Klux Klan, 49, 56
Kyle, Melvin Grove, 66, 67
Kyles, L. W., 135

language and terminology of fundamentalists, 18

Laws, Curtis Lee, 13, 59, 156
leaders of the fundamentalist movement, 10
Lewis, C. S., 109
liberalism in religion: and communist threat, 155–56; and NBC's *National Baptist Voice*, 143; warnings about, 39, 57–58, 176. See also modernism, theological
Lienesch, Michael, 11–12
Lincoln, Abraham, 167
Lincoln, C. Eric, 46, 206n17
literacy, power of, 111
literalism: about, 201n44; and anti-evolution attitudes, 41, 44; black weeklies' commentary on, 42; and doctrine of fundamentalist movement, 36, 41, 43, 54; and opponents of fundamentalism, 42; of Williams (L. K.), 47. See also biblical inspiration
Locke, Alain, 203n76
"A Lost Bible Is Found" (Berry), 103
Luther, Martin, 89, 167
lynching: and anti-lynching campaigns, 53–54, 53; and Berry's "Christian America," 171, 173

Malry, Illie E., 156, 229nn98–99
Mamiya, Lawrence H., 206n17
Manhattan Bible Institute, 123
Manna Bible Institute, 123
Marcionism, 68, 208n40
marginalization of black fundamentalists, 7–14, 187
Marsden, George: on blacks' self-identification as fundamentalists, 13, 27; and dispensational premillennialism, 200n35; and doctrine of fundamentalist movement, 36; on tenets of fundamentalism, 12, 26–27, 196n19, 196n31
Martin, Lerone A., 61
Massee, J. C., 197n42

Mathews, Mary Beth Swetnam: on American Baptist Theological Seminary, 143–44, 223n10; on anti-evolution attitudes, 44; on Biddle, 207n22; on black ministers' access to *The Fundamentals*, 207n31; and blacks in history of fundamentalism, 5–7, 195n15, 198n2; on Frank, 73–74; and National Baptist Convention's schism, 223n15

McDaniel, Eric, 194n10

McKinney, Ernest Rice: on fundamentalism's links to racism, 49; on negative impact of black fundamentalists, 30–31, 46, 50, 164–65, 187; on ubiquity of fundamentalism, 30, 33, 36, 165, 187

McKissic, Dwight, 1, 5

Mencken, H. L., 25, 199n23

Methodism, 68

military service: and American soldiers as imitators of Christ, 231n20; of blacks, 111–12

millenarianism, 9

Miller, Albert G., 122–24

Miller, Kelly, 49, 73, 98

Miller, William David, 31–32

miracles, 26, 43, 66, 78, 91, 201n44, 205n12

Missionary Baptist Church, 28–29, 38

Mitchell, Henry, 214n3

modernism, theological: accused of undermining Christian gospel, 91; and American Baptist Theological Seminary, 124, 151–52; appeal to emotions, 58; and atonement, 81; and Barbour's (J. P.) progressivism, 148–51; and Barbour's (R. C.) progressivism, 144–48; battleground issues between fundamentalism and, 30; Berry's antimodernist message, 98–112; and Berry's social message, 105–8; and biblical inerrancy, 69–70, 72–73; and black seminaries, 122, 123; black weeklies' commentary on, 27, 28–29, 38–39, 41, 42, 43; combating, with "Old Time" teachings, 29, 38–40; combating, with recorded sermons, 61; and communist threat, 155–56, 157; and conservative cultural militancy, 8, 12–13, 54; considered anti-Christian, 193n6; denial of biblical gospel, 91; and evolutionary biology, 113–14; and "false teachers" accusations, 72–73, 93, 94, 95, 96, 114, 120, 177; and Fosdick's sermon on religious tolerance, 58; fundamentalism as reaction to, 89; and fundamentalist doctrine, 60; fundamentalists' antipathy toward, 17, 18, 26, 48, 60; Garnett's antimodernist message, 145–48; gospel of compromise, 95–96; and hell, 99–101; and higher biblical criticism, 63–67, 73, 90–91, 101–4, 148–50, 217n28; as inauthentic Christians, 109; Johnson's criticisms of, 75–78, 94–98, 216n19; Mathews on, 5–6; "new theology" of, 108–9; and opponents of fundamentalism, 40; parallel perspectives of black and white fundamentalists on, 89; and progressive racial stances, 229n97; and racial advancement, 42–43, 116–17; on regressive nature of fundamentalism, 215n15; Robinson's criticisms of, 69–70, 71–73; in seminaries, 141; and Singleton's criticisms of fundamentalism, 42–43; tenets of, 26, 90–91; as threat to African Americans, 90, 118, 153; as threat to fundamentalists, 57–58; Williams's (E. F.) antimodernist message, 78–79, 91–94; Williams's (L. K.) antimodernist message, 113–19, 141, 143, 177, 180

Montgomery, William E., 202n48

Moody, Dwight L., 78

Moody Bible Institute, 62, 129

Moran, Jeffrey, 12, 45, 163, 196n33, 198n6

Morris, Elias C., 115–16, 220n67
Moses (biblical), 40, 67, 115, 210n66
Mt. Aria Baptist Church, Taylor, Texas, 116
Mullins, Edgar Young, 126
Munhall, Leander Whitcomb, 73, 206n19
Muse, A. D., 150–51

NAACP Press Service, 180
Nabrit, James M., Jr., 176, 232n31
Nabrit, James M., Sr., 39, 153, 155, 176, 232n31
Nabrit, Samuel, 176, 232n31
National Baptist Convention (NBC): and ABTS as interracial endeavor, 126, 128–34; and ABTS's founding, 122, 126; and ABTS's governance, 123–24, 128; and Barbour's (J. P.) progressivism, 149–51; and Barbour's (R. C.) progressivism, 148; doctrinal diversity in, 143, 149–50; founding of, 225n39; fundamentalist claims/impulses in, 141, 150, 151; and modernist theology, 118; and *National Baptist Voice*, 143–45, 147–51, 155; nonfundamentalist affiliations of, 8, 137–38, 143, 152; and racial uplift ideology, 134; schism in, 127, 128, 132, 223n15; and social action of the church, 117l; and textbook concerns, 152; Williams' (L. K.) leadership of, 113, 177; and Williams's (L. K.) emphasis on fundamentals, 117
*National Baptist Union-Review*, 27, 73
nationalism, Christian, 158–59, 160, 167, 168–69, 174, 182–83
nationalism, white, 185
"naturally religious," African Americans characterized as, 59, 133, 156, 204n10, 224n35, 225n38
Nebuchadnezzar, King, 170
Negro Baptist Ministers' Conference of Nashville, 127
*The Negro Church* (Du Bois), 71

*The Negro Church in America* (Frazier), 201n48
*Negro Star* (Wichita), 28–29, 38–39
neo-evangelical movement, 4, 81, 193n8
New Negro movement, 112
*New Perspectives on the Black Intellectual Tradition* (Blain, Cameron, and Farmer), 16–17
New Testament scriptures, 68–69
*New York Amsterdam News*, 27, 40, 52
Noel, Roden, 51
Noll, Mark, 14–15
*Norfolk Journal and Guide*: criticisms of fundamentalism, 45, 180–81; on prevalence of fundamentalism among blacks, 13, 25–26, 27, 28, 31, 161; and racial advancement, 25–26, 46–47, 221n74; on racial prejudice's links to fundamentalism, 49
Norris, J. Frank: belief in intellectual inferiority of blacks, 56, 59; cultural militancy of, 45; and the fundamentalist narrative, 3, 9–10, 26; as proponent of segregation, 10, 26, 56, 120
Northern Baptist Convention, 38–39, 84, 140
Nwosu, Oluchi, 219n48

Old Testament scriptures, 68–69
old-time/old-fashioned religion: and American ideals/identity, 176–77; and Berry's "Christian America," 172; and Berry's social message, 108; black weeklies on, 32–33, 37–41; combating theological modernism with, 29, 38–40; and continuity with tradition, 40–41; and Holy Spirit emphasis, 38; and opponents of fundamentalism, 40; and racial advancement, 117–18; and slavery, 162; and supernaturalist worldview, 37–40, 41; and theological giants of the past, 116; warnings about liberals' rejection of, 39; Williams's (L. K.) commitment to, 113, 116, 117–18, 183

Olivet Baptist Church, Chicago, 117
opponents of fundamentalism: and American ideals/identity, 159–60, 183; claims of intolerance of fundamentalists, 21, 41, 49, 58, 160, 180–81, 183; McKinney's criticisms, 30–31, 164–65; NAACP Press Service's attacks, 180; oppositional voices in black weeklies, 30–31, 40, 42–43; and racial advancement, 42–43, 46, 165, 179, 183; on racial prejudice's links to fundamentalism, 48–50; on regressive nature of fundamentalism, 215n15; and Scopes trial, 180; secular black elite, 163–64; Singleton's criticisms, 165–66, 212n73; Wallace's criticisms, 68–69; Woodson's criticisms, 226n52
Orr, James, 66, 67
"Our Group Are Fundamentalists in Religion" (*Norfolk Journal and Guide*), 25–26, 31, 46–47, 161–62
"The Outlook" (Johnson), 98
Overacker, Ingrid, 194n10

Paul (biblical), 72, 87–88, 91, 93, 95, 115, 167
Payne, Talmadge, 129
Peter (biblical), 115
phonograph records, sermons recorded on, 61
Pickens, William, 73
Pierson, Arthur Tappan, 74
Pinn, Anne, 221n71
Pinn, Anthony, 221n71
Pipes, William H., 214n3
*Pittsburgh Courier*, 32–33, 43–44, 49
*Plaindealer* (Topeka), 31
political parties, 9, 10
Porter, Ford, 121, 142–43, 229n98
poverty, 50, 80
Powell, Adam Clayton, Sr., 33, 51–52, 71, 199n23, 221n71
"The Practical Nature of the Christian Religion" (E. F. Williams), 78–80
prayer, practice of, 109

preachers and preaching: antimodernist messages of, 89–90, 119–20; authoritative nature of, 89; Berry's opposition to modernism, 98–112; and black ministers' access to *The Fundamentals*, 67, 207n31; as called to ministry by God, 214n3; and communist threat, 155; duty/purpose of, 96–97; Johnson's opposition to modernism, 94–98; racial progress hindered by, 165; and recorded sermons, 61; and theological giants of the past, 115–16; Williams's (E. F.) opposition to modernism, 91–94; Williams's (L. K.) opposition to modernism, 113–19
"Preachers—Modernists and Fundamentalists" (Robinson), 69–70, 72–73
premillennialism, 83–84, 200n35
presidential election of 2016, 1, 185
press/weeklies, black, 25–55; circulation of, 27, 199n8; discussions about fundamentalism in, 27–28; and fundamentalist doctrine, 60; and historical-theological perspective, 187–88; on literalism, 42; on "old time religion," 32–33, 37–41; oppositional voices in, 30–31, 40, 42–43; and prevalence of fundamentalist attitudes, 7, 27, 28, 30, 187; and racial advancement, 46–48; and self-identification of fundamentalists, 31–32; on southern racial violence/intolerance, 48–50; on theological modernism, 27, 28–29, 38–39, 41, 42, 43
Procter, W. C., 100
progressive attitudes among black fundamentalists, 4–6, 184, 195n11, 219n61
propitiation (doctrine), 30, 82, 105–6, 107, 213n84, 218n41
Protestant Reformation, 89, 211n66
public school curricula, 26

Raboteau, Albert, 15–16, 17, 18, 202n48
racial advancement/progress: and American Baptist Theological Seminary, 134;

and association of conservatism with fundamentalists, 90; and Barbour's (J. P.) progressivism, 150; Berry's messages on, 103–4, 106–8, 111–12; and black church, 48; black fundamentalists' hinderance of, 50, 165, 183–84; black weeklies on, 36–37, 46–48; and brotherhood ideal of Berry, 105–6; and democratic participation, 178–79, 221n77; and doctrine of Christ's divinity, 117; as driver of religious decisions/activity, 46; and fidelity to fundamentalist doctrines, 47, 71–72, 90, 98, 107–8, 116–17, 120, 182–83, 221n74; fundamentalism as driver of, 161–63, 182–84; and guns/military service, 111–12; interracial marriage, 107, 120; Johnson on, 217n21; and literacy, 111; and opponents of fundamentalism, 42–43, 46, 165, 179, 183; and racial prejudice/discrimination, 48; and racial uplift ideology, 134; as related to fundamentalism, 25, 36–37, 159; religious identity as related to, 46–47, 48, 182; Singleton on religion's role in, 52; and social gospel ideas, 71; Williams's (L. K.) calls for, 177–79, 182–83; and Williams's (L. K.) emphasis on fundamentals, 116–18

racial differentiation theories, 135

racial prejudice/intolerance: and antiracism resolution of SBC, 1–2, 5, 188; black weeklies' commentary on, 28, 48–50; Johnson on, 98; linked to conservatism/fundamentalism, 13, 48–50; and progressive attitudes among black fundamentalists, 4–5; and racial violence, 112; and Rauschenbusch's social gospel, 70–71; and "religious intolerance" of fundamentalists, 49, 160, 181; white fundamentalists' exploitation of, 11

Ransom, Reverdy C., 69, 71, 221n71

Rauschenbusch, Walter, 33, 70–71, 93–94, 216n19

recorded sermons, 61

*Redeeming the South* (Harvey), 124

Reformed African American Network, 185–86

Reformed Theological Seminary, 185

regeneration (doctrine), 29, 38–39, 72, 94, 108, 114, 155, 176

"Religion Worth Having" (Singleton), 42, 212n73

Republican Party, 9, 10

resurrection of Jesus Christ (doctrine), 26, 60, 80, 91–92, 131, 205n12, 206n12

*Rethinking Zion* (Mathews), 195n15

revivals/revivalism, 33, 35–36, 37, 78, 172

*Revive Us Again* (Carpenter), 9

Rhoads, Joseph J., 155

Rice, Lewis, 30

Riley, Ralph W., *154*

Riley, William Bell: antimodernist message of, 155; cultural militancy of, 45; and the fundamentalist narrative, 3, 9–10; and Scopes trial, 25; and separatist fundamentalists, 197n42

Robinson, J. G., 69–70, 71–73, 76, 82, 83, 188

*The Roots of Fundamentalism* (Sandeen), 8–9

Roundtree, Dovey Johnson, 232n31

Sandeen, Ernest, 8–9, 10

Sankey, Ira, 78

Sawyer, Mary R., 194n10

science and religion, 44–45, 118–19, 175

Scopes, John, 25, 164

Scopes trial: about, 25; and black fundamentalists, 12, 13; black weeklies' commentary on, 44–45; and opponents of fundamentalism, 164, 180; and racial violence, 49; and Williams's (L. K.) affirmation of fundamentalism, 43, 113

*Searchlight*, 56

second coming of Jesus Christ (doctrine), 21, 60, 83–84, 205n12, 206n12
secular black elite, 163–64
segregation: and Berry's "Christian America," 171; as discussed in black weeklies, 28; embraced by white fundamentalists, 58; fundamentalist institutions' relationship with, 11, 13, 26–27; and interracial marriage, 107, 229n97; Norris as proponent of, 10, 56, 120; and racial advancement, 45–46; and reunion of southern and northern denominations, 11
self-identification of fundamentalists: of black fundamentalists, 3, 7, 13; and black weeklies, 27, 31–32; as defining condition of fundamentalism, 18–20; and fundamentalist doctrine, 60; Marsden on, 13, 27
self-improvement, 111
Seminary Singers of ABTS, 121, 141–43
separatist fundamentalists, 69, 197n42, 209n42, 222n2
Sernett, Milton, 219n61
sexuality, black, 218n46
"Shall the Fundamentalists Win?" (Fosdick), 216n15
sharecropping, 171
"sight" messages of Berry, 110–12
Simmons, Roscoe, 50–51
Singleton, George A., 42–43, 46, 52, 165–66, 212n73
Sinitiere, Phillip, 222n4
*Slave Religion* (Raboteau), 202n48
Slavery: and adoption of Christian religion, 201n48; and Berry on power of guns, 111–12; fundamentalism as bedrock during, 161; and Johnson on spirit of emancipation, 163, 166–67; legacies of, 171, 173; and McKinney's criticisms of fundamentalism, 49, 164–65; old time religion's role in ending, 162–63; and Singleton's criticisms of fundamentalism, 165–66
social gospel movement, 69–72, 79–80, 82, 85, 93–94, 99, 117, 212n78
"social history of theology" perspective, 14–15
social oppression, 28
societal issues and social action, 50–54, 97–98, 105–8, 116–17, 203n76
*Something Within* (Harris), 212n77
South, American: agenda driven fundamentalism in, 11; and association of fundamentalism with white southerners, 48–50; churches as guardians of social order in, 11; exploitation of racial fears in, 58–59, 229n97; racial violence/intolerance in, 48–50; and threat of modernism, 153. *See also* segregation
Southern Baptist Convention (SBC): and ABTS as interracial endeavor, 126, 128–34; and ABTS's doctrines, 143, 150–51, 157; and ABTS's financial support, 156; and ABTS's founding, 48, 122, 126; and ABTS's governance, 123–24, 128, 133–34; antiracism/alt-right resolution of, 1–2, 5, 188; *Baptist Faith and Message*, 139, 140–41; confession of faith of, 139; and Hailey's promotion of seminary, 132; Home Mission Board of, 153, 156; and liberal affiliations of National Baptists, 137–38; and Williams (L. K.), 48
Southern Baptist Seminary, Louisville, 146, 153, 225n37
Southern Baptist Women's Missionary Union (WMU), 152
Southern Bible Institute, Dallas, 122–23, 129
Spencer, Richard, 1–2
Spurgeon, Charles, 115, 220n67
*Star of Zion*, 27, 64–65, 68, 69
Stock, John, 213n84

stock market crash of 1929, 168–69, 231n19
*Strangers in Zion* (Glass), 11, 13
Straton, John Roach, 197n42
Sunday, Billy, 99
supernaturalist worldview of fundamentalists: as discussed in black weeklies, 28; and doctrine of fundamentalist movement, 18, 36, 54; and miracles, 26, 43, 66, 91, 205n12; and modernist theology, 26; and "old time religion," 37–40, 41; and opponents of fundamentalism, 42
superstition, 40, 59, 165
Sutton, Matthew Avery, 196n20

tenant farming, 171
Texas, racial violence in, 49
theological giants of the past, 115–16
Tisby, Jemar, 185–86, 188
Toliver, I. Benjamin, 115, 116, 220n67
Torrey, R. A., 78–79, 213n84
Toussaint Louverture, 112
Townsend, A. M., 127, 145, 148, 153, *154*, 224n20
tradition: continuity with, 40–41, 54; emphasis on, 37. *See also* old-time/old-fashioned religion
Trollinger, William, 9–10
"true religion," 50–54
Trump, Donald, 185
Turner, Richard Brent, 229n99
types of fundamentalists, 209n42

*Ungodly Women* (DeBerg), 208n39
United States of America: and Berry's "Christian America" message, 167–74; and Christian nationalism, 231n20; civil liberties of, 158, 159, 169, 173, 174, 231n20; Constitution of, 173–74, 179; military service of blacks in, 112; and stock market crash of 1929, 168–69, 231n19; and Williams's (L. K.) call for education, 178; and Williams's (L. K.) call for voting rights, 178–79; and World War I, 112, 174–75, 231n20. *See also* American identity
unity, Christian, 108
University of Chicago, 148

Van Ness, I. J., 126
virgin birth (doctrine): as one of five fundamentals of the faith, 21, 60, 64, 70, 80, 205n12, 206n12; Williams (L. K.) on, 43, 47
voting rights, 116–17, 178–79

Walker's Tabernacle Baptist Church, Atlanta, 31
Wallace, Ida L., 68–69
Washington, Booker T., 30, 183, 225n45
Washington, George, 167, 172, 173
Washington, James Melvin, 225n39
Watt, David Harrington, 3, 13, 45
weeklies. *See* press/weeklies, black
Weinfeld, David, 203n76
Weisenfeld, Judith, 229n99
Wesley brothers, 167
Wesley Chapel AME Church, Houston, Texas, 32
Wheeler, Edward, 214n3
white fundamentalists: alignment of black fundamentalists with, 38–39, 76–77, 85–86; and American Baptist Theological Seminary, 126; association of fundamentalism with southern, 48–50; black fundamentalists ignored by, 24; and continuity with tradition, 41; and cultural conservatism, 48–49; cultural militancy of, 45, 186–87; and institutional support, 2–3, 121–22; and "intellectual inferiority" of blacks, 56, 59, 156; and interracial marriage, 229n97; and Jim Crow segregation, 58; and leaders of the movement, 10; portrayal of fundamentalism as exclusively white, 5–6, 187; white superiority embraced by, 125, 132

white nationalism, 1, 185
white supremacy: and American Baptist Theological Seminary, 125, 132; and antiracism resolution of SBC, 1–2, 5; Berry's criticism of, 88; cultural conservatism's links to, 48–49
Williams, Edward Franklin, 78–80, 91–94, 174–75, 212n78, 213n84, 232n28
Williams, John B. L., 215n3
Williams, Lacey Kirk: advocacy for education, 48, 178, 233n38; "affirmation of fundamentalism" of, 43; and American Baptist Theological Seminary, 48, 124, 126, 132, 202n51; antimodernist message of, 48, 113–19, 141, 143, 177, 180, 188; on communist threat, 155–56; and fidelity to fundamentalist doctrines, 120, 177, 184; leadership of NBC, 113, 177; and NBC's National Baptist Voice, 144; and old time/old-fashioned doctrines, 113, 116, 117–18, 183; and racial advancement, 51, 52, 120; on science, 118–19; on social action of the church, 47–48, 51, 116–17, 221n73; and social gospel, 117, 220n71; social/racial progressivism of, 195n11, 219n61; on voting rights, 178–79
Williams, Noah W., 29–30, 83, 200n35
Wills, Gregory, 145
Wilmore, Gayraud S., 194n9, 221n71
The Witness: A Black Christian Collective, 186
Women's Training School, 152, 223n7
Woodson, Carter G., 226n52
Woodward, C. Vann, 171
World War I, 112, 134–35, 174–75, 231n20

X, Malcolm, 183

ABOUT THE AUTHOR

DANIEL BARE is Assistant Professor of Religious Studies at Texas A&M University. He is a scholar of American religious history, focusing on Christianity, race, and the interplay between theological convictions and the formation of individual and group identities.

www.ingramcontent.com/pod-product-compliance
Lightning Source LLC
Chambersburg PA
CBHW020401080526
44584CB00014B/1126